THE GERSHWIN YEARS

COURTESY AL HIRSCHFELD

THE
GERSHWIN
YEARS

by EDWARD JABLONSKI and LAWRENCE D. STEWART

with an Introduction by Carl van Vechten

DOUBLEDAY & COMPANY, INC., GARDEN CITY, NEW YORK   1973

For our parents

From Gershwin emanated a new American music not written with the ruthlessness of one who strives to demolish established rules, but based on a new native gusto and wit and awareness. His was a modernity that reflected the civilization we live in as excitingly as the headline in today's newspaper.

IRA GERSHWIN, 1938

. . . true music . . . must repeat the thought and aspirations of the people and the time. My people are Americans. My time is today. . . .

No one expected me to compose music. I just did. What I have done is what was in me; the combination of New York, where I was born, and the rising, exhilarating rhythm of it, with centuries of hereditary feeling back of me. They ask me what I am trying to do, and I can only say I am trying to express what is in me. Some people have the ability to put their feelings into words or music. There are thousands who have the same feeling and are mute. Those of us who can must speak for those who can not— but we must be honest about it.

GEORGE GERSHWIN, 1926

I hope you are getting all the things from Ira that you asked for, because I should like to see quite a little bit about him in the book, with several of his best lyrics printed. I think they would be amusing to read and add quality to the book.

GEORGE GERSHWIN (to Isaac Goldberg), 1931

CONTENTS

PREFACE TO THE 1st EDITION

"Why 'The *Gershwin* Years'?" complained one acquaintance. And, of course, he would seem to have a point. If it's the 1920s one is talking about, they have already been labeled (allegedly by Scott Fitzgerald) "The Jazz Age"; why try to improve upon that evocation of the tinkle and talk of a celebrated day? The trouble with *that* title was that when the ticker tape floated out the windows of Wall Street in October 1929, carrying so many people with it, an age may have ended but the music did not.

Scott Fitzgerald was among the first to proclaim that the Jazz Age was dead; but George Gershwin, sitting in his Riverside Drive penthouse, took the term more literally and (in 1931) insisted: "It seems to me that we are too close to Queen Jazz and her lively era for anyone to know definitely whether her throne is already on its last legs or to forecast how long she will continue to rule." George was, after all, in the midst of finishing a second rhapsody for piano and orchestra, and he observed: "My feeling for the music I am writing today is essentially no different from what it was for the pieces I composed seven and more years ago." Clearly Gershwin music was not going to be circumscribed by the 1920s, even though it first struck into its melodic own in the day of the flapper and the jelly bean.

A great many people came of age in the American Twenties: Ernest Hemingway and Cole Porter, e. e. cummings and Richard Rodgers—it is a random grouping, but these were among the artists who made of a decade a renaissance. John Peale Bishop, who was seldom enthusiastic about "popular" culture, once wrote in his notebook: "Music: Strauss waltzes, Gershwin. Somehow in these men we are aware that while the age is mirrored, its significance is not to be found." Bishop did not mean the entry as a compliment, but those who increasingly favor creation to criticism have learned to take it as such. And Bishop's detached judgment has justified our book's point of view.

We hope that in the following pages will be created the images not only of two men but also of their times, their friends, the wonderful years that are associated with their name. It was Alfred Simon who first crystallized this feeling for us in the phrase, The Gershwin Years; and for having done so and letting us put it as title to the book we are especially grateful.

George Gershwin was among the most consistently photographed and interviewed celebrities of his day. Others, particularly movie moguls and murderers, were carried momentarily to the tops of more newspaper columns and were shot more times. But few have traveled so far so well so long as did the composer. The greatest difficulty, therefore, was not in gathering pictures of George and Ira, but in selecting those that told their story best.

To chronicle these years, we have been immeasurably assisted by the courtesy and co-operation of Ira Gershwin. Our greatest debt is to this man who, fortunately, has saved the papers, pictures, and memorabilia that tell much about the Gershwins, and who has had (for us) the grace to remain excellent copy. In giving us access to his archives he allowed us to rummage through his diaries, work sheets, and correspondence; the result is that we are here publishing for the first time a large amount of material that might well have brought him better returns if he himself had done something with it. But all of his work, published and unpublished, he let us use as we chose—gratis and unsupervised.

It would be impossible to list all the people who put themselves and their possessions to our inquiries and our camera, and always with unfailing courtesy. But we cannot leave unacknowledged the contributions of: ASCAP, Harold Arlen, Fred Astaire, Henry Botkin, Clark Bowlby, Robert Breen, Irving Brown, Philip Charig, Peter C. Clay, Alan Dashiell, Louise Dresser, Max Dreyfus, Samuel Dushkin, Vinton Freedley, Eva Gauthier, Arthur Gershwin, E. Y. Harburg, Kathleen Haven (of the Museum of Modern Art), Dorothy Heyward, Edward Kilenyi, Sr., John McGowan, Daniel I. McNamara, Emily Paley, Aileen Pringle,

Harry Ruby, Mabel Schirmer, Nathaniel Shilkret, Dr. Albert Sirmay, Carl Van Vechten, and Paul Whiteman. Jay Culver assisted with the gathering of photographs and information on the theater. Cyrus Rogers diligently prepared the index and corrected proofs. To Al Hirschfeld we are indebted for the frontispiece drawing, a favorite of ours.

Music Publishers Holding Corporation has kindly granted us permission to print the first page of the manuscript to the *Rhapsody in Blue*, the first page of the *Second Rhapsody* manuscript, the title page of the *Cuban Overture* manuscript; the lyric sketches to "Of Thee I Sing" and "Where's the Boy?" and the quotations from the lyrics of *Of Thee I Sing* and *Let 'Em Eat Cake*. Chappell's has graciously allowed the use of the lyrics to "Nevada" and "One Life to Live," and Gershwin Publishing Company has authorized the use of the manuscript pages from *Porgy and Bess*.

The New York *Times* and the New York *Herald-Tribune* must be gratefully acknowledged for their kindness in granting us permission to quote from their pages: the *Times* particularly for the Olin Downes description of the Aeolian Hall stage and the William Daly article; the *Tribune* for the use of the *Herald* article that set the composition of the *Rhapsody in Blue* in motion.

Finally we would like to pay tribute to three people: Leon Seidel (perhaps the most traditionally literary of all agents, since he is proprietor of his own coffeehouse), Barbara Ellis (our patient, tireless editor), and Edith Jablonski (mother of David Ira and Carla and invaluable and affectionate aid to both authors). They all deserve a better book; it is indicative of their especial charm that they have never once complained about the one we have given them.

E. J.   L. D. S.

New York, New York   Beverly Hills, California

PREFACE TO THE 2ND EDITION

"Why *The Gershwin Years*" indeed—and again? This echo of the query that opened our first Preface is readily answered. Since the initial publication of this book the songs of George and Ira Gershwin, and the "serious" music of George, have continued to grow in popularity or have been rediscovered. Performances and recordings proliferate although taste in popular music, since the Gershwin years, has changed to a fare-thee-well. Gershwin songs have been bent and mutilated by the style of today's "artists" beyond any recognition, much to the dismay of purists. Even gently critical Ira Gershwin was heard to say of one vocalist, "She sings like a family relative." Still the songs survive because of the classic quality of the words and music.

George Gershwin's concert works are regularly performed by important orchestras and soloists all over the world; in recorded form the works have accumulated profusely. Interestingly, both performances and recordings by European musicians with "classical" training have increased over the past two decades. Gershwin may very well be taken more seriously in Europe than he is at home.

It is well known that Ravel was a devoted Gershwin fan; so were other important musicians. During the late Twenties the Hungarian master Béla Bartók made a point of ordering all the newly printed piano music from the United States. He told one of his students, Erno Balogh, that he was most impressed with the compositions of a young American named Gershwin. Many years later, after Bartók had come to the United States, he sent his son Peter to a concert by the Pittsburgh Symphony, Fritz Reiner conducting, with specific instructions to pay particular attention to the music from *Porgy and Bess*.

"We must not make the mistake of thinking lightly of the very characteristic art of Gershwin," advised Ralph Vaughan Williams in addressing an audience of students at Yale University. Like Bartók, Vaughan Williams recognized something genuine and enduring in the Gershwin gift. Even so stern a master as Arnold Schoenberg (and his disciple Alban Berg) found much to admire in Gershwin. Perhaps Virgil Thomson expressed a consensus when, in a refreshingly uncritical moment, he said, "George Gershwin was an exquisite maker of tunes. There is life in them and grace and a wonderful sweet tenderness . . . they speak and are moving. They are music, our music, everybody's music."

And among popular songwriters he was like a young god, worthy of admiration, emulation—and by some, envy. His truly great peers—Harold Arlen, Jerome Kern, Arthur Schwartz, and others—delighted in his talent. It was another master, Irving Berlin, who said "George Gershwin is the only song writer I know who became a 'composer.'"

Recognition by one's colleagues is always gratifying, but the final evaluation comes from the uncounted, unpredictable masses and time. George Gershwin maintained that "the majority has much better taste and understanding, not only of music but of any of the arts, than it is credited with having. It is not the few knowing ones whose opinions make any work of art great, it is the judgment of the great mass that finally decides."

Since 1958, when this book was first published, there have been many signs of the continuing appeal of the Gershwins: the publication of never-before-published songs, the continuation of regular all-Gershwin concerts throughout the world after the demise of the historic Lewisohn Stadium concerts, and the recurring Gershwin "specials" on television. At least half a dozen of variable memorability come to mind, including one inspired (if that's the word) by the original edition of this book. Often as not these "specials" proved little more than the fact the songs were capable of withstanding dreary performances and stultifying productions. The viability of these unpretentious creations is extraordinary.

All of these indications, plus others, reveal a dynamic impact by these works across the generations. The Twenties are long gone, but the melodies do indeed linger on. Nothing confirms this so much as the steady flow of correspondence from young people to the door of the Gershwin home in Beverly Hills, California.

Thus did it seem appropriate, thanks to the interest and good offices of editor Harold Kuebler, to make *The Gershwin Years* available again. The authors have consequently been afforded the opportunity to make corrections, some necessary changes, and, more importantly, additions, including a discography and a bibliography of Gershwin resources. Over the past decade and a half, for example, new songs, even published ones, have come to light; so have new facts and illustrations.

At the same time the career of Ira Gershwin has proceeded with characteristic quiet distinction. He has produced his own book (*q.v.*), the delightfully erudite, informational, and entertaining *Lyrics on Several Occasions*, as well as shorter pieces, such as the introduction to *The George and Ira Gershwin Song Book*. Among other honors he has been awarded an Honorary Doctorate of Fine Arts by the University of Maryland in recognition of his contribution to our lives and times.

The authors (this note, incidentally, is being initially prepared by E.J. since L.D.S. supplied the original Preface) have, over these same years, added to their knowledge of the Gershwins and their works. One (E.J.) has written literally dozens of articles about the brothers Gershwin as well as a young people's biography of George. The other (L.D.S.) was instrumental in the creation of the rich Gershwin Archive for which he assiduously and devotedly classified and filed every scrap of manuscript, every memento, letter, drawing, painting, fact, and myth. Upon completion of that work he has returned to his first love, teaching. But not before filling several of his own notebooks with stories, anecdotes, and other rare Gershwiniana. We have drawn upon these sources for this edition.

Our revised edition of *The Gershwin Years* generally follows the form of the original, and the new material does not drastically revise our original view of the Gershwins: George, the Jazz Age Meteor, and Ira, the Contemplative Craftsman. Likewise, our evaluation of the songs and concert works remains steadfast; their own longevity says enough for them.

Those years to which we have adjectively affixed the Gershwin name traversed two world wars and a major depression—many more years than the decade of the Jazz Age. Still the name of Gershwin is most closely associated with and circumscribed by the Twenties. This is primarily because of the galvanic impact of George at the time; he basked in the limelight as to the manner born and someone or other actually dubbed him the "Crown Prince of the Jazz Age." In the United States it was an exciting, seething, and bubbling period in the arts to which George contributed his own pulsating animation. And, it is true, he did help to make the American Twenties musically distinctive—and fun. At the same time it might be remembered that some of his best work was done in the Thirties—the trio of political operettas, the *Second Rhapsody*, the last film scores, and, of course, *Porgy and Bess*.

What is particularly vivid about Gershwin's impress upon his time and his influence upon music is that they depend upon a mere handful of works, all of them created in little more than a decade: from the *Rhapsody in Blue* of 1924 to *Porgy and Bess* of 1935. And this does not touch on the songs.

The continuing Gershwin years were nurtured, after a brief hiatus, by Ira Gershwin, who returned to the musical theater scene with the brilliant lyrics for *Lady in the Dark* and went on to do several works, mainly films, reaching a peak in the now classic *A Star Is Born*. These works, done without George, revealed something few had ever taken the trouble to notice before: that while the talents of the brothers had been closely, and uniquely, attuned, both were capable of working with equal distinction apart. George had demonstrated this in the concert works; so had Ira proved himself in a number of shows (and very popular songs) even before the death of his brother.

The lyrics written in the Forties and Fifties for composers such as Harold Arlen, Aaron Copland, Jerome Kern, Burton Lane, Arthur Schwartz, Harry Warren, and Kurt Weill incited a redefinition of the genius of Ira Gershwin (who maintains the word is applicable only to his brother). That he is one of the great lyricists of American song is obvious—it was evident early in the joint career of the Gershwins and before. That it went generally unheralded for so long is one of the curiosities of our musical history.

In preparing this new edition we have, in some instances, approached those who so kindly helped us the first time around, among them Harold Arlen, Irving Brown of Warner Brothers Publications, Henry Botkin, Emily Paley, Mabel Schirmer, and Kay Swift—and, of course, Ira

Gershwin. We can't thank them enough. In addition, we should like to add a further note of thanks to Donald K. Adams, Cecelia and Milton Ager, Bernie Borak, Robert A. Beach, Jr., of the University of Maryland, Jimmie Caristia of Dayton's Records, New York, Abram Chasins, Wilson G. Duprey of the New York Historical Society, James J. Fuld, Frances Godowsky, Stanley Green, Andrea Kaufman, Katharine Kaufman, Fred Knubel of Columbia University, Chester Kopaz, Lynn Lavner, Mrs. Robert A. Levin, Linda Loving of the Museum of Modern Art, Carl Miller of Chappell & Co., Kathi and Paul Mueller, Edward Rawlinson, Don Rose, Wanda and Jerry Simpson, Richard Tooke of the Museum of Modern Art, William B. Vasels, the late Carl Williams, his sister, Gretchen, and Eddie Wilson (all three New Zealanders), Harry A. Yerkes, Jr., and two curators of the Theatre and Music Collection of the Museum of the City of New York: the late Sam Pearce and his successor, Melvin Parks, who gave us both welcome corrections and the splendid Gershwin exhibition at the Museum in the summer of 1968.

Edith Garson Jablonski, mother of David Ira, Carla, and, since the first edition, Emily, once again served as a patient and affectionate buffer for the authors. Besides contributing any number of excellent suggestions she also rejected some pretty wayward ones. To her we are grateful for the section on the final weeks of George Gershwin's life. Her affecting account of a shatteringly unexpected event, we feel, could not have been better told—so we have borrowed it for our own use. We feel too that during the formative discussions about this new edition she was a most gracious, steadying, gentle, and creative influence.

E. J.	L. D. S.
New York, N.Y.	Beverly Hills, California

INTRODUCTION

Several years ago a friend of long standing, Edward Jablonski (I number my Edwards and he is Edward XIV), wrote to inquire if I would assist him with the illustrations for a book about George Gershwin which he had planned to write. Naturally, I acceded to his request at once and XIV came over (we inhabit adjacent streets) to select the photographs by me which appear in this enchanting volume, issued to honor the celebration of the sixtieth anniversary of George's birth. It is a peculiar pleasure for me to appear in this book, not only as illustrator, but also as introducer, because I discover, in examining the records, that I played a considerable role in George's remarkable career. When Jablonski first made contact with me, his conception for a memorial volume was much more modest; neither he nor I had any idea that the book he planned would become such a rich and rewarding volume. This development from his original, more unpretentious conception was made possible by the subsequent interest of Ira Gershwin, who offered every possible mode of assistance to XIV and XIV's gifted, scholarly collaborator Lawrence D. Stewart.

George's song "Swanee" was first professionally performed at the opening of the Capitol Theatre in New York late in 1919, an occasion at which I was present. I must have encountered George, then, earlier in 1919, because he played "Swanee," a song not yet publicly heard, at a party at Sylvia Joslyn's, to which I was taken by T. R. Smith, and I had actually met him at Smith's on an even earlier date. From the opening of the Capitol Theatre on, George's career gained rapid momentum and for the March 1925 issue of the then popular *Vanity*

Fair I wrote probably the first serious article about George to appear in print, from which I would like to quote the following:

"In the Spring of 1923, in search of novelties to put on her Fall program, Eva Gauthier asked me to suggest additions. 'Why not a group of American songs?' I urged. Her face betrayed her lack of interest. 'Jazz,' I particularized. Her expression brightened. When I met the singer again on her return from Paris, she informed me that Maurice Ravel had offered her the same sapient advice. She had, indeed, adopted the idea and requested me to recommend to her a musician who might serve as her accompanist and guide in this venture. But one name fell from my lips, that of George Gershwin, whose compositions I admired and with whose skill as a pianist I was acquainted. The experiment was eventually made, Madame Gauthier singing the popular modern group between a cluster of songs by Paul Hindemith and Béla Bartók on the one hand and Schoenberg's *Gurrelieder* on the other. This recital, given at Aeolian Hall on November 1, 1923, marked George Gershwin's initial appearance as a performer on the serious concert stage."

The event did not pass uncelebrated. Newspapers and magazines commented at length on the phenomenon: Jazz at last, it seemed, had come into its own. As I had been out of the city when Eva presented this revolutionary program, she very kindly invited me, late in January 1924, to enjoy a rehearsal of the same songs in preparation for her Boston concert. It was at this rehearsal that George informed me that Paul Whiteman had requested him to compose a special piece for a concert that he (Whiteman) proposed to give, consisting of music by modern popular composers. George added, in rather an offhand manner, that it was his intention to create for this occasion a concerto in fantasia form for piano and jazz band which he proposed to name American Rhapsody. (Ira hit on the eventual title just before the concert.) On that day, a short four weeks from the date on which the composition was actually performed, he had made only a few preliminary sketches. At the first rehearsal of the program for the concert the complete score of the *Rhapsody in Blue* (orchestrated by Ferde Grofé) was not yet ready. At the second rehearsal George played the *Rhapsody* TWICE on a very bad piano. Nevertheless, after hearing this rehearsal, I did not entertain a single doubt that this young man of twenty-five had written the very finest piece of music yet to come out of America. Moreover, that he had written the most effective concerto for piano and orchestra since Tschaikowsky had conceived his B-flat minor. I escorted Rebecca West to the actual concert, February 12, 1924, when her enthusiasm matched mine.

After that George and I became intimate friends. I saw him frequently, he played at our apartment on West Fifty-Fifth Street on numberless occasions, and Fania and I attended most of the first performances of his works, including his musical shows. I invited Ernest Newman, then in New York writing music reviews for the New York *Evening Post*, to hear him at our apartment on October 16, 1924. In the *Evening Post* for November 17, 1924, Mr. Newman wrote "Mr. Gershwin's Rhapsody is by far the most interesting thing of its kind I have yet met with; it really has ideas and they work themselves out in a way that interests the musical hearer. Perhaps it is better not to prophesy. What is at present certain is that Mr. Gershwin has written something for a Jazz orchestra that is really music, not a mechanical box of tricks—such as the dull clowning of Rimsky-Korsakov's Hymn to the Sun that we had earlier in the program of some of the 'original' Jazz compositions we were regaled with."

On December 1, 1924, *Lady, Be Good*, opened. Even prior to this occasion (I have actually recorded November 5, 1922, as the first date on which we discussed these matters) I had a very considerable argument with Gershwin on two grounds: first, I objected to his choice, or easy acceptance, of books, explaining to him frankly that the best music on earth could not stand up against the inept conceptions he was faced with. On this score I made no progress: George was not a perceptive reader of literature. Many of his songs have persisted, divorced from the scores, frequently because Ira Gershwin's lyrics were so sagacious, but the only opera score of his to be revived has been *Porgy and Bess*. What became, perhaps, George's most successful song eventually, "The Man I Love," was unreasonably discarded from several musical plays almost before they opened. On other occasions I urged George to make his own orchestrations. In this direction I was most instrumental, probably *because he himself desired to learn to orchestrate*, and also because I was not the only one of his friends who tried to convince him that this would be a good idea. Eventually George learned to orchestrate very creditably. I believe he made the orchestral arrangements of all his major works after the *Rhapsody*. However, he had no quarrel with Russell Bennett's orchestrations of his musical plays, although toward

23

the end he began to work more closely with him and made many suggestions regarding the creation of certain special effects.

I find many references to George in my diaries of the period and it is interesting to remember that my interest in the Negro began in 1924–25 and that George's interest grew up parallel with mine. We met many of the same people together, attended many of the same parties, concerts and other events in Harlem together, and were equally cognizant of the same phenomena. "On July 18, 1925, Edwin Knopf brought George to his apartment at 150 West Fifty-Fifth Street where he played themes from the future Concerto in F which Walter Damrosch had ordered for production by the Symphony Society of New York." "On July 24, 1925, George dined with us and played some of the themes of the Concerto in F. He has had some of these in his mind for months, as he had intended to use them in Black Belt, but many of them are new. George started this concerto two days ago and has already written five pages." On August 27 of the same year "Alfred and Blanche Knopf gave a party for Noël Coward (who sang He Never Did That to Me and others of his songs of this period). George played several of his tunes, the Rhapsody [with cuts] and a long passage (possibly a complete movement) from the Concerto in F." "On September 2, I encountered George Gershwin at a party chez Edgar Selwyn. The other guests included Noël Coward, Francis de Croisset, Charlie Chaplin, Ann Pennington, Ralph Barton, Lenore Ulric, Walter Wanger, Gilbert Miller, Jo Davidson, Condé Nast, Percy Hammond, etc." In September, George called me to hear him play two movements of the Concerto with Bill Daly at the second piano. In October, "Fania and I met George at a dress rehearsal of Hay Fever. He tells us he has completed the Concerto lacking two bars. Noël has just taken Mae Murray's apartment at 1 West Sixty-Seventh Street and he invites us to come along to a party he is giving. Among the guests were Anita Loos, Julia Hoyt, Muriel Draper, Albert Carroll, Lynn Fontanne, Alfred Lunt, Lenore Ulric, and Eva LeGallienne." "Edwin Knopf and Mary Ellis lived on the floor above us at 150 West Fifty-Fifth Street and on January 8, 1926, Fania and I joined Edwin and George there, just returned from hearing Stravinsky's first concert with the Philharmonic at Carnegie Hall. The evening before George had played for Stravinsky and Laurette Taylor chez the Kohanskis." "On January 17, 1926, we gave an evening party 't which Adele Astaire danced, Marguerite d'Alvarez sang Gershwin songs, Paul Robeson sang Spirituals (especially Little David, Play on Your Harp), James Weldon Johnson recited The Creation, and George played the Rhapsody. Others present [and I give only the names listed in my diary] were Blanche and Alfred Knopf, Miguel Covarrubias, Deems Taylor, Marie Doro, and Otto Kahn." "On March 20, Covarrubias brought in his caricature of George, which I had asked him to draw." Some time during 1924–25 George began to express a desire to write a serious opera. Approaching me, he asked if I had any suggestions for a novel, story, or play he might use as a book. Later I had an idea of my own for such a libretto; but it was not at all what George needed or wanted; finding it presented too many problems and was much too complicated, he rejected it at once. Later he read *Porgy* and decided it was his dish. In 1926 he wrote to DuBose Heyward about this, but the opera was not completed until nine years later, when it opened in Boston at the Colonial Theatre. It was also in 1926 that I encouraged Marguerite d'Alvarez to include jazz songs in one of her programs, following Eva Gauthier's lead. This concert was given, with George Gershwin accompanying the singer, on December 4, 1926, at the Roosevelt Hotel in New York and repeated in Boston on January 26, 1927. On July 26, 1927, George made his first appearance at the Lewisohn Stadium. December 13, 1928, Damrosch conducted the premiere of *An American in Paris* at Carnegie Hall. George began to paint seriously in 1929. On August 26, 1929, he conducted for the first time at the Lewisohn Stadium and also played the *Rhapsody*. On January 29, 1932, Koussevitzky conducted the Boston Symphony Orchestra through the *Second Rhapsody*.

As most of his serious music is referred to in the preceding pages, I will only mention the fact that George was the composer of literally hundreds of popular songs before he was thirty: "I'll Build a Stairway to Paradise" (my favorite among his songs), "Somebody Loves Me," "Fascinating Rhythm," "Swanee," "I Won't Say I Will," "I Got Rhythm," "The Man I Love" are a few of these. Many of them are still popular. Most of his serious music was already in a permanent form. Only *Porgy and Bess* lingered to the last. George died in Hollywood, July 11, 1937.

A few years later I discovered a new occasion to pay my respects to George's memory. I presented my collection of musical scores, records, books, letters, and manuscripts to the Fisk University Library in Nashville, Tennessee, under the generic title: "The George Gershwin Memorial Collection of Music and Musical Literature." The collection has now grown to the point where it is one of the largest musical libraries in the South, containing, as it does, the complete works of Bach, Mozart, Beethoven, Brahms, Palestrina, and Scarlatti, together with compositions, manuscripts, biographical and critical works of and about hundreds of other composers.

N.Y., 1958

THE GERSHWIN YEARS

Morris and Rose Bruskin Gershwin at the time of their marriage. COURTESY IRA GERSHWIN

Arthur, the maid, George, Rose Gershwin, and Ira in a Brooklyn park circa 1900. COURTESY IRA GERSHWIN

Ira Gershwin in 1904. "At the age of six I was promoted from a Chrystie Street kindergarten to 1-A P.S. 20. It was either in 1-A or 1-B that I was taught the alphabet (the teacher was Miss Fagin) by learning the cute sixteen-bar tune that it was set to." COURTESY IRA GERSHWIN

Ira at Brighton Beach in 1912, when he worked for his uncle as a photographer's assistant. COURTESY IRA GERSHWIN

George, Arthur, and Ira, with their cousin, Rose Lagowitz—Coney Island, 1912. COURTESY IRA GERSHWIN

1890-1917

Ira, ca. 1907, aged around ten at his Saturday morning job, working for his uncle, Barney Bruskin, a photographer. The specialty of the house was the making of "ping-pongs," small photos on a strip—six for a quarter—of which this is a sample. Ira greeted customers and went out for sandwiches. GERSHWIN COLLECTION

When Morris Gershovitz, St. Petersburg citizen immigrating to the New World, rushed to the rail of his ship that day in the early 1890s to see the Statue of Liberty, his American troubles began. He had placed in his hatband the address of his uncle—his only American contact—but when he leaned out from the ship, the wind flipped off his hat and dropped it irretrievably into the waters of the Upper Bay. This fillip to an unformed career and embranglement of even the most careful plans foreshadowed what would frequently happen to the man who became memorable by begetting the American Gershwins.

The grandson of a rabbi and the son of a mechanic, Morris Gershovitz had presumably an orderly future before him in Russia. By his later teens he had become interested in the manufacturing of the tops of women's shoes; in his spare time he was developing a reputation for cards and billiards and a fondness for an attractive young girl, Rose Bruskin. These prosperous beginnings derived from his father's having been drafted, at the age of ten, into the service of Czar Alexander II

Ira's earliest
painting, 1911.
COURTESY IRA GERSHWIN

Ira's self-portrait,
after a "While You
Wait" photograph
taken at Coney
Island. The
wrinkled collar? Ira
was so adverse to
stiff ones he
softened his in the
bathtub in a not
completely
successful
experiment.
COURTESY IRA
GERSHWIN

and having served twenty-five years as mechanic to the artillery: this
had given the ex-soldier and his children, as Jews, the right of free
travel and free occupation in Russia. Released from the normal restric-
tions of the ghetto, Yakov Gershovitz settled near St. Petersburg and
lived a relaxed life. But his privileges would not exempt his son, Morris,
from military service. When it seemed certain that he too would have to
serve twenty-five years in the imperial army if he were to achieve any
degree of freedom, Morris slipped away to America.

His mother's brother was a New York tailor, and it was to him that
Morris was traveling when the wind blew his immediate plans away.
There was always to be a plucky matter-of-factness about him, however.
When he disembarked he immediately took a room in the Bowery, got
into a pool game, and won thirty cents. The next morning he was on the
East Side, searching for "Greenstein the tailor." He spoke no English,
but Yiddish and Russian were vernaculars in that polyglot metropolis,
and he was advised to try Brownsville in Brooklyn, a settlement popular
with immigrants. A steam-train ride across Brooklyn Bridge and three
more hours of systematic questioning brought him to his uncle. Out of
such a misdirected beginning he ultimately came to very little money
but a large reputation for whimsicality.

By July 21, 1895, when Morris married Rose Bruskin—who, with

30

her parents, had come to the States some time before—he was a foreman in a factory that made fancy uppers for women's shoes. But it was not a calling to which he listened for long. By 1916 he had moved his gradually increasing family through twenty-eight different residences, because he had moved himself through nearly as many businesses: "restaurants, Russian and Turkish baths, bakeries, a cigar store and pool parlor on the 42nd Street side of what is now Grand Central Station, book-making at the Brighton Beach Race Track for three exciting but disastrous weeks," as Ira later described them. Into this peregrinatory world Ira was born on December 6, 1896; George, September 26, 1898; Arthur, March 14, 1900; and Frances, exactly ten years to the day after Ira.

A favorite residence of the family was the brink of financial disaster. Yet they always dwelt there in style—"never without a maid," according to Rose—and they seemed inured to the possibility that something might sweep them off the cliff into economic oblivion. They carried casualness unusually far: everyone spelled the family name differently— Morris Gershovitz became Gershvin (a form Ira himself adhered to), while George used the name of Gershwin and considered even more drastic revisions. The family did not bother much with orthodox religion; only Ira had a *bar mitzvah*, but it came off impressively: dinner at Zeitlan's on Grand Street for two hundred at two dollars a plate. The family never observed birthdays, with the result that Ira was not sure of the date on which he was born, though he surmised it was "on the sixth or thereabouts." He was less certain of his first name: the parents could not remember what they had christened this, their first child; since everyone called him Izzy, Ira believed his legal name was Isidore. (On applying in 1928 for a passport he discovered it was really Israel.) On all such matters the family remained reluctant to bother with those details that, though they bog down the lives of most people, still assure them that they are part of a functioning world.

Like many Europeans who distrusted banks, the Gershwins crystallized their liquid assets in Rose's diamond ring, and it was Ira's duty to pawn and redeem this ring through the ever-changing ventures of his father; by his early teens he had maneuvered the stone through nearly half a dozen round trips, on each occasion raising approximately $400. Inevitably such a nomadic life built domestic tensions, for the parents were remarkably unlike. George once characterized his father as "a very

The sort of carney scene Ira watched a great deal in his younger years; good preparation for his future tour with Colonel Lagg's Great Empire Shows. GERSHWIN COLLECTION

easy-going, humorous philosopher, who takes things as they come"; his mother was "nervous, ambitious and purposeful":

> She was never the doting type. Although very loving, she never watched every move we made. She was set on having us completely educated, her idea being that if everything else failed we could always become school-teachers. She was against my becoming a musician, as she didn't want me to be a twenty-five-dollar-a-week piano player all my life, but she offered very little resistance when I decided to leave high school to take a job playing the piano for Remick's.

The unique self-sufficiency developed by both Ira and George perhaps is owed to this background. George's incapacity for ever knowing a fully realized and lasting emotional experience with another person probably resulted from it. And Ira's detachment, to an uncommon degree, from the anguishes other men know traces to these days. Artistically there was compensation for this colder independence: both men gained incentive for their own genius as they grew to find their greatest warmth not in personal relationships but through their own creations.

It is important to be aware of this background when we consider the *team* of George and Ira Gershwin. Their collaboration did not result because they were brothers. Having grown up almost emotionally independent of each other, these two Gershwins became a unit only when they responded to each other's talent. During their apprentice years each tried working with a number of other writers; they formed their own partnership only when they began achieving together a success they had not known apart and when they saw how remarkably well they functioned as "the Gershwins." The death of George ended a peculiarly creative relationship, where the brothers made of their name a double dividend for those who took stock in American music; but the quality of Ira's accomplishment since 1937 demonstrates that each had an independent genius.

George said of his pre-piano days "that music never really interested me, and that I spent most of my time with the boys in the street, skating and, in general, making a nuisance of myself." George's nickname was "Cheesecake," because Morris had a bakery. Ira still remembers when, as a pupil in 8A, he had to consult Miss Smith in 6A about George's disciplinary problems. George's energies always sought an explosive

The backyard view from the second-floor flat on Surf Avenue, Coney Island.
GERSHWIN COLLECTION

release. In the summer of 1914 the family moved to Coney Island, the first of their two sojourns there. (The second came in 1915, after the small chain of Morris's restaurants had broken and dropped the Gershwins into bankruptcy.) The sounds of a street fight, rising into their second-story flat that summer, would carry George off impetuously, fighting just to be fighting. He had come to music with a similar abruptness when, in 1904, he stood on Harlem's 125th Street "outside a penny arcade listening to an automatic piano leaping through Rubinstein's *Melody in F*. The peculiar jumps in the music held me rooted." (George told John McCauley in August 1929 that whenever he heard that tune, even then, "he pictures himself in overalls and barefooted outside of this arcade in 125th Street.") Later he kept a musical scrapbook, into which he glued tiny biographical sketches and concert programs; and there were several references to Rubinstein. It was not only the classics that interested George, however; during the periods of the family's Coney Island retirement he hung around outside one cafe in particular where he could listen to the ragtime of Les Copeland.

Ira's red-bearded Grandfather Bruskin, the furrier, as sketched from across the round dining room table one night in the Gershwins' railroad flat on Second Avenue.

In 1910, while living on Second Avenue over Saul Birn's Phonograph Shop, the Gershwins bought their first piano. Ira had been intended as the student, but, as he himself said, "No sooner had the upright been lifted through the window to the 'front-room' floor than George sat down and played a popular tune of the day. I remember being particularly impressed by his left hand"—that distinctive touch that would later be felt in all Gershwin compositions and performances.

George began his pianistic training with neighborhood lady teachers and quickly progressed to a flamboyant Hungarian who catapulted him catastrophically toward the "Overture" to *William Tell*. Of greater aid to his development were the concerts he began to attend, and in 1912 and 1913 he listened to recitals by Leo Ornstein, Efrem Zimbalist, Josef Lhévinne, and Leopold Godowsky. In April 1913 the Beethoven Society Orchestra had its photograph in the New York *World;* although George is not listed as being a member, it is his face that looks out to us from the piano. This P.S. 63 musical group under the direction of Henry Lefkowitz worked through such favorites as Schubert's *Unfinished Symphony* and Dvořák's *Humoresque*—the piece that George earlier at P.S. 25 had seen as "a flashing revelation of beauty" when Max Rosen had played it at the school assembly and "opened the world of music to me." One of the pianists in the Beethoven

33

Society, Jack Miller, was a student of Charles Hambitzer. And Miller introduced George to the man who, according to George, became "the first great musical influence in my life."

If George responded immediately to a genuinely great teacher, Hambitzer instantly saw the potential that lay behind his pupil's unformed ability. Hambitzer wrote his sister, "The boy is a genius, without a doubt. . . . He wants to go in for this modern stuff, jazz, and what not. But I'm not going to let him for a while. I'll see that he gets a firm foundation in the standard music first." This meant Chopin, Liszt, and Debussy, among others, and Hambitzer gave George temporarily the ambition to be a concert pianist. We do not know when George began studying with Hambitzer, but as early as April 13, 1913, he listened to his teacher play the first movement of the Rubinstein D minor concerto in a Sunday-evening concert of the Waldorf-Astoria Orchestra under Joseph Knecht. All recollected impressions of Hambitzer emphasize his remarkable sensitivity and selflessness. Having made his protégé, in George's phrase, "harmony-conscious," he turned him over to Edward Kilenyi for additional lessons in theory. Hambitzer told Kilenyi, "The boy is not only talented, but is uncommonly serious in his search for knowledge of music." Both Hambitzer and Kilenyi had been among the first in this country to champion the cause of Schoenberg and, by awakening in their student an interest in experimentation, suggested that George should build ragtime within classical forms. Although George's first song, "Since I Found You," was an innocuous ballad, his second, "Ragging the Traumerei," (both with lyrics by Leonard Praskins and written around 1913) showed an obvious intention to merge disparate styles. The early death of Hambitzer had an incalculable effect in turning George's thoughts further toward a career as a popular composer instead of as a concert pianist.

To Ira there had come no revelatory moment, as there had to George, of the beauty of one artistic form. Ira has always loved literature; his life has been a fulfillment of his desire to find solitude for reading and writing. When nineteen he reminisced in his journal:

> The first piece of literature I remember reading, outside of the school primary readers, was a nickel novel concerning the "Adventures of Young Wild West. . . ."
> Shortly after, I learned the whereabouts of a laundry store on Broome St., where the boss's son ran a nickel-novel library as a

Charles Hambitzer, George's piano teacher and the most important early musical influence in his life. GERSHWIN COLLECTION

34

sideline. For the return of a novel plus—was it two cents?—one was privileged to upset the piles of literary endeavors, and ransack until some novel attracted or appealed.

Soon I was reading four of them a day: "Fred Fearnot," "Pluck and Luck," the "Alger Series," "The Liberty Boys of '76," "The Blue and the Gray" series, and many others.

His first hard-bound volume, secured around the Christmas of 1906, was Conan Doyle's *A Study in Scarlet*, which Ira, sitting close to the stove on Chrystie Street, read through at least three times.

In October 1913 Ira Gershvin was listed as one of four art editors on the Townsend Harris Hall *Academic Herald*; he published an occasional drawing, but he devoted most of his time to being co-editor (with E. Y. Harburg) of the "Much Ado" column, a feature similar to F. P. Adams' widely admired "Conning Tower." Earlier—and for a smaller circulation (his cousin, Maurice Lagowitz, later Colonel Lagg of Lagg's Empire Shows)—he had prepared a one-page weekly newspaper, *The Leaf*, laboriously hand-printed upon laundry shirt cardboard.

"Inaccurate Conception." Ira's *Fauve* answer to the Armory Show, 1913. GERSHWIN COLLECTION

On September 26, 1914, in C. L. Edson's New York *Mail* column appeared the observation, "Tramp jokes, writes Gersh, are 'bum comedy.'" It was Ira's first publication in a regular newspaper. The following month the sports page of the same daily carried his three-quatrain poem, *Advice to a Colored Pugilist*. From this time on Ira contributed light verse and quips to local journals. He also continued his academic journalism and, in late 1915, ran with Harburg the "Gargoyle Gargles" column in *The Campus*. During this period Ira kept his hand in the Finley Club of Christadora Settlement House on Avenue B; at a club program early in 1914 George played a tango he had written for the occasion. It was his first public appearance as a pianist.

In May 1914, while he was still fifteen, George left the High School of Commerce to become "probably the youngest piano pounder ever employed in Tin Pan Alley" at Jerome H. Remick and Company for $15 a week. It was another remarkable instance when, despite his inexperience, his genuine and innate abilities were recognized. "He played all day, travelled to nearby cities to accompany the song pluggers, [and] was sent to vaudeville houses to report which acts were using Remick songs." It was an engrossing life, but George did not delight in the trips to Atlantic City with other pluggers who often embarrassed him

Must share it--Happiness was born a twin.

—BYRON.

Program

PART ONE

1. Address . . . . President
   Harry Kasper

2. Address . . . . Director
   Fred Reid

3. Piano Solo . . *George Gershvin*

4. Dialogue . . . "The Interview"
   Louis Abramovitz & Abraham Rappaport

5. Vocal Selections *Chas. Rose & George Gershvin.*

6. Recitation . . *The Old Actor's Story*

The program for George's first appearance as a pianist-composer. It took place at the Christadora House at 147 Avenue B, on Saturday evening, March 21, 1914. The occasion was "an entertainment" for the Finley Club, a literary society to which Ira belonged; he also served on the arrangement committee—as Isidore Gershvin. George's "tango" was later recorded by George with Fred Van Eps. Ira remembers it as having begun vaguely like "Stiff Upper Lip." GERSHWIN COLLECTION

George's first published song, 1916.
COURTESY HARRY VON TILZER MUSIC PUBLISHING CO.

George in his teens, not long before he became the "youngest piano pounder in Tin Pan Alley." COURTESY IRA GERSHWIN

with their loud talk and gaudy clothes; and the job offered no encouragement to an aspiring songwriter's own compositions. When George submitted one of his numbers to Remick's, he was flatly told, "You're here as a pianist, not a writer." Despite this rebuff he got "When You Want 'Em, You Can't Get 'Em; When You've Got 'Em, You Don't Want 'Em" (copyrighted May 15, 1916) published that year by the Harry von Tilzer Music Publishing Company, with a lyric by Murray Roth. For this, his first publication, George received $5.00.

The collaboration so profitably begun ended abruptly when one day George and Roth "started kiddingly to wrestle," as Ira explained it. "Both were so shaken up that they never wrote another song together." While working at Remick's, George also built a catalogue of other tunes: "Drifting Along with the Tide" (then called "You're the Witch Who Is Bewitching Me," with a lyric by Lou Paley) and "Nobody but You" owed their melodies to those days; on October 21, 1916, George and Irving Caesar copyrighted "When the Armies Disband." One of these compositions finally became published when Remick's, in 1917, consented to bring out "Rialto Ripples," a rag that George had run up with Will Donaldson.

Occasionally during these years George pumped up his income by going to East Orange, New Jersey, and making six piano rolls for $25. The first of these appeared, apparently, in January 1916, when, for the Perfection Music Company, he recorded Kahn and LeBoy's "Bring Along Your Dancing Shoes" and Morris's "Kangaroo Hop." Two months later, for the same company, he began cutting rolls under the pseudonyms of Bert Wynn and Fred Murtha. In 1917 he was turning them out for the Universal Company; far into the Twenties he continued such recordings, including one of the *Rhapsody in Blue*.

In the meantime the admiration Ira felt for columnist F. P. Adams and the pseudo-seventeenth-century style of "Our Own Samuel Pepys" encouraged him, in September 1916, to begin his own consciously archaic journal, *Everyman His Own Boswell*. (Earlier, Oscar Wilde had asked, "But do you seriously propose that every man should become his own Boswell? . . . Every great man nowadays has his disciples, and it is always Judas who writes the biography.") In his journal Ira assumed a deliberate pose, partly dictated by recollections of the *Yellow Book*, more consciously by the sights seen from the top of the "Conning Tower." Like the records of many literary adolescents, Ira's journal reveals one whose sustained shyness pushed him toward irony as a defense and self-laughter as a shield. The journals were slightly Whitmanesque, slightly reportorial with their conversations overheard; inevitably they were stylized: "Did put on my new greenish mixtured double breasted, English panted, shapely homespun new suit, and quite satisfied." Some began to view the pose as less the part and more the person; in January 1917 George fretted that Ira was not what he used to be. Ira entered in his journal George's fear "that I have become less sympathetic, that friends will leave me as soon as my 'novelty' wears off, that since I 'have become a Beau Brummell and smoke cigarettes.'" The misunderstood gestures were modified, and Ira began to think more seriously about his own writing.

To the young Gershwins in 1916, New York City had, in Scott Fitzgerald's words, "all the iridescence of the beginning of the world." The unsupervised boys wandered Manhattan's streets until early morning, bussed and subwayed up and down the island, and were equally at home in Greenwich Village, Harlem, and the East Side. So George and Ira discovered for themselves the ranges of human personality; unpredictably, because of this latitude allowed them, they both became puritans. Years later George spent more time than he needed to telling sister Frankie to pull her skirt down, and quietly turning over sister-in-law Leonore's dinner napkins so that her lipstick stains would not show. And neither George nor Ira, even as adults in the theatrical world, ever completely adjusted to the concept of the free-and-easy woman.

The 1916–18 diaries of Ira Gershvin chronicle the daily life of a young man who gave his days to the Turkish bath but his nights to occasional evening classes at City College, frequent visits with his friends, and especially vaudeville and the movies. He liked to summarize film plots, to record his impressions of the stars, and to analyze directors' techniques. (Decades later, when Ira began writing for the movies and remained one of their strongest defenders, he was merely again expressing his gratitude for these pleasures given him in the evenings of his youth). The discordant sounds of Europe's war sometimes reverberated in his thoughts, but it was typical of Ira that when he went to bed on November 7, with the newspapers blaring the "defeat" of Wilson, "who kept us out of war," Ira was thinking about the five-dollar bet he had lost—and consoling himself with the knowledge that his father, a Hughes backer, had won. (This was an early indication, by the way, of Ira's life-long attitude toward gambling: he enjoys a bet but seldom gets stirred up by the issues involved.) Thanksgiving fell on November 30 that year, and Ira had the day off from the baths. "To the Century with George and saw the *Century Girl*, a mammoth musical extravaganza. . . . Music by I. Berlin and Victor Herbert or vice versa. Evening: for a steak with Geo. and Art. G. @ Roumanian Restaurant @ 116th St. Violinist & pianist. Made horrible music. Reminded one of a Jewish East Side Wedding Music."

December 16 brought a letter from Harry Botkin, who had been living with his parents in Boston, "informing me of his impending fling at the art circles of N. York. . . . Will be here Xmas Vacation." This

A page from Ira's 1916 diary, describing the life of the Gershwins on the day before George turned eighteen. GERSHWIN COLLECTION

Irving Berlin, whose songs—exemplified by one of George's favorites, "Alexander's Ragtime Band"—were endowed with unusual vitality, a quality George hoped would become characteristic of his own. COURTESY IRVING BERLIN MUSIC CORP.

resumed the close friendship between the Gershwins and "my cousin Botkin, the painter." Harry became one of a trio of Ira, George, and Harry, and they frequently attended musicals and parties together. Harry also drifted into one channel of the music business when in March 1917 he sold a song cover to Remick's for "When Kelly Sang Killarney."

Ira's first theatrical premiere was January 15, 1917, when Kern's *Love O' Mike* opened at the Shubert. "Saw Hey. Broun. Tall. Aristocratic," Ira noted in his diary. He also recorded his introduction that night to Lou and Herman Paley, two brothers who were to have especial meaning for Ira's future. George, of course, had been taking in musicals for a long time; only four days earlier he had gone to the first night of Kern's other January show, *Have a Heart*, which starred Louise Dresser, with whom he would in another year be touring in vaudeville.

The first Gershwin to go on the road in the theater business, however, was neither George nor Ira but sister Frankie. Although she was only ten, she had nevertheless turned into something of a professional dancer. When on May 6, 1917, Ira, George, and Harry went to the Terrace Gardens on 58th Street to see her school's recital, Ira noted "Frances' Russian dance was a riot." The same night Frankie also sang "M-I-S-S-I-S-S-I-P-P-I" and then joined another girl in "a neat little double version of 'So Long, Letty,' very charming indeed." The following day Rose and Frankie took to the road to try out the act for a week in Philadelphia. Later in the month Frankie joined *Daintyland* at $40 a week—a more handsome salary than either George or Ira was to draw

Jerome Kern, who was an important early influence on George. At the wedding of his aunt, Kate Bruskin, to Abe Wolpin, George heard a Kern song, "You're Here and I'm Here" from *The Laughing Husband*, which greatly impressed him in its melodic line and harmonies. COURTESY ASCAP

for some time and one large enough to support comfortably both mother and daughter on the road.

On May 17, 1917, while working at the Lafayette Baths, Ira wrote a short satirical piece called "The Shrine." A week later he had done a whimsical song lyric: "You May Throw All the Rice You Desire; but Please, Friends, Throw No Shoes." Although this later appeared in Don Marquis's column in the New York *Sun*, he was having trouble placing his quips and verse. One Monday in May, at 5 P.M., he sent a contribution to F.P.A. "At 7:45 this morning (Tuesday) I had it again. That certainly beats all return records as far as my stuff is concerned." A month later, however, he was to write: "This morning's 'Tribune' presented in the 'Tower' a 2 line Paragraph which was credited to Gersh. This makes the 2nd contribution in as many years. Think of it!" Late in June he decided to seek a professional opinion on "The Shrine," so he stuck it in the box of Paul M. Potter, the English playwright and adapter of *Trilby*, who lived in the small hotel above the baths. Potter was Ira's first important literary friend, and he suggested that the filler be mailed to the *Smart Set*.

When they took a walk together the following month, Ira remembered that Potter "advised me to learn especially 'your American slang.' Seemed to think that a writer doesn't necessarily have to experience everything he writes about, but by being an attentive listener and observer, can gain a good deal by second hand experience." No creative suggestion Ira received was ever more adhered to. Potter's observation reinforced a conclusion to which Ira's temperament had already brought him: that one could develop talent through speculation, by imagining what was possible and assuming that it was so. George never understood how Ira could become a writer and remain so withdrawn from the world, for George was always one to be stirring the stuff of life into new forms. But Ira's work has proved Potter's theorem and demonstrates what an artist can do with emotions gained through contemplation.

Because of the uncertain direction of his literary career Ira liked to sustain himself through routine occupations. In 1916 and 1917 he had worked as desk clerk, first at the St. Nicholas Baths on 111th Street, and then at the Lafayette Baths downtown, each in turn being one of his father's unfortunate investments. After the Lafayette Baths, New York's oldest, had been surrendered to creditors, Ira looked for a job that would not evaporate so unexpectedly. He tried getting into the advertising department of Gimbel's, but unsuccessfully. Then, late in September 1917, he took a $15 a week job at Altman's, in the receiving department. On November 14 he revived his ironic style to depict one of the larger moments in his life:

> Evening: opened the door, fresh, stale rather, from the subway. Entered the flat into the dining room. "Izzy, I got good news for you," said Mamma. "Yes?" I asked easily. "What is it?" "This letter," and I was given a letter from the "Smart Set" saying they liked my little filler, would send me a cheque and wanted to read more of my stuff. I read it and felt quite elated but nothing of the supreme delight I had always coupled in imagination with the realization of my "fondest dreams"—a real acceptance. . . . It was a lucky strike and it will take lots of time and patience before is accepted another, should I immediately bombard, wherefore I must bide my time and try to attain a certain standard and distinction in all I contribute.
>   Well spoken, Rollo!

The next day brought "the munificent honorarium of 1 simoleon from the 'Smart Set' for 'The Shrine,'" the check being "full payment of all rights in America and Great Britain. . . ." (In later years H. L. Mencken explained: "The *Smart Set*, in those days, had little money in its till, but though we were thus forced to pay badly we took pride in paying almost instantly, and to the younger authors of the country that was something, if perhaps not much.")

On November 16 George told Ira that there was a possible opening on the reviewing staff of the New York *Clipper*. Ira went to the paper and met the editor, Paul C. Sweinhart, who put to him the riddle, "What's the difference between a sketch and a skit?" To one who had spent as much time at vaudeville as Ira had it was a simple test. Sweinhart closed the interview by reflecting, "You come to see me Thursday in the lunch hour and maybe I'll give you a little thing to cover Thursday night." What Ira was given to cover was, among other acts, "Wanda and Seals" at the Audubon. The aspiring critic wrote a total of three casual reviews of vaudeville acts—all without pay—before this new position did its own vanishing act.

1890–1917

Of more interest to Ira's future were his writing in December "A chorus for a melody of Geo.'s 'You Are Not the Girl,'" and working on others, unnamed. He had not yet come to think that these idle song lyrics would lift him out of the baths (to which he was soon to return) and onto the crest of the popular song. Indeed, he closed 1917 by polishing up some other verses: "I am working on a series of 'Rialto Nursery Rhymes' and I sincerely hope, oh so sincerely, that 'Vanity Fair,' which is the periodical I have designated for their destination and acceptance, thinks as 'Smart Set' thought." *Vanity Fair* did not, however. A song Ira was soon to undertake with George was to carry him farther than he expected, and he began to think of himself as a songwriter—to his amused astonishment.

THE SHRINE

By Bruskin Gershwin

FASCINATED, he would stand before it, glorying. At such times, a sublime shivery sensation . . . an incomprehensive wonder at the beauty of it all. Reverent before it, he felt invigorated with the spirit of eternal youth and happiness. Such soul absorbing devotion to the embodiment of an ideal was unprecedented. . . .

And one day it fell and lay shattered in a thousand sharp, jagged fragments.

Panic-stricken, ashen-hued, he was scarcely able to mutter, "Gawd! Seven years' bad luck!"

Ira's first published piece, written in May 1917 and published in the February 1918, issue of the Mencken-Nathan *Smart Set*. COURTESY IRA GERSHWIN

Received check for $1.00
——————
the first

During all of this time George's career moved at greater velocity. The pressure for new musicals, hastily concocted and quickly forgotten, forced Sigmund Romberg in 1916 to accept some assistance on a new Shubert production, *The Passing Show of 1916*—now remembered only for its introduction of the Van Alstyne and Gus Kahn interpolation, "Pretty Baby." George had taken five completed choruses to Romberg, and it was agreed that one of them would serve. Romberg put down his name as collaborator, Harold Atteridge set a lyric to it, and "Making of a Girl" (copyrighted June 27, 1916, and brought out by G. Schirmer) became George's second publication and the first to be associated with the stage. By mid-January 1917 he had picked up his royalties: slightly over seven dollars.

On Saturday, March 17, 1917, George gave up his job as a song plugger "in order to be able to study unhindered by the time taken at Remick's." So Ira commented at the time. In later years George said he quit because he wanted "to be closer to production music—the kind Jerome Kern was writing." He probably would not have so abruptly exchanged a certain, if uninspiring, financial security for the tenuous future as a theatrical composer, but certain of his friends had encouraged his belief that he had a genuine talent for composition, and now he wanted to see if it was so.

Sunday evening, May 27, George took Ira to call upon the Paleys, a social visit that brought together George's few devoted admirers in what was to be a lasting personal friendship; these people also formed the first important creative circle in which he was to move. Lou warmly welcomed both brothers and introduced Ira to Emily Strunsky, whom Ira immediately recorded as being "a charming miss"—an opinion that Lou himself obviously shared when, three years later, he married her. George had gotten to know the Paley brothers through Herman, who, as composer of "Billy" and "Cheer Up, Father, Cheer Up, Mother," was frequently around Remick's. Herman Paley was no ordinary Tin Pan Alley composer; a college graduate, he had studied composition under Edward MacDowell and had continued his training under Hambitzer and Kilenyi. He clearly was the sort of composer who would interest George.

If George was stimulated by Lou and Herman Paley with their talk of music, he also drew comfort and love from Emily Paley, who constitutes in herself a legend of loveliness. Ira and Lou, with their bookish

interests (Lou was an English teacher who also wrote song lyrics), became immediate friends, and Ira went away from that first evening and
duly wrote in his journal Lou's thoughts on the current young writers
around the columns—everyone from Morrie Ryskind to Newman
Levy.

This 1917 Lou and Herman Paley apartment at 19 West 8th Street
was the second of several Paley households that became homes-away-
from-home for George. The earliest of these George had come to
around 1915, while he was working at Remick's and studying with Hambitzer—this was the Paley apartment on Seventh Avenue, near 112th
Street.

"It was one of those big houses—at the time it was supposed to be
quite fancy," recalls Mabel Pleshette, a niece of the Paleys and one of
the members of the numerous (eventually no less than ten assorted
Paleys and Pleshettes) household. Perhaps they provided George with
some of the warmth he did not get at home. Certainly, for a budding
songwriter the atmosphere was stimulating. There was plenty of talk,
music and admiration. Herman Paley was a successful composer of
songs and one of his collaborators was Al Bryan, also a frequent visitor
(he wrote the words to such songs as—though not to music by Herman
—"I Didn't Raise My Boy to Be a Soldier" and "Come, Josephine, in My
Flying Machine").

Mabel, who had also studied with Hambitzer, recalls that Herman too
"played beautifully—it was a delight to hear him. And he really did have
a nose for talent. He knew it, he spotted it all the time." He had certainly "spotted" the young piano pounder at Remick's.

The Paley *ménages* thus provided George with an outlet for his gifts
and the appreciation that nourished them. Later, in 1920, when Lou
married Emily Strunsky, George gained another such warm setting; five
years later, when Mabel—who would remain a lifetime friend—married
Robert Schirmer, of the music-publishing family, there would be yet
another.

From the beginning the Paleys more than casually admired George;
it was largely their unsolicited and always-present defense that inevitably made of "Gershwin" a fighting word. Fellow musicians who studied diligently, preparing for the concert stage, resented the notion that a
young upstart, a pleasant but untutored kid, could ever be the "genius"
the Paleys asserted. They pointed out that George played ragtime in- 45

stead of the classics—and whoever heard of a ragtime composer being a "genius"? Parties at the Paleys began deteriorating into intellectual brawls: Emily dissolving into tears, Lou and Herman arguing hotly with the unconverted. Characteristically, George was indifferent to the campaigns of both his friends and his critics.

But George was not indifferent to the persuasion of Lou Paley's lyrics. Although some of the songs they wrote together were relyricized by others when they went into the *Scandals* (Lou was particularly modest about his own work and always encouraged George to do with it as he wished), there remain George Gershwin-Lou Paley collaborations that have been kept untouched. Like newly opened time capsules they release the air of another era and we can feel George's emerging talent as he worked with that witty, bookish man. One of those songs is the super-patriotic sextet, "We're Six Little Nieces of Our Uncle Sam," that was their party song in World War I. The eight-page manuscript works in musical allusions to "Over There" and "The Marseillaise," while Lou's lyric has the girls agreeing

> We think it better to
> Despatch a letter to
> A cigaret or two
> And sweater to—the Boys—
>
> We've got a notion to
> Sail o'er the ocean to
> The Big Commotion—Oh! the blow we'll hand the foe
> Over there—Over there—Over there—Over there—

Around the same time Lou provided George with a lyric that pointed out

> There is something peculiar
> About the ragtime of America
> OO-la—Oo—la-la-la
> This funny jazz musique
> It make me say
> "Encore—O kiss me queeck and right away"
> From the head down to the feet
> I start a motion indiscreet

Shake my shoulders—both my knees
Even shake my "La Chemise"
O! There is something peculiar
About the ragtime of America
     Hula—la—la

By permission of Emily Paley

1890–
1917

The most familiar of Lou's works with George remains "Something About Love." In 1919 that imperishable song was interpolated in the score of *The Lady in Red* and was sung to critical acclaim by Adele Rowland and Donald MacDonald; but the show lasted only six weeks, and the song was not again given a theatrical chance until seven years later. In 1926, when Fred and Adele Astaire took *Lady, Be Good* to London and there reduplicated its New York success, "Something About Love" was interpolated in that score and was published in England under a 1926 copyright.

Today, audiences best know "Something About Love" through its progeny. For the concluding declension of that ballad fathered "He Loves and She Loves." Isaac Goldberg attributed the new creation to George's "characteristic keenness for salvaging the happy thoughts of his youth." Emily Paley, wife of the lyricist of "Something About Love" and sister-in-law of the lyricist of "He Loves and She Loves," explains the circumstances of the recast phrase:

> I seem to remember all of us sitting around and George at the piano saying to Lou that he would like to use "Something About Love" for a special spot and would Lou mind if he used it with Ira. I can hear Lou saying "Of course, George, do whatever you want with it." Ira was there and they began to work on it. Although I don't remember Ira saying anything to Lou, recalling the spirit of the time and Ira's way of working and singing certain phrases over and over again, I can hear him singing that phrase over and over again. The phrase was so right it just naturally happened. Lou was delighted that Ira liked it well enough to keep it. As simple as that.

George's talent poured forth so generously and so independently he never worried about either "saving himself" or "justifying his work." Doing without complaint whatever came to hand, he did the best he

47

could. As for the difference between ragtime and classical, unquestionably he could make more money as a popular performer than as a potential concert artist; and he never totally ignored money. Yet he had such ability at the piano that Josef Hofmann, the hero of the prodigies, described it as "a fine pianistic talent, with a firm, clear, good command over the keyboard." Although during the summer of either 1914 or 1915 when George played duets at a hotel in the Catskills with Jack Diamond, a violinist, he got only $5.00 a week, he later made more money when he performed at parties with Fred Van Eps, the banjo player. And there was even a three- or four-week stint in 1917 when he joined a small combination at a Brooklyn night club.

George also developed ability as a theatrical accompanist: though his plans to play for Mabel Berra at Proctor's Fifth Avenue Theatre in August 1917 collapsed when she—in Ira's enigmatic term—"procrastinated," on Labor Day that year he made a public appearance. Ira went with Harry Botkin

> to see Rita Gould at Proctors 58th St. Theatre. Her accompanist being no other than George Gershvin, alias George Wynne. . . . Her songs: "Sweet Emalina, My Gal," "[Shake Hands with] Mr. Jazz Himself," "Why Did You Make Me Love You" [more likely: "What Did You Let Me Fall in Love with You For"] and a patriotic number ["Send Him Away with a Smile"]. Her accompanist played thoroughly in accord with her presentations. His solo was the "Desecration Rag" at the 1st performance, where too long, was substituted at the 2nd performance "California Sunshine."

Eddie Weber had been the accompanist for this twelve-minute act when it opened the beginning of August; the piano solos were called for by Miss Gould's rather spectacular staging: "each [song being] accompanied by a costume change made in remarkably short time," according to *Variety*.

By the middle of October "Geo. continues working at the 'Century Theatre' as rehearsal pianist" for $35 a week. The show was *Miss 1917*, which opened November 5, 1917. George's job as rehearsal pianist evidently began in July and though he had to run through the same numbers repeatedly, he kept from getting bored by imperceptibly tricking up the arrangements and making subtle improvisations of them. The resultant "refreshening" of the music kept the drilling chorus on its toes,

Vivienne Segal, who sang "You-oo Just You" and "There's More to the Kiss . . ." at the Century Theatre. COURTESY MUSEUM OF THE CITY OF NEW YORK

and George became a favorite of management. "He works quite hard," Ira noted at the time, "but comes in contact with such notables as Jerome Kern, Victor Herbert, P. G. Wodehouse, Ned Wayburn, Cecil Lean and wife, Margot Kelly, Vivienne Segal, Lew Fields, *et al.*" Despite the impressive cast and illustrious authorship, *Miss 1917* became the miss of the year and closed after only forty-eight performances. (Of its opening night *Variety* wrote: "The performance started weakly and finished worse, at about 12:20. It was an easy matter to identify those who paid for their tickets. They remained for the end.")

When *Miss 1917* began her brief commercial life, George ended his duties as rehearsal pianist. But his salary of $35 a week continued as he made a quiet transition to becoming accompanist for the singers at the Century Sunday concerts, which began November 11. The first of these was a stellar affair, with Cecil Lean, Eddie Cantor, George White, Ann Pennington, Fanny Brice, Van and Schenck, and Bert Williams; like the weekday show they replaced, however, the concerts began badly when Will Rogers appeared on opening night to pass the hat for charity—and automatically emptied half the house.

At the November 18 concert George played for Arthur Cunningham. The following Sunday "Geo. played for Vivienne Segal who took him out for a bow." She sang "There's More to the Kiss than the X-X-X" and "You-oo Just You," both songs George had done with Irving Caesar; early in December Remick's bought the second of the two numbers but did not publish it until the following year. On December 6, at the Cocoanut Grove Roof of the Century Theatre, an all-Spanish revue opened to the music of Quinito Valverde. It lasted only thirty-three performances, but for approximately half of them George served as orchestra pianist.

Clearly George's career was moving faster than Ira's. The distant war might disrupt their lives, of course. Among the immigrants who had come to the U.S.A. as refuge from service in the armies of the Czar there was little comprehension of those idealists who joined the Lafayette Escadrille or went abroad to drive ambulances. Ira, however, was of an age when he must think somewhat seriously about military service; on June 12, 1917, he registered for the state census, an action that made him eligible for the draft. Within another sixteen months he seemed to be on his military way:

In Oct. 1918 I was to go to Camp Spartenburg (in one of the Carolinas—I don't remember whether N. or S.). I was really looking forward to the trip when I reported (clutching the six pairs of sox we were told to bring along) at the Public Library on 145th Street from which we were to go to Penn Station. We waited around a bit and then were informed that because of a flu epidemic at the camp our trip was postponed a month. A month later I reported again. It was early afternoon. This time I was told to go home and wait for a telephone call at 6 o'clock as something was in the air. To this day they haven't called me. Yes, you guessed it. The date was Nov. 11, 1918—the day of the Armistice.

When George, while the family lived on 144th Street, got to wondering if he too might not have to sign up, he bought himself a saxophone and holed himself up in a closet until he had become proficient at it; he determined that if he went to war he could play the tune the others marched to.

But, as it turned out, George did not see military service either, and the war seldom inconvenienced the brothers. Ira wrote at the end of 1917 that George "is writing songs at present with Lou Paley and Caesar and myself (a couple), and Praskins also." The American dream sometimes enfolds the most unsuspecting people and turns them into legends for the rest of us. "In America everybody is but some are more than others," wrote Gertrude Stein. As we watch George and Ira Gershwin in 1918 make, for the first time, a tentative appearance as collaborators, we shall be seeing once more the development of a legend: Two young men who came from a land where everybody is. But they were to be more than others.

An early shot of Tin Pan Alley, on 28th Street just off Fifth Avenue, circa 1916–17. George worked first as a Remick's piano pounder and Ira worked fleetingly for the *Clipper*. COURTESY MUSIC PUBLISHERS HOLDING CORPORATION

1918-1923

"Some snap," Ira commented in his journal when George, early in February 1918, joined the staff of the T. B. Harms Company. George was hired as a composer; there were to be no plugging chores, no piano pounding in small cubicles. The one and only task was for George to show up occasionally and to come forth from time to time with a song.

Harry Askins, who had been the *Miss 1917* company manager, greatly impressed with George's musicianship and the songs Miss Segal had sung, found the opportunity to speak to Max Dreyfus about a young composer who "was going places." Dreyfus, with his customary uncanny perceptiveness (further proved by his earlier sponsorship of Jerome Kern, and later, of Richard Rodgers, Vincent Youmans, and other bright songwriting talents) took George into Harms, thereby furnishing him with an outlet for his expanding but still not much published portfolio. In fact George, then nineteen, had three published songs to his credit: "When You Want 'Em . . . ," "You-oo Just You," and "Making of a Girl"—this last, according to Harold Atteridge's lyric, is accomplished by clothes.

53

The elite of Tin Pan Alley about the time the Gershwins were planning
their own election. Left to right: Jerome Kern, Louis A. Hirsch, A. Baldwin
Sloane, Rudolph Friml, Oscar Hammerstein I (at the piano), Alfred Robyn,
Gustave A. Kerker, Hugo Felix, John Philip Sousa, Lesley Stewart, Ray-
mond Hubbell, John Golden, Silvio Hein, and Irving Berlin. COURTESY
ASCAP

Before signing with Harms, George had already committed himself
to a tour in vaudeville with Louise Dresser, one that turned out to be his
first extensive taste of what might be called the Big Time. The act,
which was made up of recitations and songs by Miss Dresser, opened at
the Riverside. Ira noted in the journal that she sang "My Gal Sal," by
Paul Dresser (who was not related to Louise but was the brother of
Theodore Dreiser), "Down by the Erie," from *Cohan's Revue of 1916*,
Kern's "It's a Sure Sign," from *Have a Heart*, and Herman Paley's
"Cheer Up, Father, Cheer Up, Mother." Though George had no solos,
he did accompany Miss Dresser in all her numbers.

Leaving New York, the duo barnstormed through Boston, Baltimore
(where George had a piano put into his room and practiced "inces-
santly"), and finally Washington, D.C. In the capital, during Preparedness Week, the week of March 4, Miss Dresser and George appeared at
Keith's Theatre on a program attended by President Wilson. Honored
by the presidential attendance, Miss Dresser and George just managed
to march in a Preparedness parade. Years later, Louise Dresser remembered that tour—particularly "Georgie's dislike of 'My Gal Sal'—and I
knew it, but oh! how he played it. There were times when I almost forgot the lyrics listening to Georgie trying to make that trite melody
sound like a beautiful bit of music. It wouldn't have surprised me one
bit had he banged the piano one day and walked off the stage. I wouldn't

54

Louise Dresser, a photograph taken when she and George appeared in Washington, D.C. Earlier Paul Dresser had written "My Gal Sal" for her, and it had now become her programmatic signature. Throughout his life George remained devoted to Miss Dresser, but he could never abide that song. COURTESY LOUISE DRESSER

Ira begins to work on a
song lyric in the baths.
GERSHWIN COLLECTION

St. Nicholas Baths
RUSSIAN and TURKISH

FOR
LADIES
AND
GENTLEMEN

LENOX ARCADE
LENOX AVE. & 111th ST.

NEW YORK,   191

Folk Song   2nd Verse

The Folk song hailing from foreign shore
~~Reflect a~~ traditional ~~~~ lore
They may be songs that you can't forget
They may be distinctive yet —
They lack a something - a certain snap
The tempo tickle with that makes you tap
The invitation ~~vaguette~~
And leave the rest to Fate
A baggy refrain anytime
Sends me a message sublime

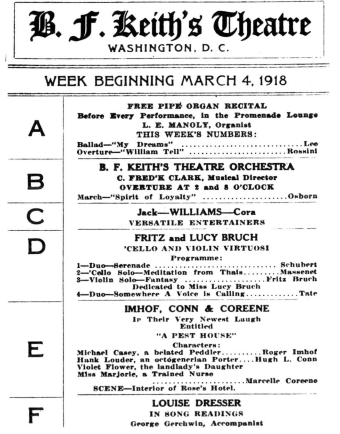

B. F. Keith's Theatre
WASHINGTON, D. C.

WEEK BEGINNING MARCH 4, 1918

A
FREE PIPE ORGAN RECITAL
Before Every Performance, in the Promenade Lounge
L. E. MANOLY, Organist
THIS WEEK'S NUMBERS:
Ballad—"My Dreams" .... Lee
Overture—"William Tell" .... Rossini

B
B. F. KEITH'S THEATRE ORCHESTRA
C. FRED'K CLARK, Musical Director
OVERTURE AT 2 and 8 O'CLOCK
March—"Spirit of Loyalty" .... Osborn

C
Jack—WILLIAMS—Cora
VERSATILE ENTERTAINERS

D
FRITZ and LUCY BRUCH
'CELLO AND VIOLIN VIRTUOSI
Programme:
1—Duo—Serenade .... Schubert
2—'Cello Solo—Meditation from Thais......Massenet
3—Violin Solo—Fantasy ....Fritz Bruch
Dedicated to Miss Lucy Bruch
4—Duo—Somewhere A Voice is Calling............Tate

E
IMHOF, CONN & COREENE
In Their Very Newest Laugh
Entitled
"A PEST HOUSE"
Characters:
Michael Casey, a belated Peddler.........Roger Imhof
Hank Louder, an octogenerian Porter....Hugh L. Conn
Violet Flower, the landlady's Daughter
Miss Marjorie, a Trained Nurse
........................Marcelle Coreene
SCENE—Interior of Rose's Hotel.

F
LOUISE DRESSER
IN SONG READINGS
George Gerchwin, Accompanist

The Preparedness Week program at
which President Wilson heard Louise
Dresser, accompanied by her "Georgie." COURTESY LOUISE DRESSER

have blamed him too much—but that lovable, shy lad wouldn't have done such a thing."

Upon his return from the Keith tour—still an unpublished Harms composer, though with a few songs already in the publisher's files—George took several jobs as a rehearsal pianist. The first show was *Rock-a-Bye Baby*, another by Kern, which opened in New York on May 22, 1918. During its out-of-town tryout George and Kern became quite friendly and George learned the word game Kern called "Guggenheim," a rather tricky contest somewhat difficult to describe. Kern was also impressed by George and offered to help him when he was ready to do his first show.

Another rehearsal-pianist job George had about this time was with the *Ziegfeld Follies of 1918*, then in preparation at the New Amsterdam Roof Garden. In another decade he was to compose songs for a star of the *Follies*, Marilyn Miller—and for Ziegfeld. Meanwhile he kept busy playing the tunes of Louis A. Hirsch.

Harms published its first Gershwin song, "Some Wonderful Sort of Someone," around September 1918. It immediately caught the fancy of Nora Bayes, who wanted it for her pending *Look Who's Here*. The full score was by A. Baldwin Sloane, but special numbers were interpolated into the customary mid-point "concerts." When the show opened at the Broadhurst on October 24, 1918, now titled *Ladies First*, another Gershwin—Ira—was represented for the first time in the annals of the American lyric theater.

George at work for "Mr. Max." GERSHWIN COLLECTION

Having given up his not very elevating job at Altman's ("Saturday March 2nd. Said GoodBye to the firm of B. Altman & Co."), Ira returned to the St. Nicholas Baths, where he had time at least to jot down song ideas between steamings: "If You Only Knew What I Thought of You, You'd Think a Little More of Me," "You're the Treasure I Treasure," and one that he and Lou Paley and George were considering, "Beautiful Bird." "Hope it turns out to be a 2nd 'Poor Butterfly,'" he notes in his journal. Another title sounded promising, "It's Such a Lovely Day for Love." But they were merely titles.

To the family Ira seemed a floating soul; he who had begun as the family scholar was now the drifter, haunting the movies and reading. "I read without plan or purpose. To tell the truth, I was at a complete loss, and I didn't care." George, on the other hand, who had once seemed destined in boyhood to delinquency and an uncertain future, was now a successful composer for "Mr. Max" at a salary of $35 a week, plus an expectancy of a royalty of three cents per copy for each accepted song.

Languishing at the baths, Ira kept his own counsel and his journal, where, the first week of June 1918, he set down with characteristic guying tone, and not without philosophic resignation, the start of an early but not the first of an all-Gershwin collaboration: "Writing songs for musical comedy consumption (embryo m. comedies, that is) certainly gives me remarkable practice in applied penmanship. I had an idea that 'American Folk Song' might be suitably developed to be classed in that category we'll call m.c. songs. Awright. Well & good & proper and unspeakably, ineffably nice. So I started on the chorus. I wrote one. Discarded it. Wrote another. Started a third. Waste-basketed all. Finally after several sporadic starts came to some agreement with myself somewhat on this fashion.

The Great American Folk Song is a rag
A mental jag.
Captures you with a pure melodic strain.
Its aboriginal odd refrain
Has been innoculated
With an ultra syncopated
Rhythm
And with 'em

There's a happy, snappy, don't care a rappy sort of
I don't know what to call it.
But it makes you think of Kingdom Come.
You jazz it
As it
Makes you hum.
Concert singers say that they despise it.
Hoary critics never eulogize it.
Still—it's our national, irrational folk song
It's a masterstroke song
It's a rag.

1918–
1923

Courtesy Ira Gershwin

"Not good, not bad. Passable with a good rag refrain. Geo. liked it. So we sat down on, (at, rather) the piano & Geo. started something. Something sounded good so we kept it. It was a strain for the 1st 2 lines. That in our possession we went along and Geo. developed the strain along legitimate or illegitimate (if you prefer) rag lines and with a little editing here & there the chorus, musical, stood forth in all its gory. But unhappily the musical lines were of different lengths from the lyric, so after having sweated & toiled & moiled over 20 or so different versions, it now devolves upon me to start an entirely new one keeping the 1st 2 lines as a memento of a tussle strenuous and an intimation of a struggle heroic to materialize."

The more or less final version, with further changes—even Max Dreyfus had suggested that "aboriginal" was not the right word and Ira obliged by substituting "old traditional"—was sung for the first time at a tryout of *Ladies First* at the Trent Theater in Trenton, New Jersey. To hear his newborn in its first public performance, Ira took the afternoon off from the baths to attend the audition. He arrived in New Jersey poetically attired in a self-designed vesture consisting of purple shirt, dark blue knitted tie, and a mottled green tweed suit (with European-styled horizontal pockets in the front of the trousers). But this aesthetic apparition had somehow disembarked at the wrong station—Princeton Junction. Too shy to ask directions, Ira arrived at the Trent Theater only after a detour through Princeton and a wild trolley ride through the rugged New Jersey terrain. To hear his own creation sung in a real show was worth the travail and travel.

But eventually "The Real American Folk Song" was dropped from the show during the New York run and reached publication only some forty years later. Across an early version of the song Ira scrawled, "Too much like an essay." A typical self-criticism, for even after making numerous variants of a lyric he continued to appraise a song with dis-

Nora Bayes, the vaudeville headliner, who brought the Gershwins to Broadway when she put "The Real American Folk Song" in *Ladies First*. COURTESY MUSEUM OF THE CITY OF NEW YORK

comfort and not without misgivings, parting with it only under pressure and protest.

When *Ladies First* went on a six-week tour, George went along as accompanist for Nora Bayes. It was not a very happy or compatible combination. Miss Bayes was a stormy personality as well as the star; she could do no wrong. So whatever did go wrong was generally laid to George. The climax came when Miss Bayes suggested to George that he change the ending of one of his songs—a favor, she was quick to add, tendered her by Berlin and Kern.

But not, it seems, by Gershwin. George returned to New York in an agitated mood. This resulted in the main from his battle with Miss Bayes; but also, along the way, he learned of the royalties being collected by composer Sloane. Mere interpolation was not enough; George was ambitiously out for greater returns aesthetically, financially, and in terms of personal prestige. It was "m. comedy" he wanted despite the uncertainties so amply proved by the *Miss 1917* fiasco.

In the office at Harms, Max Dreyfus had good news for George: a musical comedy and, while it would not require a full score, there was room for more material than the usual interpolations. This first Gershwin musical comedy was less than a triumph. Though in later years George tended to forget about it, he did manage, once, to recall some of the facts of this incipient, tentative venture into the magical world of musical comedy.

"Several months after I signed up with T. B. Harms a chap named Perkins came to Mr. Dreyfus and said he wanted to produce a revue. Mr. Dreyfus, who always encouraged young producers, offered to help Mr. Perkins by giving him an advance and offering to pay for the orchestrations for the show. He also told Perkins about a young composer he had signed up recently and wondered if it would not be a good opportunity for him.

"To make a long story short, I got the job.

"Perkins had brought some songs and effects from Paris and wanted me to write additional songs for his revue. We got together, Perkins and I, and wrote five songs, for which he wrote the lyrics [Ira also worked on some of them].

"Mr. Perkins, who was a friend of Joe Cook—the comedian—induced Cook and his vaudeville troupe to appear in the show. With Joe Cook and myself, and about $1500 in cash, Mr. Perkins set up shop and went into rehearsal. The rest of the cast consisted of a Clef Club orchestra of about twenty-five colored musicians, a bicycle act, Sibyl Vane and one or two other people, with no chorus."

Half Past Eight, an inaccurate title as it turned out, opened at the Empire Theatre in Syracuse, N.Y., on Monday, December 9, 1918. Perkins was particularly jubilant because one organization had bought out the first night for $800.

"*Half Past Eight*," George continued, "had come to its premiere—the curtain went up at a quarter to nine—the first act was over at nine thirty. Intermission of half an hour and the second act started. The final curtain rang down at a quarter of eleven—not much of a show from the standpoint of running time, you must admit."

The audience agreed, for the curtain came down to hisses from the house. And the press was equally critical with the consensus best expressed by *Variety:* "$2 SHOW NOT WORTH WAR TAX," read the headline though it was pointed out that "Sybil Vane, who sings four delightful songs, is . . . not to blame for the poor entertainment."

George continues the narrative of the fate of the show: "On Wednesday afternoon—the first matinee—some of the cast began to worry

George around the time of *Half Past Eight*. GERSHWIN COLLECTION

about not getting paid at the end of the week. One of the acts refused to go on unless they collected. I happened to walk back-stage at the moment, dressed in a blue suit and unshaven. Perkins rushed up to me and said, 'You've got to go on—one of the acts just refused to appear and we must have something to go on while we make a change of scene.'

" 'What will I do?

" 'Play some of your hits.'

"I should loved to have played my hits—except that I didn't have any.

"But I walked on the stage to a very small and innocent audience, and made up a medley right on the spot of some of my tunes. The audience must have thought it very queer. I finished my bit and walked off—without a hand!

"Another funny incident happened in connection with the show. It was advertised as having a Broadway chorus. There was no chorus in the show so I, being the ripe age of around nineteen-and-a-half, suggested to Perkins that in the finale of the show, we send all the comedians out dressed in Chinese pajamas, holding umbrellas which would hide their faces from the audience. The audience would then say, 'Ah, here's the chorus'—and, at least would keep their seats until the finale was over."

But George, whose innocence equaled the audience's, hadn't reckoned with the management's enforced frugality. Perkins had bought cheap paper umbrellas and the Gershwin-inspired finale was, shall we say, a little spoiled for the boys from Syracuse when three of the umbrellas failed to open.

George fared a little better. "I managed to get my fare back to New York and the show closed on Friday night of that week. It was good experience for me and, anyway, I got a thrill on seeing on the billboards, 'Music by George Gershwin.' "

By the spring of the following year, May 1919, he was to experience a similar but more substantial thrill from the same legend on the billboards heralding the successful musical, *La-La-Lucille!*, his first full-scale show. It was produced by Alex A. Aarons, who advised George not to take up Kern's long-standing offer to help on the first musical. Aarons was put out over an action by Kern that the producer had interpreted as a snub. George, in complying with Aarons's orders, only succeeded in making Kern angry at him. This estrangement ended by 1922, when Kern announced that he would retire and present George with his unfulfilled show contracts (neither of which he did). In one of his more ungracious moments, Kern said of George, "And here's Gershwin, who showed a lot of promise." Ira, who witnessed this rudeness, alway wished he had replied, "And here's Kern, who promised a lot of shows."

A happier professional friendship began for George early in 1919 when Irving Berlin considered changing his own publishing affiliation. Berlin had recently responded to the Russian Revolution with "The Revolutionary Rag," and he took its lead-sheet to Max Dreyfus, thinking that perhaps Harms would be a better firm for him. George Gershwin was around the office at the time, and Dreyfus called upon him to give the rag a run-through. Berlin remembers: "He sent this kid in. I couldn't hear my own tune—but it was brilliant." Clearly George was up to his old harmonics and plugging a number—even to its own

MAURICE B. LAGG
General Agent

HERMAN AARONS
General Manager

ROBERT H. LESLEY
Sec.-Treasurer

HIGH CLASS SHOWS

MONSTER RIDING DEVICES

Lagg's Great Empire Shows

SENSATIONAL FREE ATTRACTIONS

ROYAL ITALIAN CONCERT BAND

A World's Fair on Wheels

We do not tolerate
Immoral Shows or Gambling
Devices

Every Show on Midway for Ladies and
Children as well as for the
Gentlemen

Ladies and Gentlemen
at all times and in
all places

We Please all the Committees
Letters of Recommendations from
all of them.

OUR MOTTO
TREAT EVERYBODY SQUARE

Look us over, you will be
glad you did

Ira, now working as treasurer in his cousin's carnival, writes about *his* first tour. GERSHWIN COLLECTION

```
                                        9 P.M.Sun.July 6th'19
    EN ROUTE East Pittsburgh,Pa.

    Since the law prohibits my using anything
stronger than 2.75,my overflow of affection
will have to content itself with
    Dear Moxie,
             as an initial greeting.(Notice re-
markable self-restraint in not indulging in any
variation of"spirits").
    I've grown so accustomed to the speech
of the Punks (foreigners)in this part of the coun-
try,that the first question that shapes itself is,
Moxie(my love),how are you feel?
    The parenthesis is my own.
    Oh,how I miss you,dear old town of
mine.(You'll pardon my jumping from topic to top-
ic,but emotion surges strongly within me.)
    This is quelque helluva town.Here it
is Sunday,and the three movie palaces are closed
as tightly as Frank Tinney's purse is reputed to
be.Talk of a feller needing a friend!
    ****Of course all the girls in the '49
show are just dying to fall into my arms,but Hell!
as sec-treas of this outfit the bosses told me
they expect a certain dignity of bearing,an exter-
nal contempt     for the charming vices of the
Sirens,so demmit,the gals'll just have to swear
and bear it.
    And there ARE GALS.
    But as I said before,it's a great life
(and a bum typist),and I'll try not to weaken.
    Thanks for the puff,which George
clipped and sent me.Like Izzy Halperin,I now be-
long,I see,to the ranks of Brothers Of The Great.

    It's getting late,and I've got to
finish the "Times" and "Tribune"that I had to go
to Pittsburgh to buy this afternoon,
```
So I'll lay off—

composer! "This kid" then asked the famous Berlin if he (George) could play him (Berlin) a couple of Gershwin songs. And Berlin listened appreciatively to two which soon after were heard in *La-La-Lucille!* (undoubtedly "Tee-Oodle-Um-Bum-Bo" was one). Before long, George was being offered a job as Berlin's musical amanuensis. George decided No, and Berlin agreed: "Why work for somebody else when you can be doing your own?" Thus commenced the mutual respect and warm friendship that continued the rest of George's life.

It was during the period of work on *La-La-Lucille!* that George would become the most intrepid composer in America. For some reason, now lost to history, he accompanied Al Jolson and Buddy DeSylva, the show's major lyricist, to Dixville Notch, in the northern tip of New Hampshire, to spend a few days resting and working at a hotel owned by the father of composer-conductor Paul Lannin. It was not an excursion to be taken lightly, encompassing as it did a trip each way of about a day and a half by train.

J. Clarence Harvey, Alfred Hall, Eleanor Daniels, John E. Hazzard, and Janet Velie (the last two the stars) in *La-La-Lucille!*, George Gershwin's first full-scale musical. "For candor of speech it is rivaled only by the disease columns of the daily newspapers, and its wily influences are even more luxuriant," wrote Percy Hammond in Boston. "'Up in Mabel's Room' is to 'La-La-Lucille!' as a crocus is to poison ivy. . . . There was pretty music by someone named George Gershwin, and several pretty girls to dance to it." CULVER SERVICE

Before the weekend was up George, a city boy, had tired of the woodsy setting and became obviously bored and anxious to return to his native haunts. He heard then about the two planes that flew the mails and newspapers between New York and Dixville Notch. These were obviously surplus aircraft of the First World War, either the Curtiss "Jenny" or the De Havilland DH-4, chillingly known as the "Flaming Coffin," although not to George.

The thought of returning to New York in a few hours (it took about four) instead of spending more than a day on trains appealed to George and he spoke about it. It was Jolson who triggered the final decision for he promptly dared George to make the flight. Arrangements were made for George to occupy the second cockpit (with the returning mail), although he was not outfitted in the proper gear of the intrepid pilot. His most vivid recollection of the flight, thanks to the time of year—spring—the altitude, and his lack of proper flight clothes, was, "It was very cold!"

La-La-Lucille!, "The new up-to-the-minute musical comedy of class and distinction," enjoyed a good run despite its pre-summer opening and an actors' strike. Brooks Atkinson found the music "now vivacious and surprising of detail, and again harmoniously pleasing." Surprising of detail may have been the osculatory sound in the lyric, by Irving Caesar, "There's More to the Kiss than the X-X-X." George, never a waster, salvaged from *Half Past Eight* a couple of numbers, one now retitled "The Ten Commandments of Love." "From Now On" has a decided Kern flavor, but his own distinctive touch is evident in the very "harmoniously pleasing" "Nobody but You," a souvenir of his piano-pounding days at Remick's. Still four months from his twenty-first birthday, George had come of age in the musical-comedy world with his first solid success.

The "interpolated song," which made up the composite score of so many of the musicals, especially revues, in the pre-World War I years and after, was the major outlet for the aspiring young composer. Until George had really built a reputation for himself as a production composer, he continued to write individual songs, sometimes tailored to specific talents, that were used in shows. Before *La-La-Lucille!* had come to the Henry Miller the brother-sister team of Charles and Millie King was singing the graceful "I Was So Young, You Were So Beautiful" in *Good Morning Judge* with much success; this was George's first song to achieve some kind of popularity. "Some Wonderful Sort of Someone" went from *Ladies First* to *The Lady in Red*, to be sung by Adele Rowland; for the same production George and Lou Paley did "Something About Love."

Irving Caesar, ever-fertile and industrious lyricist, came up one day with an idea for a song: "At that time there was a raging one-step sensation 'Hindustan.' I said to George that we ought to write a one-step and give it an American flavor. That evening we had dinner at Dinty Moore's, discussed the song, boarded a Riverside Drive bus, got up to his home on Washington Heights, and immediately went to the piano alcove, separated by the inevitable beaded curtain of the period from the dining room. There was a poker game in progress at the time.

"In about fifteen minutes we had turned out 'Swanee,' verse and chorus. But we thought that song should have a trio and for a few minutes were deciding about this addition. The losers in the game kept saying, 'Boys, finish it some other time' and the lucky ones urged us to complete the song right there and then. This we did, and old man Gershwin lost not a moment in fetching a comb, over which he superimposed some tissue, and accompanying George while I sang it over and over again at the insistence of the winning poker players. . . ."

"Swanee," sung "over and over," was to become a national reality within a few months. When the new Capitol Theatre, a movie house, opened, a *Capitol Revue* was devised, to which George contributed two songs: the auspiciously launched "Swanee" and "Come to the Moon," with a lyric by Ned Wayburn and Lou Paley. But nothing happened with either song at the Capitol. Running at the nearby Winter Garden was Al Jolson's successful revue *Sinbad*. At a party Jolson heard George play "Swanee" and was all for interpolating it into the score of *Sinbad* (most of which was by Sigmund Romberg). After this happened, by February 1920 Gershwin and Caesar found themselves hit songwriters. Though not exceptional Gershwin, "Swanee" is a good popular song by the standards of the time: irresistibly rhythmic, with an unusual change of key (from minor to major) from verse to chorus, and a typical humorous Gershwin touch in the quotation from "Old Folks at Home" in the last bar. The sale of Jolson's phonograph record went into the millions; similarly, sheet-music sales jumped, reaching a peak in February–April of 1920. By the values that prevailed—and still do— George was accepted as an important man in Tin Pan Alley: he had

"Swanee" brought fame and fortune to George Gershwin. Instrumental in the recognition of the song and its composer was Al Jolson, shown here with George—in a snappy bowler—and two friends. GERSHWIN COLLECTION

practically tossed off with Caesar, in less than an hour, a "commercial" song hit. Ironically, he never did it again.

At about the peak of the "Swanee" popularity George traveled to Detroit to see George White about doing a score for the *Scandals*, White's challenge to Ziegfeld. With Gershwin's name practically everywhere White needed little convincing that George should do his second production of the series; and, as it turned out, the following four.

Although he was fluent at the keyboard and spontaneously inventive, he had by this time begun jotting down musical ideas in small notebooks for possible future use. Typical of these books, which were kept up during his entire career, is one, probably the first, labeled "Tunes 1921—" with his name as "Geo. M. Gershwin." The significance of the middle initial is not clear, unless it was a mildly humorous allusion to another and at the moment more famous Geo. M.

The forty pages of the notebook contain more than sixty ideas, some fragmentary, some complete with verse and chorus, and others choruses only. Most are melodic lines without the bass or harmonization. The earliest date (though preceded by eight melodies) is July 26, 1921, and the song is "We're Here Because," which appeared in *Lady, Be Good* about three years later. The final dated entry (excepting one or two strays obviously out of chronology) is September 25, 1922, a "One Step." The page also holds a "Theme" and an undated, untitled fragment of definite musical interest. The book, in fact, contains several such quite advanced ideas.

68

B. G. "Buddy" DeSylva, lyricist of many Gershwin songs, plus those with Brown and Henderson. Eventually DeSylva became head of Paramount Pictures. PHOTO BY JOHN MCGOWAN

The first half-dozen pages or so are carefully notated in green ink—several complete "Melodies"; the first rather Jerome Kernish, one is untitled; likewise the second. The third is "Beautiful Bird," which had existed, as a title at least, as early as 1918. Another completed tune is entitled "Ain't Love Grand" and is not particularly distinguished, nor is "Moonlight" which follows. However, on the same page is a fragment, "He's Gone," which is memorable. The source of the title, though not the melody, is obviously "He's Gone Away," George's favorite American (actually Anglo-American) folk song. But this was never developed, as was true of many of the sketches, because later books were equally, or even more, copious.

Not that several of the ideas were not used: "We're Here Because" was joined by "Jazz Bird" (as it is titled in the notebook) in *Lady, Be Good*. "Isn't It Wonderful," which would eventually be heard in the London production, *Primrose*, is complete and dated September 25, 1921. What is "American Blues" (October 5, 1921) in the notebook eventually emerged as "Yankee Doodle Blues" the following year. Both a snatch of a waltz and "Walking Home with Angeline," composed in the spring of 1922, were heard in the score of *Our Nell* in December.

When the tune book was begun it was a most active summer for George for, besides being involved with writing the songs for his second *Scandals*, he was enrolled in summer courses at Columbia University's music department. His instructor was Rossetter G. Cole, head of the department, and a composer and teacher with a high reputation (though his own music was heavily influenced by Franck); in the winter months he taught theory at the Cosmopolitan School of Music in Chicago. George took two courses with Cole, "Nineteenth-Century Romanticism in Music," which began with Schumann and Berlioz and continued on through Debussy and the nationalists "especially in such countries as Russia, Scandinavia and Bohemia." The other course, which met at for what must have been to George the ungodly hour of 8:30 A.M., was "Elementary Orchestration"—". . . the historical development of the orchestra, the study of the technical possibilities and tonal qualities of each instrument of the modern orchestra, the principles of tone combination, and the arranging of given compositions for various groups of instruments and for full orchestra." With all this going on it is remarkable that George was able to keep up his jottings in the tune book during that summer of '21.

John McGowan, who sang the Prologue to *Blue Monday* in the *George White's Scandals of 1922*. McGowan also hoped to become a songwriter but gave it up when Jerome Kern told him that a new McGowan tune was fine, but that Kern had written it first, under the title of "They Didn't Believe Me." McGowan gave up singing to go into the writing of musical-comedy books. COURTESY JOHN MCGOWAN

69

The book is not a musical diary; the entries are not made with any regularity. The first dated jotting was made about two weeks after the opening of the *Scandals* of 1921—thus the period before would have been too hectic for jotting ideas in the notebook. The next date, "Sept. 25, 1921," though preceded by "If I Only Had Somebody Like You," reveals that nearly a month went by between entries. There is a date for "Melody—Sept. 27, 1921—(For Aarons or Way-burn)," a curious notation. There being no melody notated between these two, it is clear that George was too busy on his twenty-third birthday for jotting down melodies.

An especially fascinating entry—March 21, 1922—is obviously an instrumental, a piece for piano built on an ostinato idea in the bass. It is untitled and may have been regarded by the composer as one of his little "novelettes" for which he chose to do nothing. In many of the pieces are little snatches and figures, intimations of ideas that were fully developed in the *Rhapsody in Blue* and the *Concerto*.

Two final observations: the fact that George dated his entries reveals an early sense of history. It reveals also an appreciation of his own work, an objective judgment and critical faculty that rejected some ideas and employed others. Some melodies were marked "GT," meaning Good Tune. Even so, of the three entries near the end of the book so marked, not one was ever developed and used. It may have been that some of the songs were a bit offbeat for the time. Despite the few Kernish entries there are some strikingly Gershwinesque ideas. But such material as George White would want for the *Scandals* could not, as so many of these pieces do, present any challenge to Bald Head Row.

George's first *Scandals* contained some interesting ideas, especially in "Idle Dreams" and his first attempt at handling the blues in "On My Mind the Whole Night Long." This song is remarkably close to an authentic blues construction, complete with breaks between phrases. The next year there were a couple of good songs again in the sprightly "She's Just a Baby" and the relyricized "Drifting Along with the Tide." For the 1922 *Scandals* there were "Where Is the Man of My Dreams?" sung by Winnie Lightner, and "I'll Build a Stairway to Paradise," a vibrant production number that had grown from Ira's "New Step Every Day," which was revised by the lyricist for the show, Buddy DeSylva.

For the *George White's Scandals of 1922* George made his initial public attempt at a "serious" work in the one-act opera titled *Blue Mon-*

Ann Pennington, the dancing star of George's first *Scandals*.
MUSEUM OF THE CITY OF NEW YORK

The first published song of George and Ira Gershwin (Arthur Francis).
COURTESY T. B. HARMS AND CO.

Some *Scandals* song covers. USED BY PERMISSION NEW WORLD MUSIC CORPORATION

Vincent Youmans with Ira

day. The music is often groping (except in the really "jazzy" passages), though it does point toward developments to come. The title song is good, so is "Has Anyone Seen Joe?" (which was the theme of his early string quartet, later published as *Lullaby*), with an interesting melodic line that has not become dated. The spiritual "I'm Gonna See My Mother," sung in true "operatic tradition" by a dying man, is not distinguished.

George always felt that the tension and excitement that went into the composition of *Blue Monday* left him with his famous "composer's stomach." He and DeSylva had discussed their idea with White, who at first vetoed it for production reasons (costumes, sets, etc.), then changed his mind just three weeks before the show was scheduled to open. In five days and nights George and DeSylva composed their opera, which was planned to be the second-act opener (the first act had closed with the elaborate "Stairway to Paradise" number).

To the pleasure-loving *Scandals* devotee *Blue Monday* came as a jolt. "The most dismal, stupid, and incredible blackface sketch that has probably ever been perpetrated," was the reaction of Darnton of the *World*, the morning after the New York opening on August 28, 1922, and he echoed to a great extent the feelings of the audience. In the minority was the more perceptive and tolerant "W.S.," who noted that White and company "have given us the first real American opera in the one-act piece called *Blue Monday Blues*. Here at last is a . . . human plot of American life, set to music in the popular vein, using jazz only

72

at the right moments, the sentimental song, the Blues, and above all, a new and free ragtime recitative. True, there were crudities, but in it we see the first gleam of a new American musical art." George liked to remember, too, the prediction of the critic who had seen the New Haven opening: "This opera will be imitated in a hundred years."

But the producer, with his eye on the box office and not on history, withdrew the sketch after that first night's performance in New York and the *Scandals* returned to its more congenial frivolity. Paul Whiteman, whose orchestra was featured in the revue, never forgot it or its

Ira's first show-song sheet.
COURTESY T. B. HARMS AND CO.

composer. Whiteman, who had only shortly before come out of the west, where he once played in a symphony orchestra, was coming into vogue. He became a great champion of *Blue Monday*, which he presented periodically in later years under a title he gave it, *135th Street*, in an arrangement and orchestration by Ferde Grofé (the original having been done by George's friend Will Vodery).

The 1923 *Scandals* offered no novelties or any deviation from the conventional, not even in the music. But there was an affecting song, "Where Is She?", a metropolitan blues that was neither jazz nor a typical popular song, a style of which George was becoming the master.

Lyrically, Ira continued to toil away. *The Sweetheart Shop* (1920) had "Waiting for the Sun to Come Out," music by George. The show's lyricist and author, Anne Caldwell, had liked the song enough to have it interpolated despite the fact that the full-score composer's contract stipulated no interpolations. But the major distinction of "Waiting for the Sun to Come Out" is that it is the first published George and Ira collaboration, though Ira chose to be known as Arthur Francis, an appellation sprung from the names of his younger brother and sister. He felt that the pseudonym would discourage the usual imputations of slipping into the act by virtue of a family connection, since George was by 1920 considered an important influence in Tin Pan Alley.

Arthur Francis also supplied lyrics to George Gershwin's songs for *A Dangerous Maid*, an effort that expired in smoky Pittsburgh. Vinton Freedley was the handsome leading man whose fortunes were soon to be combined with those of the brothers. Freedley had met George for the first time during rehearsals of *Dere Mable*, when it was found that a very special kind of song was required for a spot. The protagonist was based on the famous letter-writing soldier, Bill, who was fond of his dog. The show's composer was at a loss to come up with a song that Bill was to sing to his dog. George was then sent in. The result was "We're Pals" (lyric by Irving Caesar) which served very well.

Sometime after Ira ended his stint with the carnival in September 1919, George suggested that his brother begin writing songs with Vincent Youmans. The first venture of the new team was *Piccadilly to Broadway*, a revue being produced by Ray Goetz and directed by Ned Wayburn. The show was rehearsing in Atlantic City and starred Helen Broderick, Clifton Webb, and Johnny Dooley when Ira and Youmans went down to join it. But Goetz was not about to spend money unnecessarily for a new lyricist and a new composer. Ira remembers that "when Youmans asked for money—I think $15 a week (a lyricist for a successful show was paid approximately $25 per week)—Goetz replied that we were lucky to be having anything in the show." What they were having was four songs, including "Who's Who with You" and a title song, "Piccadilly's Not a Bit Like Broadway." (The latter they had supplied overnight, to Goetz's astonishment; Ira said it was not difficult —they had the title and "that's 60% of the problem.")

By October *Piccadilly to Broadway* had gotten to Detroit and St. Paul, and "Who's Who with You" was still being programmed (the program was also crediting songs to William M. Daly and George Gershwin). Ira remembers seeing the show in New York: he recalls a comedy scene of falling bricks and he can still hear the "title song," "Piccadilly's Not a Bit Like Broadway," in the revue that by then had a different title. (Evidently only two of the four Youmans-Gershwin songs got to Broadway.)

George Gershwin was familiar with the songs from the revue and the next year he played them for Alex Aarons, who decided that this was the team he wanted. Youmans had recently been signed by Harms; and Max Dreyfus could not understand why Aarons would want to take a chance on Ira (an unknown) when Irving Caesar was available. (Even George was puzzled at Aarons's choice: were not he and Buddy DeSylva a better risk for the assignment?) But Aarons was adamant. The new show was *Two Little Girls in Blue*, taking its title from a turn-of-the-century song, and was to have two composers: Paul Lannin as well as Youmans.

The first conference for the show was held at the Garden City Hotel, where Lannin was working. Ira, Youmans, and Ned Wayburn would work together and Lannin, in chef's costume, would pop in from the kitchen. "His father wanted him to learn every phase of the hotel business," said Ira, "—which didn't include composing." While the show was in production, Aarons ran short of money and A. L. (Abraham Lincoln) Erlanger, formerly of Klaw and Erlanger, took over. Erlanger was a small and difficult man, and Wayburn urged Youmans and Ira to keep in the background: If Erlanger saw that his writers were so young, there would be trouble. Ira was standing in the wings at one rehearsal when Oscar Shaw on stage was singing "Who's Who with You" to a girl. The melodic line descended at the end of the title.

Erlanger rushed down the aisle: "What's the name of that song?" Shaw told him. "It's a question!" exclaimed the producer; "it should go UP!" Shaw winked to Ira and repeated the song, raising the end of the line an octave. The appeased producer left; the song descended to as-written.

Two Little Girls in Blue opened on May 3, 1921, at the George M. Cohan Theatre. *The Clipper*'s next-day review said, "The lyrics written by Arthur Francis are of the best, and seem to show that there are some lyricists who are still able to write a lyric that rhymes and also means something." But working with Youmans was not entirely a pleasure. "The trouble with Youmans," Ira later remembered, "was that he wanted to do everything: write, publish, produce, conduct, and show people down the aisle." It was not an uncommon theatrical ego. Even before *Two Little Girls in Blue* opened, Ned Wayburn was complaining publicly to *The Clipper:* "I am not satisfied to retire from the calling of Producing Stage Director with the reputation of being 'the world's greatest buck dancer.'" Consider his true worth: "I have personally supervised every detail of the production of 'Two Little Girls in Blue' including the staging of the play and musical numbers; have coached the Fairbanks Twins for many weeks in their arts and dances; have devised all of the stage settings, color schemes and scenic effects, and used my own taste in selecting the materials and costumes as well as engaging the beauties which they adorn."

Once Ira was asked if the show had not been a hit. "No, but Erlanger hated Ziegfeld so—he had stolen all his girls, and My God they were beautiful girls we had in that show—and he was determined to keep the show running, even at a loss, through the summer." Erlanger was a Napoleon buff and had assumed some of the Little Corporal's hauteur: in his own building, for example, when he stepped into an elevator everyone else had to step out and wait for the next car: the emperor rode alone. When *Two Little Girls in Blue*'s sheet music was published, Max Dreyfus thought he would capitalize on Erlanger's vanity and win the producer permanently to Harms: so, for the first time in theater history, the producer's photograph—and no one else's—appeared on the sheet-music covers!

The next year, 1922, there were Gershwin interpolations in two shows that opened on the same night, February 20. *For Goodness Sake,* starring Fred and Adele Astaire, friends of George from the piano-pounding days at Remick's, had in it a spirited song, "Tra-La-La"

The Astaires in *For Goodness Sake*, one of their earliest musicals. They had been in vaudeville since 1908, and Fred—two years younger than his sister— was once ruled off the New York stage in 1912 as under age. CULVER SERVICE

Irene Bordoni, "The French Doll," who sang "Do It Again" and signed this picture to George "très sincèrement." COURTESY ARTHUR GERSHWIN

(which was rewritten to good advantage in the film musical, *An American in Paris*, almost three decades later). At the Lyceum, Irene Bordoni was singing Buddy DeSylva's quasi-naughty lyric "Do It Again" in *The French Doll*. The innocently sensual "Do It Again" is one of the finest of George's early songs, achieving a quite un-Tin Pan Alley harmonic distinction by subtly changing from bar to bar with each phrase repetition, an effect that was to become a part of the Gershwin style. The following year Miss Bordoni was again singing another Gershwin-DeSylva-Arthur Francis song along similar suggestive Gallic lines: "I Won't Say I Will but I Won't Say I Won't," which was interpolated into the score of *Little Miss Bluebeard*.

S. N. Behrman, in his *People in a Diary*, has perfectly captured the effect of George's sound: "I felt on the instant, when he sat down to play, the newness, the humor, above all the rush of the great heady surf of vitality. The room became freshly oxygenated; everybody felt it, everybody breathed it." "*Oxygenated*": a technical word, almost so technical as to alienate the literary mind. But according to writer Cecelia Ager, "That *is* the word. For forty years I have been looking for the word that would describe George's effect upon a room, and that is it. You cannot imagine what a party was like when he was expected and he did *not* appear."

The parties that Behrman and Mrs. Ager remember most vividly were those at 18 West Eighth Street, where Emily Paley poured tea and Lou Paley moved among his books and thoughts; and everyone gathered to hear the busy George relax and play. One of Lou's whimsical notes to George re-creates those days and nights:

George,
    I've taken an accurate census of the various theatrical managers, producers, sages, etc. with the following results:

1. Klaw offices   — 4 extravaganzas with music to be written by Geo. G.—next Monday—

2. Gest   "   — 12 pantomimes with incidental music composed by G. Gershwin—next Tues.

3. Shubert "   — 1⅓ shows with music—interpolated by Mr. George Gershwin—next Thursday at least

4. Selwyn "   — 2.003 Music Review Melodies by Mr. G. Gersh—next Friday—

5. T. B. Harms   17 checks—to be handed to George Gershvin—All next Saturday A.M.

6. Gushwin—familye— 26 hours—to be occupied by George (himself) at piano and vicinity for benefit and pleasure of the pop & mom and neighbors—

And
Next Wednesday—At the Paley's
    Feb. *16*, 1921—Bring Caesar—Iz—Vinc.—all & sundry

No wonder that when George and Emily ate together, George was so unconcerned about food that he had to ask her if he had eaten enough—he couldn't remember. What he would later remember and tell Mascha Strunsky, Emily's mother, however, is: "You gave Emily to Lou and Lee to Ira, but who do you have for me?" One of the loveliest of those early stories is from Sam Behrman—one which he forgot to put in his memoirs. Late one Saturday night Sam was leaving 18 West Eighth Street with George. They stopped outside, and a bedazzled Sam asked: "What *is* there about Emily that makes her so wonderful?" George was puzzled at the question: "Why, Sam, don't you know? She's the perfect circle."

Snapped by a photographer on the Bowery: Joseph Meyer, Bela Blau, and, seated, Ira. GERSHWIN COLLECTION

In December of 1922 George formed a professional partnership that was to develop into a warm friendship with William Daly, excellent musician, conductor, and composer. Bill Daly—people rarely called him William—eventually abandoned composition (as well as the editorship of a national magazine) in favor of conducting. Unlike George, Bill was heedless of appearance, favoring scuffed, comfortable shoes, old clothes with character, including a sweater with the elbows out. With an unruly shock of hair and his fair complexion he was a striking contrast to the dapper, dark George. Bill's understanding of George's music made him a trusted adviser as well as interpreter (he conducted many shows), which eventually led to a charge that it was Daly who wrote the music to which George merely signed his name. But in 1922 this sophistry was in the future; the show at hand was *Our Nell*, "A Musical Mellowdrayma" (for a while it was known as *Hayseed*), for which George and Bill collaborated on a song, with a lyric by Brian Hooker, "Innocent Ingenue Baby," a delightfully delicate, graceful song. Most of the show's songs were divided between George and Bill

Daly, George supplying the rhythmic and musically witty "Walking Home with Angeline." There was also a genre number, "Gol-Durn," but antiquity has obscured the author. *Our Nell* was presented by Hayseed Productions and, though it was no great hit, did run well into 1923.

"Swanee" had gone on to sweep England after the United States and Canada had had its fill of Dixie sentiments. "Every club has its jazz band on the American style and every dance number seems to be an American product," said a London dispatch, January 18, 1921: "The prize number is 'Swanee.' You can't get away from it. Every night, everywhere, 'Swanee' has been played for months and months, with no sign of exhausting its popularity. And London keeps dancing to it." Such success brought George to the attention of English producers, who offered him an inducement ($1500 plus a round-trip ticket) to do an English score. As *The Rainbow*, a revue, turned out, the return ticket came in handy. George was not aware of his impending British disaster when he wrote to Ira the day after he had arrived in London:

Sunday, noon.

Dear Iz,

Well, ol' boy, here I am in London almost 24 hours, or rather only 24 hours & the rain is coming down in the manner we've heard about for years. It is not raining hard — but hard enough to keep one from going out It will not however, keep me from going to C. Grey's house in a few minutes to start on a show that begins music rehearsals Tuesday. Writing the Scandals in a month, will seem an eternity compared to the time allotted us to write what will probably be called Silver Lining

A funny thing happened yesterday which made me very joyful & for the moment very happy & came here. The boat was in dock at Southampton & everyone was in line with their passports & landing cards. When I handed my passport to one of the men at a table he read it, looked up & said, "George Gershwin writer of Swanee? It took me off my feet for a second. It was so unexpected, you know. Of course I agreed I was the composer & then he asked what I was writing now etc. etc. I couldn't ask for a more pleasant entrance into a country. When I reached the shore a woman reporter came up to me & asked for a few words. I felt like I was Kern or somebody.

Last night a man called me on the phone & said he was from the weekly Dispatch & would like to have an interview. I met him & spoke a while to him. He asked my opinion about the possibility of a rag-time Opera & when I thought it would come about. I told him my opinion & when it is published I'll send it along to you.

Last night we went to see Jean Bedini's "You'd be surprised" a Revue. It's a fast show with many scenes from burlesque & music by Melville Morris. I wonder what he wrote as all I heard were popular american songs. George Robey, a famous comedian is in the show & I think he is a fine artist. He puts over a lyric song

as good as anyone I've seen. The hit of the show is an orchestra. The Savoy orchestra. And who do you suppose is the leader? Bert Ralton the sax player who recorded my Mexican Dance with me. He's got a great band and is a riot over here.

From what I can see america is years ahead of England theatrically both in wealth of material & money. They're shy of Ingenues, leading men, composers etc. They have a half dozen good lyric writers however.

The English are the politest people I've yet met. Even the taxi drivers are polite. How different from the Yellow Cabs of New York.

I'm finding a little difficulty in understanding the money system here. They go by 12's instead of 10's. For instance a penny is equal to two cents. A six pence piece is, of course

12 cents. A shilling is 24. This is their par value. At present they are under par as you know. The cars drive on the left of the street which is also a bit befuddling.

I could go on & tell you more observations of my first 24 hours here but I must trot along to Chappells. Did you notice "trot along"?

Give my love to Mom & Pop & Frances & Arthur & tell them to drop a line to their bro'.

Am stopping at above Hotel but only for a few days. Until I can find a suitable apartment for Foster & myself. Address my mail to Chappell mus. Pub. 50 New Bond St. London, until I find out where I shall definitely

stay.

Give my regards to the 'boys' individually.

Write heaps & heaps.
(notice? heaps & heaps?)

your brother,

George.

Note: "Mexican Dance" to which George refers above was "Tomale (I'm Hot for You)," which George had written with Buddy DeSylva. Frank Saddler orchestrated the number, changing it from major to minor and introducing it with an extensive vamp.

George and Clifford Grey, certainly one of the "half a dozen good lyric writers," finished their songs on time. On opening night, April 3, 1923, some unprogrammed comedy was supplied by an unhappy comedian, whose part had been cut to almost nothing because he had not been able to learn it. Just before the finale the comic stepped to the footlights and began an impromptu soliloquy of an ostensibly patriotic nature, his major thesis being that English performers were superior to Americans. In a cast full of aliens, he declaimed, an Englishman was not given due recognition. At the climax of the peroration the speaker was forcibly assisted from the stage. Had this ad lib business been retained, it is still doubtful that *The Rainbow* would have survived, for, after meeting his first impolite Englishman, George was introduced to others in the guise of critics. One of the revue's many authors was Edgar Wallace, who deserted the theater for more compatible mysteries.

George's London portrait, 1923, made during his trip that resulted in the *Rainbow* fiasco.
GERSHWIN COLLECTION

George's songs for *The Rainbow*, possibly because of the little time there was for actual composition, have a tossed-off quality. He did "Sunday in London Town" for local consumption, as well as "Eastern Moon," the lively "Oh! Nina," and interpolated his and Bill Daly's "Innocent Ingenue Baby" with the lyric altered a little by Clifford Grey and the title changed to "Innocent Lonesome Blue Baby." When George left England, he was still best remembered for "Swanee."

Over this period, roughly from 1918 to 1923, the techniques of both George and Ira were developing, and experience gave them confidence and the willingness to try different approaches to the art of songwriting. They continued to experiment (as a form of study) with off-beat material in their respective crafts. Ira turned out and reworked his ideas without much more than a hope that any of them would be used, and George kept on writing tunes he would eventually put to use when the right vehicle came along.

George also continued to study music when his show assignments gave him time. With Edward Kilenyi, Sr., he studied harmony, counterpoint, and form. "Many a time," Kilenyi has written, "our lessons consisted of analyzing and discussing classical masterpieces. George understood that he was not to learn 'rules' according to which he himself would have to write music, but instead he would be shown what great composers had written, what devices, styles, traditions—later wrongly called rules—they used. Consequently he enjoyed the contents of our

Some of George's study sketches in harmony and orchestration done with Edward Kilenyi from 1919–21. Work on successful shows eventually interfered with these lessons, although George never stopped studying music.
COURTESY EDWARD KILENYI, SR.

textbook, *The Material Used in Musical Composition*, by Percy Goetschius." After September 1921 the exigencies of his success in the musical-comedy field sometimes created breaks in George's more or less systematic studies, but he did call on Kilenyi (Hambitzer was dead by this time) from time to time to discuss the more technical aspects of music. Kilenyi, who recognized George's natural gift, never stopped encouraging him to compose as he felt rather than according to conventional "rules."

Some time later, probably in 1923, George began to study with Rubin Goldmark (a teacher of Aaron Copland), a hard-cored traditionalist who had no sympathy for modernistic nonsense. George gave up after three lessons because it was obvious that he and Goldmark were incompatible. It may have been after the lesson to which George had brought along a copy of *Lullaby*, the early string quartet dating from around 1919 and written while he was studying with Kilenyi. Goldmark studied the piece for a few moments, then said, "It's good. Yes,

Eva Gauthier. Always in the vanguard of modern music, Mme. Gauthier introduced George to the concert world in New York in her "Recital of Ancient and Modern Music for Voice." PHOTO BY CARL VAN VECHTEN

very good. It's plainly to be seen that you have already learned a great deal of harmony from me." The publication of *Lullaby* in 1968 made it apparent to us all as pure and early Gershwin.

Something even less harmonious was entering the American consciousness; this was jazz. An American folk art, of New Orleans polyglot origins, thought by many to be the only indigenous American folk art, jazz became a commercial commodity after King Oliver brought his band north to Chicago. In 1916 an all-white group calling itself The Original Dixieland Jazz Band opened at Reisenweber's, off Columbus Circle in New York, and caused a sensation—once the mystified patrons were informed that it was possible to dance to the music made by the band.

Jazz soon became "the latest thing," gave a name to a music and an age. Paul Whiteman formed an orchestra featuring "jazz arrangements" (a contradiction in terms) and soon was crowned, by a press agent if by no one else, "The King of Jazz." Before long the intelligentsia and society discovered jazz and the controversies began. Jazz was denounced from the pulpit, by educators, by editorialists. It entered the burgeoning world of the stock market when Vincent Lopez announced that he would incorporate a jazz orchestra and sell shares in it. The New York *Times* somberly found it fit to print the fact that Queen Victoria's cornettist had died on hearing "American jazz." Jazz was blamed for drunkenness, suicides, sexual orgies, and by one historian, through a not too clearly explained process, for the fall of the Roman Empire.

But not all concert singers, Ira to the contrary in "the Real American Folk Song," said that they despised it. Late in 1923 Eva Gauthier announced a "Recital of Ancient and Modern Music for Voice," and though the program did not present any actual jazz (as it was labeled by the critics), a part of her recital was devoted to popular American songs in an American group. Encouraged in this venture by the always-interested Carl Van Vechten—probably the first champion of American popular music as a source of inspiration for more ambitious music—who felt that Mme. Gauthier's recital would prove to be "one of the very most important events in American musical history," she lined up, with her customary flair for the exotic, George as her accompanist for the American songs. Her accompanist for the ancient, modern Hungarian and German, Austrian, British, and French songs was Max Jaffe.

Constance Binney in *Sweet Little Devil.* CULVER SERVICE

The contrast of the composed Jaffe, as he placed his sedate "black and white" covers on the piano, with George, who nervously darted from the wings to place the garish giant popular song sheets before him, brought titters from the fashionable audience.

For dramatic effect Mme. Gauthier wore a long-sleeved, black velvet evening gown backward (with the décolletage in the back, contra the current style), accented further by enormous diamond earrings. Against the black backdrop only her face, hands, and the earrings were visible as Mme. Gauthier, having finished with Bartók and Hindemith, began the American song group with Berlin's "Alexander's Ragtime Band" to George's crackling accompaniment. Three numbers later, into his own "Do It Again," George inserted a phrase from *Schéhérazade.* "The audience howled," Mme. Gauthier recalled. George had made his concert debut and had stolen the show. Encores were demanded and the request was filled with "Do It Again"—sung twice.

86   The next day's reviews made very little of the fact that Schoenberg's

"Lied der Waldtaube" (from *Gurrelieder*) had received its American premiere, but much was made of the so-called jazz songs. George's playing, too, had made a hit. It is best summed up by Henry Taylor Parker after a Boston repeat of the recital: "He diversified them with cross-rhythms; wove them into a pliant and outspringing counterpoint; set in pauses and accents; sustained cadences; gave character to the measures wherein the singer's voice was still . . . He reins or loses sentiment as in Swanee with a discriminating will. Humor tempts him in Ingenue Baby and Do It Again. With accent and color he is making conscious strokes of the theater as he builds the Stairway to Paradise."

Thus George had arrived on the stage of Aeolian Hall, November 1, 1923. But he had little time to consider the implications of his concert-hall debut and triumph; he was, as usual, busy with something. He was at work on a new show that was heralded as the one that was bringing Constance Binney back from Hollywood, *Sweet Little Devil*. Even though he aspired to the higher reaches symbolized by Aeolian Hall, and had opinions on ragtime opera, George never forgot his first love, the lyric theater, where both he and Ira were hoping to make their mark. And they were ready now.

The first page of Gershwin's manuscript of *Rhapsody in Blue*. COPYRIGHT
1924 BY NEW WORLD MUSIC CORPORATION. USED BY PERMISSION

1924-1929

Perched atop a tall stool in the Ambassador Billiard Parlor, on Broadway at 52nd Street—a favorite hangout for songwriters—Ira was reading the morning's *Tribune*. It was about 11 P.M., January 3, 1924.

At a nearby table, engaged in a three-cushion tournament, were George and Buddy DeSylva. The two had practically finished their songs for *Sweet Little Devil*, due to begin its Boston tryout run soon.

Ira, ever the careful reader, caught a small item on the amusement page:

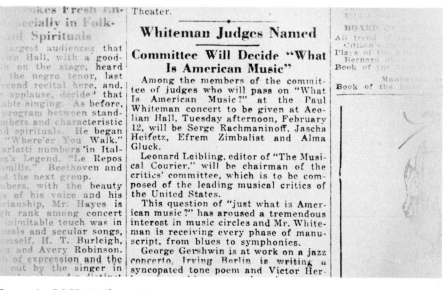

Theater.

Whiteman Judges Named

Committee Will Decide "What Is American Music"

Among the members of the committee of judges who will pass on "What Is American Music?" at the Paul Whiteman concert to be given at Aeolian Hall, Tuesday afternoon, February 12, will be Serge Rachmaninoff, Jascha Heifetz, Efrem Zimbalist and Alma Gluck.

Leonard Leibling, editor of "The Musical Courier," will be chairman of the critics' committee, which is to be composed of the leading musical critics of the United States.

This question of "just what is American music?" has aroused a tremendous interest in music circles and Mr. Whiteman is receiving every phase of manuscript, from blues to symphonies.

George Gershwin is at work on a jazz concerto, Irving Berlin is writing a syncopated tone poem and Victor Her-

From the N.Y. *Tribune*, January 4, 1924

After the game (George had lost) Ira read the piece to him. Through his ever-present cigar smoke George didn't show that he was particularly mystified. "So he's really going through with it." George and Whiteman had talked of a possible "jazz concert" for which he might work up a serious composition. Whiteman had never forgotten *Blue Monday* of the '22 *Scandals* and, with jazz so big in the world of commerce, it seemed a timely and worthy idea, in terminology of the times, to set the musical world on its ear. But when they had talked about the proposed concert, its date was an indefinite point in the future.

Now here was an announcement—and a concert no more than a month away. George was a speedy craftsman, but, with all the work still to go into putting *Sweet Little Devil* into shape for the New York opening on January 21, turning out a "piano concerto" seemed highly improbable.

When he called Whiteman, he learned that the concert's date had been advanced because a rival conductor, also hoping to exploit the jazz fad, was talking about a serious jazz concert of his own and had even announced his date. Whiteman was forced to advance his own and begin hectic preparations for the concert. More importantly, he was able to convince George that he could produce the so-called jazz concerto. All George needed to do was to supply a piano copy of the piece to Whiteman, who would turn it over to his orchestrator and arranger, Ferde Grofé. As George's experience with orchestrating up to this time was limited, this proposition seemed reasonable to him, and, when he recalled the glamour and hullabaloo of the Eva Gauthier Aeolian Hall experience, the Whiteman experiment took on attractive and challenging dimensions.

On the train to Boston and the tryout of *Sweet Little Devil*, George began to sketch out the piece. George had already begun to call it a rhapsody (he was thinking of *American Rhapsody*) when Ira, freshly returned from seeing an exhibition of Whistler's colorfully labeled works, suggested *Rhapsody in Blue*, which would be in keeping with a concert of jazz. Also the freer rhapsody form would prove easier to work with for him than the strict book-defined concerto form. Ross Gorman, Whiteman's clarinetist, was famous for being able to play a glissando upon an instrument supposedly capable of producing only individual tones. George decided that this tricky effect would be a good

Ferde Grofé, Whiteman's arranger and orchestrator of the *Rhapsody in Blue*. Grofé later left the band business and composed such works as *Mississippi Suite* and *Grand Canyon Suite*.
COURTESY ASCAP

90

one to open the *Rhapsody;* the desired jazzy whoop immediately sets the mood of the piece.

When he returned from Boston with the framework of the *Rhapsody* set in his mind, and some of the actual themes chosen, George began the final writing on January 7. He worked in the Gershwin apartment on 110th Street, in which a back room with an old upright piano was set aside for the songwriting Gershwins. George composed the *Rhapsody* for two pianos with some indications as to the scoring. From this manuscript Grofé orchestrated the piece for the Whiteman band. He practically haunted the Gershwin house, drinking Mamma's delicious Russian tea, engaging in charming *non sequitur* conversations with Pop, and taking George's rhapsody from him page by page.

Grofé's scoring was conceived in so special a manner that he often did not indicate the actual instrument in the score, but only the name of instrumentalist, many of whom played several instruments.

Four days after *Sweet Little Devil* opened in New York, George had more or less finished the *Rhapsody;* on February 4 Grofé completed the orchestration. Rehearsals were held at the Palais Royal, on 48th Street, where Whiteman and band could be heard nightly. During the off-hours the band would reassemble to play the *Rhapsody in Blue* for critics, friends, and curious musicians. The whole atmosphere was rather tawdry in the night club, empty by dawn, the chairs upturned on tables, dim lighting, and stale air. Five days were spent rehearsing the *Rhapsody*, which proved to be the main event of what Whiteman had chosen to call "An Experiment in Modern Music."

Despite the preparation in advance George had not decided on the final piano part up to the afternoon of the concert; he filled in the blank pages during the performance itself.

Though he described the *Rhapsody in Blue* as for "Jazz Band and Piano," he never conceived of it as an example of what was later called "symphonic jazz." Nor was Whiteman's a true jazz band, but a large dance orchestra. Whatever jazz was contributed by it came from individuals who were members of it from time to time such as the Dorsey brothers, or Bix Beiderbecke, who came after 1924.

The *Rhapsody in Blue* is actually a Lisztian rhapsody, loosely constructed, and achieving its contrasts, which serve to compel interest, mainly in tempo changes. Its important breach with convention lies in

George's treatment of the materials of popular music, the blue-tinged harmonies, and its jazz-like, but not jazz, rhythms. Also, the *Rhapsody in Blue* is a tricky piano piece reflecting George's marvelous piano technique. But its truly American flavor can be attributed to George's training in Tin Pan Alley and the theater rather than to the work's rather stilted quasi-jazz effects. In its original piano form the *Rhapsody in Blue* is much less dated, for all its period flavor, than in the orchestral version, which Grofé later reorchestrated for symphony orchestra.

Snow was falling the afternoon of February 12, but it apparently did not discourage anyone from journeying to Aeolian Hall on 43rd Street. Many, in fact, were turned away. The auditorium was filled with the elite, seated and standing, of the musical world—from 57th Street to Tin Pan Alley. As Whiteman remembered it, "It was a strange audience out in front. Vaudevillians, concert managers come to have a look at the novelty, Tin Pan Alleyites, composers, symphony and opera stars, flappers, cake-eaters, all mixed up higgledy-piggledy."

Olin Downes described the setting: "Pianos in various stages of *deshabille* stood about amid a litter of every imaginable contraption of wind and percussion instruments. Two Chinese mandarins, surmounting pillars, looked down upon a scene that would have curdled the blood of a Stokowski or a Mengelberg.

"The golden sheen of brass instruments of lesser and greater dimensions was caught up by a gleaming gong and carried out by bright patches of an Oriental backdrop. There were also lying or hanging about frying pans, large tin utensils, and a speaking trumpet later stuck into the end of a trombone—and what silky, silkly, tone came from that accommodating instrument. This singular assemblage of things

Paul Whiteman's announcement
for a Lincoln's Birthday concert.
GERSHWIN COLLECTION

THE MORNING TELEGRAPH, SUND____

PAUL WHITEMAN

:: AND HIS ::

PALAIS ROYAL ORCHESTRA

WILL OFFER

An Experiment
in Modern Music

ASSISTED BY

ZEZ CONFREY and
GEORGE GERSHWIN

*New Typically American Compositions by VICTOR
HERBERT, IRVING BERLIN and GEORGE
GERSHWIN will be played for the first time.*

AEOLIAN CONCERT HALL

ENTRANCE AND BOX OFFICE   34 WEST 43rd STREET

Tuesday, February 12, 1924

Lincoln's Birthday, at 3 P.M.
Tickets on Sale Now: *From 55c to $2.20*

Victor Records Exclusively
Chickering Pianos   Buescher Band Instruments

The Paul Whiteman orchestra as it was expanded for the Aeolian Hall concert. COURTESY PAUL WHITEMAN

was more than once in some strange way to combine to evoke uncommon and fascinating sonorities."

Into the hall had come, on Whiteman's invitation, the celebrated of the musical spheres, among them, Walter Damrosch, Victor Herbert, Jascha Heifetz, Sergei Rachmaninoff, Ernest Bloch, William Mengelberg, Leopold Stokowski, Fritz Kreisler. From the other arts came Carl Van Vechten, Gilbert Seldes, Heywood Broun, and Fannie Hurst.

Even though Aeolian Hall was packed, Whiteman lost $7000 on his experiment. He spent lavishly on a finely printed program booklet, the best seats were given away, though not to flappers and cake-eaters, and for the concert the orchestra was augmented from the usual nine of the Palais Royal (which was used for the first portion of the program) to twenty-three for the more elaborate part, which included the presentation of the *Rhapsody*.

What resulted was a rather drawn-out concert. In a pronunciamento Whiteman had said, "The experiment is to be purely educational." And so it began, with an exemplification of jazz of a decade before—a five-piece band accomplishing this with an animated rendition of "The Livery Stable Blues," complete with barnyard sound effects made with the help of a bowler hat and a tin can. After which the Palais Royal orchestra proper, all wearing gray spats, came on stage to give "melodious jazz" treatment to "Mama Loves Papa." Following that were some "Comedy Selections," among which was an anthropological tracing of the origin of "Yes, We Have No Bananas." Then came "Whispering" in legitimate *vs.* jazzing guise—and so on, and on and on.

Zez Confrey came out to play his "Kitten on the Keys" in a medley of his flashy piano pieces just before intermission.

More of same followed: "Semi-symphonic" arrangements of some Irving Berlin songs, the "symphonic tone poem" never having materialized. Victor Herbert's attractive *Suite of Serenades*, especially written for the concert, did not contribute to the excitement and by this time the listeners were beginning to lose interest in the experiment. The next selections didn't pep things up: "Pale Moon," "To a Wild Rose," and "Chansonette" played in dance rhythm.

The audience was becoming restive, bored. The overfilled hall was hot, standees began to slip through the exits. Of the twenty-three numbers on the program George was slated to come on in the twenty-

second.

He practically darted to the piano on stage, sat down at the piano, shot Whiteman a quick glance. Whiteman signaled to Gorman, who electrified the entire hall with the *Rhapsody*'s opening whoop. If George's composer's stomach was troubling him, it was imperceptible, for he played with aplomb and steely assurance. He improvised brilliantly in the blank passages. The haste with which the *Rhapsody in Blue* had been prepared resulted, not only in several blank piano pages, but also in rather unorthodox musical directions in Whiteman's conductor's score. One, following pages of unwritten piano solo, instructed the conductor to "wait for nod," before cuing the orchestra.

The audience wasn't nodding. When the *Rhapsody* came to the final passages, the hall broke into spontaneous, loud and long, applause. George was called upon to take several bows acknowledging the recognition—the arrival—of himself as a serious composer.

Not by all critics, however. Some had noted what they called "structural deficiencies" in the rambling *Rhapsody*. Those for outnumbered those against, however. Whatever the critical appraisal, the *Rhapsody in Blue* has outlived them, its own viability having greater strength than the comments of the critics. In the *Times* Downes's impressions proved as viable: "This composition shows extraordinary talent, just as it also shows a young composer with aims that go far beyond those of his ilk, struggling with a form of which he is far from being master." Downes then went on to observe that "the audience was stirred, and many a hardened concert-goer excited with the sensation of a new talent finding its voice, and likely to say something personally and racially important to the world."

Lawrence Gilman's reaction to the *Rhapsody* is representative of the opposite view: ". . . weep over the lifelessness of its melody and harmony, so derivative, so stale and so inexpressive. And then recall, for contrast, the rich inventiveness of the rhythms, the saliency and vividness of the orchestral colors." This was one of the few notices of Grofé's contribution to the impact of the *Rhapsody in Blue*.

The rather surprising success of the concert, with its attendant discussion in the press and publicity, and the particular attention given the *Rhapsody*, encouraged Whiteman to repeat the concert, a month later —March 7, 1924—at Aeolian Hall and on April 21 at Carnegie Hall; this last as a benefit for the American Academy in Rome.

By this time George was beginning to prepare the score for what

Zez Confrey, composer of "Kitten on the Keys," who also appeared as piano soloist at the Aeolian Hall concert in 1924.

George and his first large work—the *Rhapsody in Blue*, in the original cover. COURTESY ARTHUR GERSHWIN

Carl Van Vechten wrote George two days after the Aeolian Hall concert: "The concert, quite as a matter of course, was a riot, and you crowned it with what, after repeated hearings, I am forced to regard as the foremost serious effort by any American composer. Go straight on and you will knock all Europe silly." COURTESY CARL VAN VECHTEN

Victor Herbert, whose *Suite of Serenades* was introduced in Aeolian Hall along with the *Rhapsody in Blue*. It was Herbert who suggested that George write a short introductory passage for piano leading into the slow melody. (And it had been Ira who urged George to put that slow melody into the *Rhapsody;* George had thought of making it an entirely rhythmic work). COURTESY ASCAP

was to be his last *Scandals* production. When it opened, June 30, George was making plans for another trip to England to work on *Primrose*, starring the comedian Leslie Henson. The lyrics were mostly by Desmond Carter, but Ira assisted on many, and contributed a typically Gilbertian take-off, mixing the Mikado with the Rhine maidens, in the sprightly 2/4 number "Four Little Sirens," rewritten from a score originally provided for *A Dangerous Maid*.

Ira dropped the Arthur Francis disguise when he collaborated with Lewis Gensler and Milton Schwartzwald on *Be Yourself*, which boasted a book by George S. Kaufman and Marc Connelly (who produced the hit *Beggar on Horseback* this same year). *Be Yourself* was moderately successful.

Finding a proper professional name had taken Ira some time. His friends called him Iz—for all, including Ira, thought his name was Isidore. But neither Iz nor Isidore had ever appeared above his lyrics. Forty years later he was still not certain he had replaced it properly. "I wanted to keep the 'I'—and I didn't like 'Irving'—there were so many Irvings. (The reason I wanted to change my name in the first place was that Isidore was too common.) And Ira seemed kind of uncommon. It was new then and distinct—but there are a lot of Iras around now, and I sometimes think I helped popularize the name."

It is a name that continually turns out to have new meanings. He was working a crossword puzzle and found, to his astonishment, that the synonym for "watchful" is "Ira." "I always thought it meant 'sweet' or 'gentle,' but the puzzle's right: the dictionary does say Ira means 'watchful.' " He remembered the misdefinition from the late Twenties: "I had gone with George to a party at Crosby Gaige's—Ethel Barrymore was there—and when I got there, Crosby met me at the door and said he had been looking up my name and it meant 'kind' or 'gentle'—something like that. Crosby had subscribed to the Oxford Dictionary and was getting it in fascicles as issued, so I thought he knew what he was talking about." It is not a name, however, that others have always been sure about; and Ira has been told many tiresome jokes about its sexual confusions. One sorry misidentification occurred when he was sent a magazine that contained an article, "Ira Gershwin, Gent." Both the envelope and the accompanying letter from the deluded publisher were addressed to "Miss. Ira Gershwin." The

Studying a score with the, at the time, ever-present cigar, not long after the completion of the *Rhapsody*. GERSHWIN COLLECTION

period newly puzzled him—but only temporarily. "Maybe they think it's Mississippi Gershwin," he speculated—"like Tenn. Williams."

In London *Primrose* was a smash; so popular was the music that Chappell's published the full score, the first of George's to be so preserved. But George had little time to enjoy the success of *Primrose*, for he and Ira had agreed to furnish music and lyrics for the new producing team of Alex A. Aarons and Vinton Freedley. Aarons, who had a deep passion for music, was the son of the successful producer Alfred E. Aarons. Freedley had given up acting. Both combined their divergent talents and interests in the common interest of producing musicals.

On the return trip to New York George met Otto Kahn aboard ship and with very little coaxing played some of the new score for him. In London George had begun what was to become "Fascinating Rhythm," which Aarons, who was with him, wanted for the coming show. (Ira's original lyric, "Little Rhythm—Go 'Way," had in May 1923 been set musically by Bill Daly and Joe Meyer, but nothing had happened to it.) Kahn was asked to put money in the forthcoming musical, which would star the comparatively unknown brother-sister team of Fred and Adele Astaire, but he demurred until George played another song also planned for the production. When he heard "The Man I Love," Kahn is supposed to have decided then and there to invest $10,000 in *Lady, Be Good*. After the first week in Philadelphia, where *Lady, Be Good* opened on November 17, Freedley insisted that the song be taken out because it slowed up the show. (The song was published, however, in the *Lady, Be Good!* cover; in the rare first issue it was "The Man I Loved.")

Lady, Be Good was the first complete George and Ira Gershwin scored musical to open on Broadway, which it did on December 1, 1924. With the Astaires, Walter Catlett, and Cliff Edwards, known as "Ukulele Ike," in the cast *Lady, Be Good* was well received in New York. The songs were a delight, literate, many a cut above the conventional musical fare. The character of the songs, particularly musically, was pointed up by the presence in the pit of the duo-piano team of Phil Ohman and Victor Arden. Their weaving in and out of the orchestrations endowed the interpretations with an authentic Gershwinesque flavor. George liked the effect so much he retained it for most of his succeeding shows and in later years had Ohman and Arden play between the acts.

The early weeks of 1925 were devoted by George and Ira, collaborating with Buddy DeSylva on the lyrics, to the composition of the songs for *Tell Me More*, an earlier title of which had been *My Fair Lady*. (Thirty years later, when Frederick Loewe and Alan Jay Lerner were adapting *Pygmalion* and thinking of calling their musical *The Talk of London*, they were reminded of this earlier title which the Gershwins and DeSylva had considered and discarded.) Whatever the title, the Gershwin-DeSylva show survive barely a month, by which time George was again bound for England. There *Tell Me More* opened on May 26, to begin a long, successful run. While still in London, George began sketching ideas for a piano concerto that had been commissioned by the New York Symphony Society upon the suggestion of the conductor Walter Damrosch. George accepted the commission and then went out to acquire a book that would tell him precisely what a concerto was. He planned, too, to do his own orchestration, which he had tried his hand at in some of the numbers in *Primrose*. So he also fortified himself with a copy of Forsythe's *Orchestration*.

After attending a party in Paris given by Jules Glaenzer at 5 Rue Malakoff, where he was introduced to Francis Poulenc and Jean Wiener,

Fred Astaire surrounded by Beauties in *Lady, Be Good.* CULVER SERVICE

George left for home in early June. By July he was giving full attention to what he called "New York Concerto." Working in the crowded Gershwin apartment became difficult even for the usually gregarious George, who was heard now and then to complain about his need for a little privacy. His friend, Ernest Hutcheson invited him to come to Chautauqua, where he might compose in peace. However, Hutcheson's piano students were so fascinated by George, and particularly by his playing, that they too tended to gather round while the concerto was set aside temporarily.

By September it was finished except for the orchestration. George worked on this at the same time he collaborated with Ira on the score of *Tip-Toes*, and with Herbert Stothart, Oscar Hammerstein II, and Otto Harbach on *Song of the Flame*. In desperation for uninterrupted working periods George rented a couple of rooms in a nearby hotel away from the family activities and the almost constant attendance of friends, acquaintances, and strangers.

The *Concerto in F*, George's final choice for a title, was completed on November 10, 1925. Shortly thereafter George acquired the Globe Theatre from Charles Dillingham for the afternoon, plus sixty musi-

Queenie Smith in *Be Yourself*.
CULVER SERVICE

George and his friend Ernest Hutcheson, teacher at the Institute of Musical Art (later Juilliard School of Music), discussing music on the El.
GERSHWIN COLLECTION

cians and Bill Daly to conduct. In the nearly deserted theater sat Walter Damrosch and the usual group of friends. With George at the piano the *Concerto* was played and revised. Revisions were few, only six actually, and then the *Concerto in F* was considered ready for more formal rehearsal in Carnegie Hall. At one of them George showed up very tweedily dressed, smoking an enormous briar pipe that was in action even while he played.

The premiere of the *Concerto in F* took place at Carnegie Hall on December 3. From Aarons, George received a typical message:

UNDERSTAND CON CONRAD HELPED YOU WRITE AND ORCHESTRATE
NEW CONCERTO IF SO I CANNOT HANDLE AUSTRALIAN RIGHTS

Irving Berlin's was more conventional, saying, no doubt, what Aarons really meant but could not say because of his reputation as a wit. Berlin said:

I HOPE YOUR CONCERTO IN F IS AS GOOD AS MINE IN F SHARP
STOP SERIOUSLY GEORGIE I AM ROOTING HARD FOR THE SUCCESS
AND GLORY YOU SO RICHLY DESERVE.

Chautauqua, July 1925. In this unusual setting (for him) George worked on his "New York Concerto," later the *Concerto in F*. COURTESY EMILY PALEY

At Chautauqua, July 1925, with Ernest Hutcheson and students: standing, Jerome Rappaport, George, Oscar Wagner, and Abram Chasins; seated, Mary Huggins, Hutcheson, and Muriel Kerr. GERSHWIN COLLECTION

George going over the *Concerto in F* with Walter Damrosch prior to the performance in Carnegie Hall. COURTESY ARTHUR GERSHWIN

Possibly those of George's devotees who expected a sensational sequel to the *Rhapsody in Blue* were disappointed in the *Concerto* (the critics, as is their wont, were), for the *Concerto in F* in George's own orchestration is definitely not for jazz band and piano. Scored for symphony orchestra, the *Concerto* marks a decided advance over the *Rhapsody* both in the form as well as in the handling of the orchestra. George had put a great deal of work into the *Concerto*, five months as against the few weeks of the earlier work. He was somewhat conscious of history, too, for he dated each movement: the first, July 1925, the second, August–September; the third movement was also dated September. The orchestration was done in October and November.

In keeping with his highly developed sense of showmanship George again came up with a striking "icebreaker." (In musical comedy formula the icebreaker is the opening number of the show serving to put the audience in the proper frame of mind by bringing on the girls to lively music.)

The kettledrum opening of the *Concerto in F* sets the metropolitan scene, reflecting George's original intention of calling it a "New York Concerto." The first piano theme that follows is ingenious in its simplicity; it is actually a syncopated manipulation of a mere three notes that hold up under development and variational treatment exceedingly well.

For the *Tribune* (Sunday, November 29, 1925) George prepared a brief analytical description of the *Concerto in F*:

> The first movement employs the Charleston rhythm. It is quick and pulsating, representing the young enthusiastic spirit of American life. It begins with a rhythmic motif given out by the kettledrums, supported by other percussion instruments, and with a Charleston motif introduced by bassoon, horns, clarinet and violas. The principal theme is announced by the bassoon. Later, a second theme is introduced by the piano.
>
> The second movement has a poetic nocturnal atmosphere which has come to be referred to as the American blues, but in a purer form than that in which they are usually treated.
>
> The final movement reverts to the style of the first. It is an orgy of rhythms, starting violently and keeping to the same pace throughout.

George once described the first movement more succinctly when he said it "was in sonata form . . . but." This typical Gershwinism (another: when an interviewer asked him, "Didn't you play anything when you were a boy?" George replied, "Only hooky.") implied that George was treading warily in the halls of the academy. Actually the *Concerto in F* is really a concerto; its first movement is in the accepted first-movement form, complete with the conventional number of themes and contrasting themes, development, and recapitulation, all in keeping with what could be found in the books.

The second movement, which took George the longest to compose, is one of his loveliest creations and is probably one of the finest pieces of writing by an American composer. Aside from a slight harmonic debt to Debussy this movement is invested with an unmistakable American sound as a muted trumpet sings the blues in a beautifully sustained atmophere that is "nocturnal" and "poetic."

The last movement is the most conventional of all, a rondo that recapitulates some of the earlier themes and introduces new material in a brisk, rhythmic finale.

Actually the *Concerto in F*, or any of George's "serious" works, does not lend itself to the typical (and generally meaningless) musical

The Gershwin house at 316 West 103rd Street. COURTESY IRA GERSHWIN

When the house on 103rd Street became too crowded to work, George took
a couple of rooms in the Whitehall Hotel on 100th Street and Broadway,
where he worked on the *Concerto in F, Song of the Flame,* and *Tip-Toes.*

analysis. His gift, first of all, was a natural one that gives his music an improvisatory and sometimes effortless quality. He did not write by the book, although he was thoroughly familiar with its contents.

One of the favorite indoor sports of George's friends at this time was to argue the merits of his natural ability as opposed to study. Some advised him to stick to songwriting and others implored him to abandon popular music for a career in serious composition. George listened to these arguments, but in a detached manner, for he did not intend to give up one for the other. In fact his success in the popular field helped pay for the time spent in writing the large-scale works. Still, he never lost his keen taste for knowledge about the more technical aspects of his craft; happily, however, he continued to write as he felt. He stated his own case when he observed, "To me feeling counts more than anything else. In my belief it eventually determines the greatness of any artistic effort. It means more than technique or knowledge, for either of these without feeling is of no account. Of course, feeling by itself is not enough, but it is the supreme essential."

That George did not divide himself up into a "popular" and a "serious" Gershwin is no better exemplified than by his work, during the period of the *Concerto*'s composition, for the theater. Three weeks after the premiere of the *Concerto*, *Tip-Toes* opened at the Liberty, boasting a graceful score by George and excellent lyrics by Ira. The latter's work, in fact, inspired a fan letter from a distinguished contemporary:

Lorenz Hart, who sent Ira a cherished letter. COURTESY LYNN FARNOL

When, the other night at the Guild's menagerie, Joe Meyer told me a departing guest was Ira Gershwin, I should have brushed aside your friends, grasped you by the hand, and told you how much I liked the lyrics of "Tip-Toes," but, probably because the circus-clowns inspired a speedy retreat from a too acute consciousness, I had imbibed more cocktails than is my wont, and so when the coffee-loving Mr. Meyer pointed you out, all I could only say, "Zat so!"

Your lyrics, however, gave me as much pleasure as Mr. George Gershwin's music, and the utterly charming performance of Miss Queenie Smith. I have heard none so good this many a day. I wanted to write you right after I had seen the show, but—well I didn't rush up to you at the Guild circus either.

It is a great pleasure to live at a time when light amusement in this country is at last losing its brutally cretin aspect. Such delicacies as your jingles prove that songs can be both popular and intelligent. May I take the liberty of saying that your rhymes show a healthy improvement over those in "Lady Be Good."

You have helped a lot to make an evening delightful to me—and I am very grateful.

Thank you! And may your success continue!

Lorenz Hart

Ira had not been involved in the concoction of *Song of the Flame*, which opened on December 30, two days after *Tip-Toes*. The pseudo-Russian setting did not inspire George to contribute anything authentically Russian, nor for that matter anything typically Gershwin. Actually the authorship of the songs was shared, for both George and Herbert Stothart wrote the music, sometimes in collaboration, sometimes independently.

After resting a little following the stimulating but strenuous series of first nights that brought 1925 to a triumphant close, George left for England again with Alex Aarons to prepare *Lady, Be Good* for London. George wrote an additional song for the Astaires—"I'd Rather Charleston" (the dance was at the height of its popularity in 1926)—with a lyric by Desmond Carter. "Something About Love," with Lou Paley's lyric, a song going back to 1919, was interpolated. *Lady, Be Good* proved to be as pleasing to Londoners as it had to New Yorkers.

There was to be even a greater dividend from the 1926 trip. After George had seen to the Liverpool tryout on March 29 of *Lady, Be Good*, he had some free time before the London opening. So he went to Paris to stay a week with Bob and Mabel Schirmer. Evidently George already had it in his mind to write something about Paris, and he worked on it at the Schirmers': "He had only the original, the walking theme—that first theme, the way *An American in Paris* starts," remembers Mabel. "And I know that after that first theme, he was a little stuck. He said,

109

'This is so complete in itself, I don't know where to go next.'" Where he and Mabel would go daily was shopping and sight-seeing. And thus it was that one day he wanted to go to the Avenue de la Grande Armée. "It's not a very chic street," laughs Mabel. "In those days it had nothing but automobile parts and all the things that you need for automobiles. And so we went, up and down." George, it turned out, was looking for taxi horns; and that shopping solved his thematic problems. On April 11, when he was getting ready to leave Paris and take the Schirmers back to London with him for the opening of *Lady, Be Good*, he inscribed a studio photo to them: "Many thanks for a wonderful week in Paris. Love, George." He wrote out his customary signature (including some measures from the *Rhapsody*), and then he wrote something special: the opening measures (marked "Very Parisienne") for his work-in-progress and signed it *An American in Paris*. He would not complete the work until two years later, when he returned to Paris. But this photo was a series of promissory notes to the Schirmers that there would indeed be someday such a composition which would have a special meaning for them all.

George and Alex returned to New York at the end of April. Already plans were laid for a new Gershwin musical to be produced by Aarons and Freedley and starring the radiant Gertrude Lawrence, who had captured the Gershwins and all of New York as well when she made her American debut in *Charlot's Revue* in 1924.

It was late in 1924, incidentally, that one of George's least-known compositions was put together. "Put together" is apt in this case, for it happened that Samuel Dushkin, the violinist, was visiting George on

Oscar Hammerstein II and Jerome Kern. Hammerstein collaborated with Otto Harbach on the lyrics for *Song of the Flame*.
COURTESY LYNN FARNOL

The Astaires around the time of the London production of *Lady, Be Good*. COURTESY ARTHUR GERSHWIN

110th Street and noticed some short sketches for piano. These were some "Novelettes" that George had been writing off and on. Dushkin suggested that he and George work them into a piece, which struck George as an interesting idea. They took two of the "Novelettes," a slow one and a more rhythmic one, out of which they made *Short Story* for violin and piano. The piece, though quite charming, never proved to be popular or very effective and George tended to dismiss it in later years. He did work up other "Novelettes" as a suite of *Preludes*, composed in 1926.

Alex Aarons and George returning from England after launching the London *Lady, Be Good*. CULVER SERVICE

With Ira's fine lyric George turned out one of his best songs, interpolated into the 1926 edition of *Americana*. The song was "That Lost
Barber Shop Chord," a masterful but gentle satire. With Phil Charig,
Ira wrote a number that enjoyed popularity, "Sunny Disposish," in
which Ira indulged his fancy for adapting current linguistic fads to the
needs of his more pointed lyrical observations. The 1926 *Americana*
was notable, too, for being the occasion for the first appearance of
Helen Morgan *sur le* piano.

The major energies of George and Ira were now being given over
to the Gertrude Lawrence musical, once known as *Mayfair*, then *Miss
Mayfair*, later *Cheerio*, and, finally, *Oh, Kay!*

During the last stages of the rehearsals, October 1926, George came
home one night too keyed up to sleep. Hoping to relax, he took up a
slim novel that was then on the best-seller lists. The opposite occurred;
George was excitedly writing a letter at four in the morning to the
author of the affecting novel, DuBose Heyward, suggesting that they
collaborate on a musical version of *Porgy*.

What had struck George was not only the simple but powerful story,
and the dignified characterization of the Negro, but the importance of
music to the plot. In it Heyward worked snatches of folk songs, and his
descriptions of musical effects displayed an unusual musical sensitivity:

> . . . instruments that glittered in the sunshine, launching daring
> and independent excursions into the realm of sound. Yet these
> improvisations returned always to the eternal boom, boom, boom
> of an underlying rhythm, and met with others in the sudden weav-
> ing and ravelling of amazing chords.
>
> Copyright 1925 by George H. Doran Company

Heyward further described several voices "singing drowsily, as
though burdened by the oppression of the day. In another part of the

Dorothy Heyward about the
time she was secretly con-
verting her husband's novel
into a play. COURTESY MRS.
DUBOSE HEYWARD

Rose Gershwin, mother of the successful song-writing team, George and Ira Gershwin. GERSHWIN COLLECTION

A pre-holiday gathering of friends and family at Belmar, New Jersey, with George in the foreground. To the left of the left-hand pillar are, top row: Milton Ager, Cecelia Ager; second row: Marjorie Paley, Morris Strunsky, and Elsie Payson. In the arch, top row: Lou Paley, Bela Blau, S. N. Behrman, Mrs. Arthur Caesar, English Strunsky, Harold Keyserling. Second row: Mrs. Bela Blau, Mischa Levitzky, Henrietta Poynter, and Jim Englander. Bottom row: Howard Dietz, Cecelia Hays, Arthur Caesar, Emily Paley, Phil Charig, Leonore Gershwin, Ira, George Backer, and Harold Goldman. Behind George Backer are Anita Keen and Barney Paley. On the porch is Albert Strunsky, father of Leonore, Emily, and English. GERSHWIN COLLEC-TION

building someone was picking a guitar monotonously, chord after chord, until the dark throbbed like an old wound." Or "The rhythm swelled, and voices in the court and upper rooms took it up, until the deeply-rooted old walls seemed to rock and surge with the sweep of it."

Thus inspired, George quickly mailed off the letter. Heyward, who was not aware that his wife, Dorothy, was secretly preparing a dramatic adaptation, expressed an interest in the idea. But by the time he traveled north to visit George, she had confessed, and he explained that he did not want to disappoint his wife. George agreed and said that he would want to postpone the project until he had made more serious study of music, for what he had in mind was to create an opera out of Heyward's story.

At this time the Gershwins were living in a five-story house on 103rd Street near Riverside Drive. George had the top floor to himself, the rest of the family scattered on the other floors. The pride of the entire establishment, as far as Pop Gershwin was concerned, was the self-service elevator, in which, at the beginning, he spent a great deal of time. When Heyward called on George, it was Pop who escorted him to the fifth-floor sanctuary, pushing the button in so professional a manner that Heyward mistook him for a rather informally attired butler. But Heyward was due for another surprise. When time came for lunch, he and George sat down at the table, to which was brought a bowl of white liquid that Heyward assumed was potato soup. His southern palate was given a slight jolt when he tasted, for the first time, a local delicacy: sour cream.

On October 18, 1926, Queen Marie of Rumania descended upon New York to get her first glimpse of America (and, incidentally, to give William Anthony McGuire and Guy Bolton a plot for a later Gershwin

Ira and Lou Paley at Belmar, New Jersey. GERSHWIN COLLECTION

Leonore Strunsky (later Gershwin), Ira, and Emily Strunsky Paley. GERSHWIN COLLECTION

115

musical, *Rosalie*). Her disembarkation epitomized the giddy madness of a ticker-tape decade; but the Gershwins missed this international frolic, absorbed as they were by a felicific enterprise of their own.

Down in Philadelphia the U.S.A. was commemorating its hundred fiftieth birthday with a Sesquicentennial Exposition; and in this same city on the same October 18 the Gershwins tried out *Oh, Kay!*— a show whose title could almost have been the proclamation of well-being in the world of the Twenties. The show enchanted the audience at the Shubert; but success seldom immobilized the Gershwin brothers. The next day they—the "they" now being a trio including the former Leonore Strunsky, whom Ira had married on September 14—were re-packing their bags and heading for an Atlantic City rendezvous with Edgar Selwyn and the first discussions on what subsequently became *Strike Up the Band.* Selwyn was going to produce the as-yet-unwritten show, but first he intended celebrating his birthday on October 20, and the Gershwins were going to help. Soon afterward the newspapers had it that the next Gershwin musical would be *Strike Up the Band*, that George S. Kaufman would supply the book, and that the entire pro-duction would belong to "an entirely new genre."

While the Gershwins were in Atlantic City they happened to meet the Heywards, who were waiting for word from the Theatre Guild on the production of their play, *Porgy*, then finished and ready for the boards (production had to wait another year, however). George and DuBose walked apart and discussed again their proposed opera.

Oh, Kay! opened in New York on November 8, with raves for the Gershwins and Gertrude Lawrence, and proved to have the longest run of any Gershwin musical up to that time. The songs matched the Lawrence sparkle and loveliness. There is a wonderful "icebreaker" in "The Woman's Touch," which may surprise those who believe that

Gertrude Lawrence as Kay in *Oh, Kay!*, her first American-produced show (her first American appearance was in *Charlot's Revue*, an English import), in which she appeared as the sister of a titled English bootlegger. Miss Lawrence had hard-boiled New Yorkers at her feet when she wistfully sang "Someone to Watch over Me" to a little rag doll. CULVER SERVICE

integrated songs furthering the plot belong to a day long after the Twenties came to an ignominious end. Another fine song, a lovely melody with a lyric that keeps it away from the sentimental, is "Dear Little Girl." Some of the songs gained lasting popularity: "Someone to Watch over Me," "Do-Do-Do," "Maybe," and "Clap Yo' Hands."

During the writing of *Oh, Kay!* Ira had been rushed to Mt. Sinai Hospital, where his appendix was removed. Howard Dietz came in then to help complete the lyrics, most notably the title song and "Heaven on Earth."

In an attempt to repeat the furor of the 1923 Gauthier recital George and the Peruvian singer Marguerite D'Alvarez programmed a "Futurist" musical concert at the Roosevelt Hotel on December 4, 1926. Mme. D'Alvarez sang, in addition to the selections from her standard repertoire, Kern's "Babes in the Wood," George's "Nashville Nightingale," "Clap Yo' Hands," from the current *Oh, Kay!*, and as an encore "Oh, Lady Be Good." George played one of the pianos in a two-piano arrangement of the *Rhapsody in Blue* and, solo, presented for the first time five *Preludes for Piano*, of which three were eventually published and dedicated to Bill Daly. One of the unpublished preludes is in song form and has been given the title "Sleepless Night" by Ira,

Marguerite D'Alvarez,
Peruvian singer who once
said: "When I die, I want
Gershwin's jazz concerto
played over my grave." For
a joint recital with her
George prepared the *Preludes
for Piano*. PHOTO BY CARL
VAN VECHTEN

though no lyric has been written for it; it is #17 among the unpublished manuscripts.

The *Preludes* are attractive miniatures comprising a balanced little suite, two rhythmic pieces placed on either side of a haunting blues. In these pieces, and especially in the second prelude, George is revealed at his most sensitive.

He then toured with Mme. D'Alvarez, appearing in Buffalo and Boston. The return to New York catapulted him into his usual round of activity. With Bill Daly he prepared a Gershwin medley, which he played at the Imperial during an intermission of *Oh, Kay!* to perk up the box office. In April of 1927 he made a new recording for RCA Victor at Liederkranz Hall of the *Rhapsody in Blue* with the Whiteman orchestra, now counting among its members such jazz men as Bix Beiderbecke and Jimmy and Tommy Dorsey. On July 26 George made his first appearance at Lewisohn Stadium as soloist in the *Rhapsody in Blue*.

Among those whom strikes, political unrest, and—as Lady Bracknell would have it—"a revolutionary outrage" brought to the height of their power in the late 1920s and early 1930s was Ira Gershwin. He owed this rise specifically to an outbreak of three operettas: *Strike Up the Band, Of Thee I Sing,* and *Let 'Em Eat Cake.*

In April 1927, George, Ira, and Leonore took a country house at Ossining, New York, where they promised themselves uninterrupted quiet for their work; there at Chumleigh Farm they had occasional guests: George Kaufman for a day, Franklin P. Adams for a weekend.

A regular visitor to the farm was Harry Ruby, of the Kalmar and Ruby song-writing team. Ruby's passion was baseball and he would frequently show up with the proper equipment, trying to get someone to toss a few. Only George agreed to don a glove and throw the ball. When they met some weeks later in their publisher's office, George allowed that Ruby threw very well, adding "I could do very well also, if I tried, but I must be careful of my hands." Further adding, in the words of Ruby, "in his sweet and natural way, with no insult intended, 'With you it doesn't matter.'"

When he chided George about this remark at one of Jules Glaenzer's parties, George didn't even remember it. Ruby repeated it, George listening intently, and when the tale was told, George merely said, "Well, it's true, isn't it?"

George in Ossining, April 1927, when he and Ira were at work on the first *Strike Up the Band.*
COURTESY ARTHUR GERSHWIN

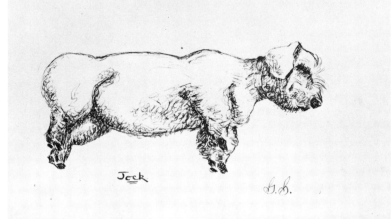

One of George's earliest drawings, made at Chumleigh Farm. Incidentally, Jock is reclining—he was not deformed. GERSHWIN COLLECTION

On their way to Boston, George and Alex Aarons stopped off at Vinton Freedley's farm near Pomfret, Connecticut. George wanted some exercise, so Freedley sent him into the hayfield with pitchfork in hand—and, contrary to rules of agriculture, with a pipe in his mouth. Freedley relates, "It took a bit of persuading to convince him that farmers did not smoke pipes in hayfields, so it was half-hour on, and half-hour off (for the pipe)." Freedley is on the left, George in the middle, and Aarons on the right.

A pencil sketch by Ira
Gershwin of his brother-in-
law, English Strunsky.
COURTESY ENGLISH STRUNSKY

English

4/25/27

Ira Gershwin

After the hay-pitching on one of the
hottest days of the year, Aarons,
George, and Freedley cooled off in
the pool. GERSHWIN COLLECTION

The Ossining house, set on forty acres of farmland, was so successfully remote that gregarious George and Ira began dabbling with water colors to fill in the long evenings. They also bought automobiles; George settled for a used Mercedes touring car that a mechanic, supplied by the company, taught him to subdue as they careered along the Old Post Road. Lee had learned to drive the preceding summer, and now her brother, English Strunsky, went up to give her a refresher course and to endeavor, unsuccessfully, to put Ira too behind the wheel. (Ira did get a license that summer, but once he left Ossining he never took the wheel of a car again; he gave as one of his reasons for abandoning motoring that he could not abide the dirty looks from other drivers.) Ossining became a fine place to write a score, and the brothers often worked far into the morning hours. By July, however, with *Strike Up the Band* in rehearsal, they were commuting almost daily to the city. Consequently they gave up their lease, abandoned the country retreat, and settled for a hot summer back on 103rd Street to put the show in shape.

Strike Up the Band opened on August 29, 1927, in Long Branch, New Jersey at the Broadway Theatre. On September 5 it began playing the Shubert in Philadelphia. After two weeks there, of small business and larger rewriting, it abruptly folded, for the first week's business was around $17,000; the second week was under nine. It seemed unlikely, therefore, that the show could pull through the six weeks scheduled for that city, but Selwyn would have given it a try if he had had the money. *Variety* said: " . . . although the critics raved, there wasn't a chance. Attendance dwindled gradually every performance until the last few days there wasn't a handful of people in the big theatre." Once again, a *succès d'estime* was not big box office.

Today it is difficult to understand why *Strike Up the Band* was such a failure its first time out. It certainly had an ingenious plot: because Switzerland had protested the 50 per cent American tariff against Swiss cheese, Horace J. Fletcher, owner of the American Cheese Company of Hurray, Connecticut, persuaded Colonel Holmes (modeled upon Woodrow Wilson's Colonel House) to force Switzerland into war. Fletcher happily agreed to bear the financial burdens of the campaign as long as a grateful country christened the struggle The Horace J. Fletcher Memorial War.

In this milieu the leading man is Jim Townsend, a newspaperman, who loves (inevitably) the leading lady, Joan Fletcher, the cheese

From the scrapbook: a clipping commemorating the turning of tables—a recital at which the critics performed and the performers criticized. Standing are pianist-composer-author John Erskine, critic Olin Downes, pianist Josef Hofmann, Ernest Hutcheson, flutist Georges Barrere, and George. At the piano, Erskine's daughter and critic Ernest Urchs.

maker's daughter. Through the efforts of a secret-service agent Townsend discovers that Fletcher has watered his cheese with Grade B milk; this knowledge turns the reporter into a pacifist. When patriots, who have already barred the *Swiss Family Robinson* and *William Tell* from libraries and schoolbooks, find that Townsend has a Swiss watch, they label him un-American. War is declared, Townsend is drafted, and Joan Fletcher gives her affections to another.

The second act opens in Switzerland, where the war is being waged. (The Swiss hotels had offered attractive rates to encourage the tourist business; after all, khaki-clad or otherwise, a customer is still a customer.) In the background reverberates the roar of battle, but on stage sit the American soldiers, knitting for the poor folks back home.

> Oh, this is such a charming war,
> Whoops! What a charming war!
> Whoops! What a charming war!

123

It keeps you out in the open air.
　　Oh, this is such a charming war!
　　Whoops! What a charming war!
　　Whoops! What a charming war!
　We're glad that we're over here over there!
We sleep in downy feather beds—we never see a cot;
Our contract calls for ice cream sodas when the weather's hot;
And a helluva lot of publicity if ever we get shot!

Courtesy Ira Gershwin

A yodeling maneuver of Jim's captures the Swiss Army; providentially an unmasked Swiss spy confesses that it was he who had pumped the Grade B milk into Fletcher's cheese. Despite Jim's protests that his feelings about the whole mess are unchanged he becomes a hero. The soldiers return home triumphant, getting much praise—but losing their jobs. Then comes the grand celebration of the Peace with Switzerland; matters have gone so well that when Russia protests the tariff against caviar, all agree that she too should be taught a lesson, and as the curtain bangs down, we hear again "Strike Up the Band."

Variety sourly observed that the American Legion wouldn't like it. Not even Ira's whimsical, palliative lyrics and George's rollicking music could conceal the deeper scars cut in the audience's awareness by the whiplash cynicism in the book. During those moments when the Gershwins held the stage, however, *Strike Up the Band* was frequently a lyrical show. The charming duet "Seventeen and Twenty-One" established the idyllic quality of the play, later developed by "The Man I Love" (and its masculine reprise, caroled by Morton Downey: "The Girl I Love").

To avoid too many Savoyard echoes in the programmatic lyrics, George cleverly revised Ira's patter song, "The Unofficial Spokesman," which had been written in the strict Gilbertian tradition—even to the extent that for once Ira's words came before the music. By having the lyric stutter on "unofficial," George endowed it with unique charm. But the ghosts of D'Oyly Carte hovered in the wings of Ira's imagination; one night, while the show was floundering in Philadelphia, the three authors stood in front of the Shubert. They were looking disconsolately down the street when a cab drew up and two elegant Edwardian clubmen, dressed to the nines, got out, bought tickets, and entered the thea-

Portrait, 1927. COURTESY EDWARD STEICHEN

Poster for the London production of *Funny Face*, with Leslie Henson in the Victor Moore role. GERSHWIN COLLECTION

ter. "That must be Gilbert and Sullivan," said Ira, "coming to fix the show." "Why don't you put jokes like that in your lyrics?" complained Kaufman. The show did not fail because of too few lyrical jokes, however, or even the heavy influence of Gilbert and Sullivan. The outspoken satire against the War Profiteer was too grim for the musical-comedy audience who wished their train of thought diverted but not upset. It was 1927, the height of Coolidge well-being, and the aficionados of musical comedy didn't want to study about war.

A good number of problems afflicted the next show, *Funny Face*, especially tailored for the Astaires, who were returning from England after the run of *Lady, Be Good* ended. For some reason *Smarty* (the original title) did not gel out of town. The producers laid the blame on the songs, which were discarded mercilessly. This not only cost the Gershwins time and hard work; George was also charged for the copying of the new orchestrations. He did this without complaint; similarly he and Ira came up with new songs. In six weeks an almost entirely new score and show were assembled; about half the original songs were thrown out—one of them being the excellent "How Long Has This Been Going On?"

Betty Compton, Adele Astaire, Gertrude McDonald and Fred Astaire in *Funny Face*. CULVER SERVICE

When *Funny Face* finally arrived in New York it had the earmarks of a hit further enhanced by the gala occasion of the simultaneous opening of a new theater, the Alvin—the name a combination of the first syllables of Aarons's and Freedley's first names. *Funny Face* began a run on November 22, 1927, and racked up a total of 244 performances, thanks to the songs, the Astaires, and Victor Moore's appealing characterization of a quite ineffectual jewel thief.

After *Funny Face* was safely and surely settled in the Alvin, George got himself involved with some of the songs for a Ziegfeld show, *Rosalie*. When Vinton Freedley attended the first-night performance, on January 10, 1928, he felt that he had already seen the show, or at least had heard it. This may be a slight exaggeration, but George did not put much effort into the score of *Rosalie*, which also had songs by Sigmund Romberg. The lyrics were the joint effort of P. G. Wodehouse and Ira.

Into *Rosalie* from *Funny Face* went "How Long Has This Been Going On?"; from *Oh, Kay!* came the discarded "Show Me the Town"; 127

from *Primrose* came "Wait a Bit, Susie," newly titled "Beautiful Gypsy"; and finally, from the temporarily demobilized *Strike Up the Band*, "Yankee Doodle Rhythm." The new songs, including "Oh Gee! Oh Joy!", "New York Serenade," and "Say So!" (with its fine, delicate rhythmic effect), are very good indeed. The success of *Rosalie*, which starred Marilyn Miller, was assured by the reception of the first night's glittering audience; and Mayor Jimmy Walker, during intermission, stood up to deliver a brief address on *Rosalie*'s virtues, with some added remarks on his own city budget, only recently signed.

After a steady run of musicals George became a bit restive and anxious to begin work on another extended composition. Also, he and Ira agreed that it would be a good time for them to take a vacation abroad.

Added impetus was given to George's idea for a "serious composition" at the special party given by Eva Gauthier for Ravel on March 7, the French composer's fifty-third birthday. Ravel was finishing a long tour of the United States, and his good friend Mme. Gauthier wished to send him off in style; she asked him what he wanted most before

Jack Donahue, George, Sigmund Romberg, Marilyn Miller, and Florenz Ziegfeld at a rehearsal of *Rosalie*. CULVER SERVICE

Marilyn Miller as *Rosalie*.
CULVER SERVICE

leaving for Paris. Ravel asked for two favors: 1. He craved to have an
un-American steak—RARE—and, 2. To meet George Gershwin, which
of course was arranged after Ravel had enjoyed attending *Funny Face*.

At the party George took the opportunity to ask if he might become Ravel's pupil, but Ravel declined, insisting that George was perfectly fine the way he was. As so many other composers with a reputation in the world of "serious" music, Ravel was captivated by
George's gifts as a composer and, also, as a pianist. Gershwin's boyish
eagerness to please and delight in his own creations made him a target
for good-humored envy.

George, Mme. Baton, Rhené Baton,
and Alexandre Tansman in Paris.
GERSHWIN COLLECTION

The Ravel birthday party given by Eva Gauthier. Standing around Ravel
at the piano are Oskar Fried, a conductor; Eva Gauthier, Tedesco of Naples,
conductor of the San Carlo Orchestra; and George. WIDE WORLD PHOTOS

"I wonder," he is supposed to have mused while at the keyboard of someone's piano, "if my music will be played a hundred years from now."

According to Oscar Levant (who was occasionally credited with the quip), it was Newman Levy who retorted, "Yes, if you're around to play it."

George's winning personality, a combination of diffidence and gregariousness, won him many friends, though few actual close ones. The role of the celebrity, of being in the limelight, sought after by the smartest hostesses, by the newspapers, by the small as well as the great, was one that George unabashedly enjoyed.

Even so towering a personality as Ravel recognized George as a remarkably talented young man and gladly gave up his role of guest of honor at the party to have George play until dawn. Ravel later paid his tribute to George, and recalled his trips to Harlem's hot spots in his two piano concertos composed after his return to France.

The New York *Times* announced on March 9, 1928, that George was to leave for Europe, where he would study and work on a new composition. On the eleventh George, Ira and Lee, and Frankie left for London and points on the Continent. In London, a week later, they arrived early enough in the day to get Phil Charig out of bed. He and Ira had written the songs for *That's a Good Girl*, which was to be produced in London in the summer. The show had been on the agenda of Kern and Hammerstein, who were involved with *Show Boat*. Max Dreyfus then asked Ira and Phil to fulfill the commitment.

In London the Gershwins saw the closing performance, on March 24, 1928, of *Oh, Kay!*, then they crossed the Channel and settled down for a stay in Paris. George had brought with him the initial sketches for a new orchestral piece. Ira was content "to see the sights and drink beer," but George, between parties, interviews, and meetings with the musically important in Paris (including Milhaud, Ravel, Stravinsky, Prokofiev, Poulenc), worked on a tone poem that he decided to call *An American in Paris*, the idea and title for which had come during the 1926 trip to Paris.

Concert-going, too, was another important activity, though often as not it turned out that in honor of his presence in the city Parisians were playing his music quite regularly. The Gershwins heard a Paris performance of the *Rhapsody in Blue* at the end of March. The piano part was shared by Wiener and Doucet (who had served Bach similarly in the preceding number in the program); the Pasdeloup Orchestra was conducted by Rhené Baton. Ira noted the event in his journal, March 31:

3/31 Paris (Rain, most of day) Saturday. Up at 8 (don't know what wakes me so early and suddenly). Found no papers so to bed again. Woke at 9. Found papers. Sinclair Oil 29. Breakfast. At 2 Adolph Block came up. Lunch at 4. Then at 5 with George to the Saturday concerts Pasdeloup at the Théatre Mogador. (Rose Marie is in its 2nd year here.) The theatre smelt beery and the air was close. We got a box in the middle of the orchestra floor. There were several women musicians in the orchestra. Rhené Baton, a large, bearded man with a ring on his left hand, conducted. 1st they played Cesar Franck Symphonie en Ré mineur—2. Mikhail (1st performance altho written in 1909) by R. Brunel, wishy washy Oriental moving picture music, 3. Le Chant de Migamon—Honegger (1917) based on American Indian themes. Good. Intermission. 4. Concerto en Ut Mineur—J. S. Bach pour deux pianos et orchestra (3 short movements—charming—the soloists Messieurs Wiener et Doucet. 5. Rhapsodie in Blue—George Gershwin. I alternately giggled & squirmed during this performance. It was at times almost unbelievably bad. The solo part had evidently proved too hard for M. Wiener, the premier soloist, so he got an assistant to oompah. Some of the fast tempi were taken at a funereal pace, and the rhythms were terrible in spots. A banjo played the same chord almost all thru the piece. The middle theme couldn't be spoiled of course and came like a violet ray on a bald spot. And yet I realized that since probably 95% of the audience had never heard it before they might take the occasional sour notes as a true reading and find it all interesting. Sure enough at its conclusion that was real spontaneous applause all over the house & lots of cheers & bravos. George had left quickly for the bar to wait for us but when I saw Wiener on the platform looking anxiously over the audience & then gesticulating to the conductor I knew they wanted G. So I called him & he was rushed backstage—and on his appearance the house gave him another big hand. So the 2 pianists played for an encore "Do! Do! Do!" a verse & 3 choruses they had evidently arranged and practised for it went with great eclat and the house wanted more. It was the 1st time I had heard of an encore by soloists to a symphony program. In the lobby G. told us Baton had apologized for the performance saying they had only rehearsed the piece ½ hour, and he had only the piano score etc. At any rate despite the almost laughable performance George was thrilled by the reception. In the

George and Gertrude Lawrence in London. GERSHWIN COLLECTION

Frankie Gershwin, who
sang Gershwin songs at
Les Ambassadeurs in
Paris. GERSHWIN
COLLECTION

lobby met Deems Taylor & Mary Kennedy; then Fekerte, Salabert
and Yvain, a tall and hicky looking Frenchman. Adolph left us and
G., F., Lee, Mabel & myself drove to Mabel's apart. to get Bob who
had been golfing, and all of us to L'Aperouse a restaurant on the
Left Bank where we had a good dinner for about 550 Francs.
Then to hotel, where we spent a wild hour in Paris playing
"Ghost." And to bed about 2. Finished "Transition" about 4.

George, on the other hand, found the French manner of playing different from the American and rather enjoyed the performance because
of the entirely "different effect from the French method of being exact
with every note."

On Tuesday, April 3, Ira, Lee, Frankie, and Leopold Godowsky
Jr., went to the Louvre, where they spent an hour "doing the wing
nearest the river, mostly Italian primitives, Davincis, Hals, Van Dycks,
Reubens, Tintorettos. A Membling near the entrance I loved . . . I
wanted to stay on, but the girls were tired so to the Hotel Chatham."

After dinner the Gershwins went to the apartment of Alexandre Tansman, where they met "E. Robert Schmitz & wife, Ibert & wife, a couple of other composers & wives and 3 critics. George played about 2 hours without stopping to the success & enthusiasm he is accustomed to."

Ira found it curious that the "refreshment consisted of cake, candy & orangeade. Not a drop of liquor in any form—a state of affairs possible only in a country where there are no Prohib. laws." They stayed late; Ira noted marginally that also present at the party were Dimitri Tiomkin and his wife Albertina Rasch, both of whom were to perform Gershwin music professionally.

Tiomkin's opportunity came first, for on May 29 he appeared as piano soloist in the European premiere of the *Concerto in F*, with Vladimir Golschmann conducting. The *Rhapsody*, however, became the Gershwin leitmotiv; the Gershwins heard it practically everywhere they went: at the Champs-Elysées Theater, where the Ballet Russe performed a ballet by Anton Dolin, or, when they later traveled to Vienna and entered the Café Sacher in the company of Emmerich Kalman, the little orchestra struck up the *Rhapsody* as entrance music.

One evening Frankie and George accompanied Mabel Schirmer to a party and before it ended George was at the piano, but with a difference—Frankie was asked to sing. In her small but true and charming voice, she sang several of her brothers' songs. Elsa Maxwell was enchanted and spread the word to Cole Porter, whose own revue was then in preparation at the night club Les Ambassadeurs. Porter, too, was so

Announcement of the first European performance of the *Concerto*. Aaron Copland's name is misspelled, incidentally—and Dimitri Tiomkin has moved to Hollywood, where he composes film scores. GERSHWIN COLLECTION

135

taken with Frankie's singing, and no doubt not underselling the presence of George, that he talked Frankie into appearing in his show. She would sing what in the program was listed as a "Gershwin Specialty." For the opening, on May 10, she wore a simple but beautiful gown with a bouffant skirt and sang to George's accompaniment. As Mabel Schirmer recalled it, "Frankie literally stopped the show." She remained with it, in fact, though without George, for a full two weeks.

In the Hotel Majestic George worked on *An American in Paris* and readily played it for the usual stream of callers, among them the young British composer William Walton, Vladimir Dukelsky, Dick Simon, the publisher, pianist Mario Braggiotti. One day Leopold Stokowski dropped by and became greatly interested in the work in progress, but this lasted only until he heard that the first performance had been promised to Damrosch.

Another day George and Tansman walked along the Avenue de la Grand Armée until they were able to take back to the Majestic more French taxi horns that George had decided would be worked into the score of *An American in Paris*.

While in Paris he received a cable from Ziegfeld:

WILL YOU WRITE THE MUSIC FOR A NEW PLAY FOR EDDIE CANTOR
REHEARSALS START SEPTEMBER FIRST BOOK BY MCGUIRE IF NOT
CAN I DEPEND ON YOU TO WRITE THE MUSIC FOR ONE SHOW REGARDS
                                                    ZIEGFELD

George and Ira were already committed to do another Gertrude Lawrence show for Aarons, so any thought of another Ziegfeld show was put off momentarily. When they did begin work for Ziegfeld in early 1929, they were planning what might have proved a most interesting undertaking in setting a hit play of 1918, *East Is West*, to music. They began writing the songs even before all arrangements were completed, but *East Is West* never did materialize. An original and interesting reminder is the art song "In the Mandarin's Orchid Garden," which was eventually published. An unpublished "Yellow Blues" (in two keys) (#42 among the unpublished mss.) is also a Gershwin highlight. Other songs were, of course, salvaged for future shows and a film.

The Gershwin party made plans for their return to New York, with the public press closely reporting their activities and plans. On June 6, the *Times* announced that George's new piece, *An American in Paris*,

1924–
1929

136

George in Vienna,
April 1928.
CULVER SERVICE

Ira's manuscript
for an early
version of the
verse for a
memorable song
from *Treasure Girl*.
It has been
suggested that this
verse is the essence
of the plot of every
Twenties musical.
COPYRIGHT 1928 BY
NEW WORLD MUSIC
CORPORATION. USED
BY PERMISSION

Where's The Boy?

There is no doubt
About
The fact that life without
A lord and master
Is a disaster.
Is there a "he"
Who'd be
The world and all to me
But fate decided
We be divided.
There's just this man and it's high time
He came to take up my time.
Will he appear?
Oh dear!
Each day seems like a year.
But who knows whether
We'll get together.

was to be played the next season by the New York Philharmonic-Symphony Orchestra. On the twentieth the *Times* noted the return of the Gershwins to New York, and the fact that George and Ira had returned to go to work on the Gertrude Lawrence musical.

On August 1, George finished the piano sketch of *An American in Paris*, then began the orchestration. That is, when work on *Treasure Girl* did not interfere. *Treasure Girl*, starring Gertrude Lawrence and Clifton Webb, despite the show-saving graces of the stars and one of the brothers' best scores, did not survive beyond the new year. The real tragedy is that it took its score with it, including such songs as "Oh, So Nice," "Where's the Boy?," "I Don't Think I'll Fall in Love Today," and "Feeling I'm Falling."

On November 18, 1928, ten days after the unheralded opening of *Treasure Girl*, George completed the orchestration of *An American in Paris*. "This new piece," he explained, "really a rhapsodic ballet, is written very freely and is the most modern music I've yet attempted. The

Franz Lehar and George in Vienna, May 1928.
GERSHWIN COLLECTION

Ira, Lee, George, and Emmerich Kalman in the Café Sacher, Vienna.
GERSHWIN COLLECTION

opening part will be developed in typical French style, in the manner of Debussy and the Six, though the themes are all original. My purpose here is to portray the impression of an American visitor in Paris, as he strolls about the city, and listens to various street noises and absorbs the French atmosphere.

"As in my other orchestral compositions I've not endeavored to represent any definite scenes in this music. The rhapsody is programmatic only in a general impressionistic way, so that the individual listener can read into the music such as his imagination pictures for him.

"The opening gay section is followed by a rich blues with a strong rhythmic undercurrent. Our American friend perhaps after strolling into a café and having a couple of drinks, has succumbed to a spasm of homesickness. The harmony here is both more intense and simple than in the preceding pages. This blues rises to a climax followed by a coda in which the spirit of the music returns to the vivacity and bubbling exuberance of the opening part with its impressions of Paris. Apparently

139

the homesick American, having left the cafe and reached the open air, has disowned his spell of the blues and once again is an alert spectator of Parisian life. At the conclusion, the street noises and French atmosphere are triumphant."

For the premiere, under Walter Damrosch at Carnegie Hall, December 13, Deems Taylor prepared a more elaborate program for the *American*, which has come to be closely identified with it ever since, and is frequently quoted in concert programs and other likely places. However, enjoyment of the direct appeal of *An American in Paris* is not dependent upon a programmatic crutch (though it is skillfully written); George's less polished prose (which seems never to be quoted) sufficiently covers his own intentions in the piece.

Not that he did not have a story in mind. In his two-piano copy of the score, dated only "January 1928," from which he worked in preparing the orchestration, there are also included some of the original pencil sketches. Written into these sketches are a few narrative ideas he originally considered when he first began thinking about his "tone poem." For example there is the phrase, "Old World Wanderings," and an indistinct word that appears to be "Drunk" followed by the notation, "possibly two octaves lower." Then this:

Sees Girl
Meets Girl
Back to 2/4–Strolling Flirtation
Into Cafe
Mix Love Theme with 2/4
Conversation leading to Slow Blues

(This section is readily identifiable, since it occurs just before the well-known blues in the work; the "conversation" is held by two violins.) The two-piano manuscript is of especial significance not only because of the annotations of plot and the indications of instrumentation but also because of the various alterations and cuts. It was clearly very carefully edited before George began final work on it.

In the orchestration especially he evidences a remarkable growth since the *Concerto;* the handling of the strings is particularly ingenious. Exactly what he meant by saying that his opening is in the manner of Debussy and the Six is difficult to say, unless, rather than Debussy, he actually meant Satie, the spiritual leader of the Six, who were actually

Dorothy Rodgers wrote in *My Favorite Things:* "Elsa Maxwell's parties were huge and elaborate and always had a theme . . . We took great pains with our get-ups and always had make-up men put on the finishing touches. I still have a picture taken at one of Elsa's 'Come as Somebody Else' parties in 1929, just after Dick and I announced our engagement. In it, Jules Glaenzer, George Gershwin, Justine Johnson and Dick look startlingly like the four Marx brothers. Jules was Chico; George, a remarkable Groucho; Dick was Zeppo; and—with the wig and horn she borrowed from Harpo— you'd certainly never guess that Justine was one of the world's most beautiful women." GERSHWIN COLLECTION

in revolt against Debussy. The opening "walking theme" is in the spirit of the Six—saucy, spirited, full of good humor, delightfully insouciant. Humor is an often-overlooked quality in George's music, whether in song or larger work, and a reflection of his intellectual side is most evident in his tricky rhythms and harmonies far afield from Tin Pan Alley.

As a change of pace George chose not to furnish *An American in Paris* with a piano part for himself. But, to retain that jazzy touch, he scored the blues for trumpet. Vladimir Dukelsky, when he heard this section at the Hotel Majestic, considered it saccharine, but George chose not to alter it, particularly after William Walton expressed pleasure in the blues as it was. It was, of course, partly autobiographical, for despite the round of European activity George missed the more familiar excitement of New York, the opening nights, the parties at Glaenzer's, or Condé Nast's, or Sidney Fish's—or at 33 Riverside Drive at 75th Street, where, with Lee and Ira, he shared adjoining penthouses that became a meeting place for the talented and would-be talented, of musicians from both sides of the musical track, writers, beautiful women (George's taste), members of society whom George had met at the Glaenzer, Nast, Fish ménages. Another party center was Carl Van Vechten's.

George working on his water color
"Me." UNITED PRESS PHOTO

George and friends on a Canadian
skiing trip. GERSHWIN COLLECTION

Kay Swift Warburg, gifted composer
and good friend of the Gershwins.
GERSHWIN COLLECTION

George on the Warburg farm in Connecticut, where he liked to go "horse riding." "Not *horse* riding, George," Kay Swift Warburg would gently remind him: "horse*back* riding." But George stuck to his own terminology. He had one lesson from a groom on the proper way to seat his mount; thereafter he rode (frequently in bowler hat and with cigar) chanting *sotto voce*, "Tummy in, tummy out, tummy in, tummy out."
GERSHWIN COLLECTION

Here George met mainly personages in the arts, including brilliant Negro artists such as Bessie Smith, who was one of the few people for whom George would desert the piano to hear. He was not a little impressed, too, by her ability to down a stiff jolt of gin before she sang the blues.

Jules Glaenzer's role as host to parties that were referred to as either "swank" or "fabulous" was to bring together an assorted group, with an emphasis on songwriters, and society folk and financiers who might give aid to young talent. It would not be unusual to have at a single party such richly endowed composers as George, Vincent Youmans, Harry Ruby, and an impressive showering of musical-comedy stars including Gertrude Lawrence, Beatrice Lillie, the Astaires, and Ohman and Arden, who played, as they were generally doing in the current Gershwin show, on the two pianos.

It was after the premiere of *An American in Paris* that Glaenzer held a party in honor of the occasion for George. A humidor covered with the signatures of George's friends was to be presented by Harry Ruby, but he was trapped in Boston with an ailing show and his place was quickly filled by Otto Kahn, who made the presentation with an appropriate speech.

After comparing George to Lindbergh as a leader of American youth, 143

Ruby Keeler in *Show Girl* when she was billed as Ruby Keeler Jolson. CULVER SERVICE

Kahn, whose son was leader of a "jazz" band, felt that George's powers would be deepened by a bit of suffering, something, as far as Kahn knew, he had managed to evade in his rise to the position of leader of young Americans. Kahn wished for "an experience—not too prolonged —of that driving storm and stress of the emotions." For some reason there were those who felt that somewhere in Kahn's speech there was a veiled invitation for George to write an opera for the Metropolitan.

George, suffering or not, had already considered tackling an opera. He had spoken with Van Vechten about it and had even rejected a rather complex idea for a Negro opera, a sophisticated book along the lines of a Svengali motif. George's own choice still was Heyward's *Porgy* or possibly the Jewish folk tale *The Dybbuk*.

Though the critics were not in agreement about *An American in Paris*, the work proved most effective and popular from the beginning. Nathaniel Shilkret, an old friend from the student days with Hambitzer, was a successful conductor in radio. He performed the tone poem in its

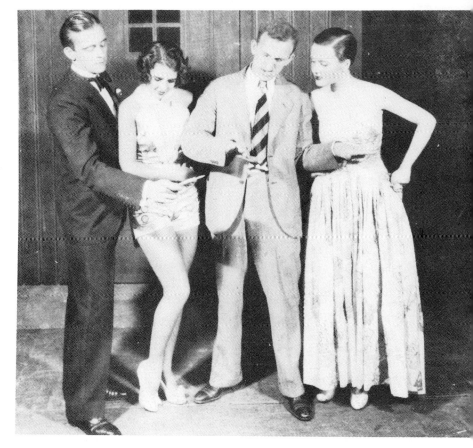

Eddie Foy, Jr., Ruby Keeler, Jimmy Durante, and Kathryn Hereford in *Show Girl*. CULVER SERVICE

radio premiere on January 9, 1929. In February a date was set for a complete recording in the studios of RCA Victor, the first full-scale recording of a Gershwin composition.

George was quite excited about this and in fact managed to get into Shilkret's way during the rehearsals. Shilkret asked George to leave the studio for a while and George did, though he was a bit miffed by this action. When George returned to the studio the orchestra was ready to record and he was drafted to play the brief bridge passages for celeste. In his excitement he missed one cue, but he can be heard in the remaining passage. This first recording is undoubtedly the most authentic interpretation of *An American in Paris;* it is in a sense a period piece. The small orchestra used in the recording gives the work a particularly muscular character that is right for it.

Ziegfeld was, finally, to have another show from the Gershwins. Wanting to produce a summer show, he talked the brothers into writing the songs for *Show Girl,* in which the Great Glorifier wished to star a girl who not only was graduate of the Texas Guinan school of dance (the slogan of which was, of course, "Hello, Sucker!") but, more importantly, had just married Al Jolson; and so she was billed too: Ruby Keeler Jolson.

Ziegfeld never got along very well with his composers, and where the Gershwins were concerned he had a disconcerting habit of dropping in on them, unannounced, just to check up, and likely as not find George at his easel instead of the keyboard, for he was spending much time at painting.

But the score of *Show Girl* was completed in time for rehearsals and the July 2 opening at the Ziegfeld. It seemed to have sure-fire hit ingredients: the songs by George, Ira, and Gus Kahn, a good book (to begin with) by J. P. McEvoy, adapted by William Anthony McGuire—plus Ruby Keeler, Eddie Foy, Jr., Jimmy Durante, and even Duke Ellington and orchestra. And on the gala opening night—with a "Who's Who" audience from society, stage, screen, and music—Al Jolson sprang from his seat to serenade his wife with "Liza."

An American in Paris was adapted to ballet by Albertina Rasch, and a song, "Home Blues," was devised from the blues section. An unusual song, "Feeling Sentimental," seemed years ahead of its time, being built along a lovely curving melody over unique, sophisticated chords. Years ahead indeed, for it was cut. "Do What You Do" was contemporary in tempo, and "So Are You!" was effectively jaunty. But to no avail. When it dawned upon Ziegfeld that *Show Girl* would not be the last rose of summer, he refused to pay the Gershwins their royalties and began to barrage them with profuse telegrams. Finally the Gershwins were forced to sue; Ziegfeld countered by suing them for not writing a hit show. But, as was the case with *Show Girl* itself, nothing came of it.

Preferring not to become involved in Ziegfeldian altercations, George and Ira gave their attention to a new version of *Strike Up the Band*. Even while they were in Paris in April of the previous year Edgar Selwyn had written to George of his plans to revive the anti-war operetta. Selwyn had lost out on one version of *Strike Up the Band*, but he was convinced that the operetta could be patched up and turned into a hit. Morrie Ryskind was called in to popularize the Kaufman book. And, of course, wholesale shifts in the score were made.

Before *Strike Up the Band* opened, George made his debut as conductor at Lewisohn Stadium on August 26, 1929, when he was soloist

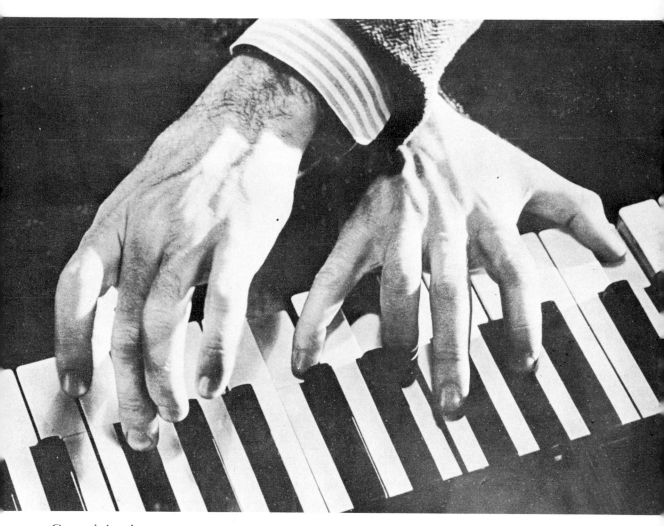

George's hands. COURTESY ARTHUR GERSHWIN

147

GEORGE GERSHWI
GUEST CONDUCTOR & SOLOI
STADIUM CONCER
AUGUST 26, 1929

A panoramic view of Lewisohn Stadium, August 26, 1929, when George
made his conducting debut. GERSHWIN COLLECTION

McCullough and Clark in
Strike Up the Band. <small-caps>CULVER
SERVICE</small-caps>

in the *Rhapsody*. He conducted "for the first time in my life" *An
American in Paris*, and the *Times*, in noting the event, reported that "he
could hardly contain his enthusiasm," and that George "showed a clear
and admirable sense of rhythm." In November George conducted the
American again at the Mecca Auditorium, sharing the podium with
Henry Hadley leading the Manhattan Symphony. The *Times* observed
on this occasion that, though *An American in Paris* was "well known,
its effect upon the audience seemed as fresh and novel as if it were being
heard at a premiere. The piquant rhythms, the dramatic entrances of solo
violin and trumpet, the bizarre strokes in the percussion section, all intrigued the auditors once more. . . . The composer-conductor was recalled many times and prevailed upon the orchestra players to rise and
share the honors with him."

Around this time George was thinking again about an opera, and in
terms of the Metropolitan. He wrote to his friend Isaac Goldberg on
October 11, 1929: "I have been doing a lot of thinking about the
Dybbuk. . . . I have also spoken to Otto Kahn about my idea and he is

very eager to have me do the opera. I think something will come of it. I will let you know first hand if anything does. In the meantime do not mention it to anyone."

George wrote to Goldberg again on October 23: "The *Dybbuk* news broke out on the front page of the *Morning Herald* a few days ago and has caused quite a bit of excitement. Other papers writing the news afterward." The New York *World* headed its item: GERSHWIN SHELVES JAZZ TO DO OPERA.

George felt ". . . my arrangement with the Metropolitan Opera House is, I believe, as good as settled. I am seeing Mr. Kahn this week."

He was so certain that he began to sketch out thematic ideas and to consider going to Europe to study Jewish music. The rights to the original play, however, were not available and George was forced to abandon the work. For a while he also considered doing an opera with a New York setting.

By this time *Strike Up the Band* was in the tryout stages. In Boston the Gershwins looked in on the *Nine-Fifteen Revue*, also in its pre-Broadway throes; its score was largely the work of Kay Swift and her husband, the financier James Warburg, who wrote lyrics under the name of Paul James. George was particularly impressed with a song by a new, young composer, Harold Arlen, whose "Get Happy" George considered one of the best first-act finales he had ever heard. The *Nine-Fifteen Revue* expired in Manhattan after seven performances, but it did serve to launch the gifted Harold Arlen, and for it Kay Swift had written one of her best songs in "High Among the Chimney Pots." And George and Arlen became friends who on the spot formed an enduring mutual-admiration society. This was typical of George, who was popularly considered to be self-centered; he was quick to recognize, and more importantly to speak for, new composers, and to aid in publication of their songs. Later, when he had his own radio show, he introduced the new songwriters to the wide audience the networks provided.

The revised *Strike Up the Band*, which began its Boston tryout on Christmas night 1929, importantly differed from the original. The program credited the idea to Kaufman, but Morrie Ryskind supplied the new libretto. Imaginatively a far weaker book, commercially it was a more successful one. Ryskind, however, had as much of a reputation for mordant revelations of man's absurd militarist passions as had Kaufman.

Indeed, as early as April 3, 1917, Ira was writing in his journal: "From morning papers gleaned fact that Morrie Ryskind expelled from Columbia S.O. Journalism ac't insubordination & insults to powers that are & be." In those days Ryskind had been the hero of the girls at Hunter College, both because of his pacifist views and his independent assertion of them. But Ryskind was willing to modify his thoughts for the stage, which Kaufman, with what Isaac Goldberg called his "obstinate integrity," would not do.

In the revised show the War against Switzerland took place only in Horace J. Fletcher's dreams (staged as a fantasy), and even there it turned so disastrously against him that when he awoke he was a man reformed. At Ira's suggestion the Cheese Factory had been closed down in these years between versions and a Chocolate Plant built on the spot—a further attempt to sweeten the play's atmosphere. (It seemed an obviously simple change to him, since milk was the principal ingredient of both products.) But if the book had lost its message and the pacifist theme become merely a device for getting the singers and dancers upon the stage, the Gershwin score had gained in sophistication and memorability. George and Ira discarded nearly half of the numbers in the original version (including "The Man I Love," which by 1930 Gilbert Gabriel was calling "that radio-scarred old war-horse"); among the numbers that brightened the new score were: a fine ballad, "Soon," a whimsical ditty, "I Want to Be a War Bride," one of the best Gershwin patter songs, "If I Became the President," and a recapitulation finale that summed up the dream play in sprightly lyrics and tinkling music.

When the revised *Strike Up the Band* opened at the Times Square Theatre on January 14, 1930, the critics agreed that Selwyn was a shrewd showman, but many wondered if the original version would not have been a superior show. As for the Gershwins, they had finally gotten to write a show that totally delighted them. For the first time in his career George got into the pit and conducted the orchestra on the out-of-town and New York opening nights. (On the latter occasion he hummed, sang, and whistled so loudly that one reviewer called him the star of the show. "My voice," George admitted, "is what is known as small but disagreeable.") Even after *Strike Up the Band* settled down for its comfortable run, George returned again and again to look it over; the man who usually found pleasure in the act of creating was now learning to relax and enjoy his music as performed by others.

"My voice is what is known as small but disagreeable." INTERNATIONAL
NEWS SERVICE

The first-act finale of *Strike Up the Band*. CULVER SERVICE

1930-1932

In April 1930, George and Ira signed their first movie contract with the Fox Film Corporation to do a screen musical, a cycle then in vogue shortly after the advent of sound. All of the best of the Broadway composers were then entraining for "the Coast to work on pictures." The motion-picture editor of the New York *American* reported, with undisguised relish, "The Gershwins both are staunch in their loyalty to the screen and its potentialities. Each refuse to take Hollywood with the tongue-in-cheek sneering that has come to be considered the smart attitude along Broadway."

George himself announced to an always-attentive press: "I go to work for the talkies like any other amateur, for I know very little about them. I am not a film fan, a movie addict; neither am I crazy about shows. . . . Because I am inexperienced with films, I am approaching them in a humble state of mind." Such humility may have puzzled the movie-makers, who were accustomed to dodging brickbats from Broadway, but, remembering the Gershwins' successes, they took no alarm. After all, wasn't the movie George pretended to approach so humbly

John McGowan,
co-author with Guy
Bolton, of *Girl
Crazy*. COURTESY
JOHN MCGOWAN

Alex Aarons, musical half of the producing team of Aarons
and Freedley. PHOTO BY JOHN MCGOWAN

Eunice Healy, Willie Howard, and Olive Brady in *Girl
Crazy*. CULVER SERVICE

Delicious? And wasn't *Delicious* a sure-fire musical hit? Consider: a cast with Janet Gaynor, Charles Farrell, and El Brendel. A Guy Bolton plot of poor-Scotch-girl-immigrant meets (and marries) Long Island-polo-aristocrat.

The brothers looked forward to their western trip, but before they left, George and Ira had an Aarons and Freedley assignment to fill. George managed to crowd in a little more activity, however, as on May 1 he wrote to Goldberg: "I am resting at the moment in anticipation of a very hard week; as, tomorrow, I begin an engagement to play at Roxy's Cathedral with Paul Whiteman's band. You see, *The King of Jazz*, Whiteman's picture, has its premiere there tomorrow, and I have been engaged as soloist for the week. Oh Baby, that sounds like a lot of work."

In between, George and Ira toiled away at the songs for *Girl Crazy*, the Aarons and Freedley show. It was being written by John McGowan, who had given up the stage and songwriting to write books; in this he

George taking part in an experiment intended to measure the touch differences between the ordinary pianist and the virtuoso. The seat of the chair is on rollers and George's feet are on a bathroom scale.
PHOTO BY DR. AVROM BARNETT. COURTESY MILTON A. CAINE

was joined by Guy Bolton. Their story was a far cry from the unconventional *Strike Up the Band*. From their *East Is West* score the Gershwins revived "Embraceable You" and still managed to write brilliant production songs like "Sam and Delilah," "Boy! What Love Has Done to Me!" (both sung by a new name to musical comedy, Ethel Merman, who managed to make every syllable of her songs heard in the last row, particularly in "I Got Rhythm"); other well-wrought songs were the wistful "But Not for Me," and the wonderfully worded "Could You Use Me?"

Two days after *Girl Crazy* opened, George was writing, on October 16, to Isaac Goldberg, then at work on George's biography: "I am just recuperating from a couple of exciting days. I worked very hard conducting the orchestra and dress rehearsal and finally the opening night, when the theater was so warm that I must have lost at least three pounds, perspiring. The opening was so well received that five pounds would not have been too much. With the exception of some dead head friends of mine, who sat in the front row, everybody seemed to enjoy the show tremendously, especially the critics. I think the notices, especially of the music, were the best I have ever received. Did you see them, by any chance?

"The show looks so good that I can leave in a few weeks for Hollywood, with the warm feeling that I have a hit under the belt. When are you coming down to see the show and me?"

Gingerly claiming a good catch—in Florida, resting after the opening of *Strike Up the Band*. GERSHWIN COLLECTION

Leopold Godowsky, Jr., and Frances Gershwin Godowsky.
GERSHWIN COLLECTION

Though George had previously sold the film rights to his *Rhapsody in Blue* for $50,000 and had, with Ira, as early as 1923 improvised a song to be plugged alongside Thomas H. Ince's silent *Sunshine Trail,* this was the first time the brothers had become answerable for a complete film score. Their theater-chain promoter and salesman friend, A. C. Blumenthal, got George seventy—and Ira, thirty—thousand dollars for the few weeks' work; and there was even no agent's commission. Amid scurryings to help sister Frankie and Leopold Godowsky, Jr., get married on the morning of November 2, 1930, and the senior Gershwins off that same afternoon for a Florida holiday, George, Ira, and Leonore left for the Coast the evening of the fifth on a train that also carried Guy Bolton, the brothers-in-law Nicholas Schenck and Edgar Selwyn, and a cortege of film personalities. The movie-makers had their own car, and nightly the diner was cleared for cards as they pokered and partied their way across the continent.

For their 1930–31 California sojourn the three Gershwins took a house together at 1027 Chevy Chase, Beverly Hills, a two-story Spanish structure that earlier had given temporary shelter to Greta Garbo. "I am sleeping in the bed that she used," George noted. "It hasn't helped my sleep any." George and Ira did most of their work in this house, but occasionally they went to the Fox lot, where the DeSylva-Brown-Henderson cottage had been reserved for them. Guy Bolton and Sonya Levien, who were collaborating upon the screenplay, also used it; and

George with Gene Sarazen, Thomas Meighan, and William Gaxton. CULVER SERVICE

George in a Valentino
dressing gown before the
Hollywood-Spanish
fireplace at 1027 Chevy
Chase. WIDE WORLD
PHOTOS

the brothers found it a convenient place to drop in for a few hours'
work after they had picked up the mail. It was also their best retreat
when the social pressure got so great that George was forced even to
disconnect the telephone.

Six weeks after they reached the Coast, George reported:

> Our picture is practically written, with the exception of a Man-
> hattan Rhapsody—or Fantasy—which I am going to write for it.
> We had a meeting with Winnie Sheehan [head of Fox Studios
> and producer of *Delicious*] the other night and read and played
> him what we had written. He and the director of our picture
> [David Butler] seemed more than pleased.

George patched together the songs in his score largely from pieces unused in earlier works—melodies to which Ira now had to set new and
appropriate lyrics. So their witty "Blah, Blah, Blah" came from Ziegfeld's abortive *East Is West;* the song "Delishious" had been played in
New York for visiting journalists as early as the previous April; and
Guy Bolton and Sonya Levien contrived their script to utilize (temporarily) even the Gershwin parlor piece "Mischa, Yascha, Toscha,
Sascha." George's principal musical inventions were not to be songs but
a long dream sequence and a rhapsody.

George stepped briskly into the athletic tempo of California life: going for daily hikes up Franklin Canyon with his trainer, shooting an 86 one day at Rancho Golf Course, playing tennis, going for swimming and golfing weekends to Palm Springs. There was also merriment: on New Year's Day the three Gershwins drove to Caliente, Mexico, where Joe Schenck gave a Hollywood party, and two Spanish dancers (legend has it that one was Rita Hayworth) gyrated to the *Rhapsody in Blue*. In those days Caliente was a favorite destination for weekending Californians and was famous for its hot springs, gambling casino, race track, and "longest bar in the world." Before their return to New York the Gershwins went back to Caliente at least once more.

In Los Angeles on January 15, 1931, Artur Rodzinski and the Los Angeles Philharmonic, in a program of American music by Daniel Gregory Mason and Emerson Whithorne gave *An American in Paris* so enthusiastic a local premiere that George had to step to the stage for his bows. There was a lot of Gershwin played that week in Los Angeles. When the Carthay Circle Theatre premiered *Lightnin'*—starring Will Rogers and Louise Dresser—Abe Lyman and his "International Band" nightly opened the performance with a concert that included "I Got Rhythm" and a popular tune Ira had concocted with Billy Rose and Harry Warren, "Cheerful Little Earful." Ira encountered a different sort of fame when one day he went to visit a producer who lived high in the hills of Bel-Air; the mistress of this pseudo-Roman villa (complete even to the extent of a classical frieze, decorated with portraits of the producer and wife) told Ira that she had been taking elocution lessons. One of the recommended texts: "Somehow by fate misguided, a buttercup resided in the Mandarin's Orchid Garden"—the recently published and already obscure Gershwin art song.

In his free time George worked on his *Manhattan Rhapsody*. (The final script called it *New York Rhapsody*, but George had begun to think of it as *Rhapsody in Rivets*. Later he simplified it to *Second Rhapsody*.) The house on Chevy Chase filled with the sounds of George's piano; and Ira grew to feel closer to this than to any other of his brother's orchestral compositions. In 1924 he had prevailed upon George to include the slow, romantic theme (*Andantino moderato*) in the *Rhapsody in Blue*; now once again he made incidental melodic suggestions that George encased in a couple of his measures. For by the time that George had set to work on his rhapsody, Ira had finished his lyric-writing

Delicious triangle: Raul Roulin (as a Russian composer), Janet Gaynor (a Scots girl on her way to America), and Charles Farrell (a polo-playing rich man). GERSHWIN COLLECTION

chores; his main diversions were golf and reading and ever listening to the work in progress.

When the Gershwins left for New York on Washington's birthday in 1931, they took back not only the first draft of George's rhapsody. In Hollywood they had done some preliminary work on *Of Thee I Sing*, including a complete "The Illegitimate Daughter" and a roughed-out "Of Thee I Sing (Baby)." Though George claimed that his first movie score went easily because, as he explained to the press, "the screen executives allowed him free rein," it took him some time to realize that, once he had completed writing his film music, he had automatically broken his connection with the picture. One of the last things he did before he left California was to record at Winnie Sheehan's request all of the songs so that the studio would be unmistaken about the tempi. (At the same recording session the lyrics were crooned by one of Paul Whiteman's singers whom George had hired for the job; so the comparatively unknown Bing Crosby earned an unexpected $50.) Back in New

Dream Sequence from *Delicious;* how the little girl from Scotland imagines she will be welcomed in the United States. Although it held potential, this film never rose above mediocrity and wasted the Gershwins. GERSHWIN COLLECTION

York, George told friends that he would return to California in July "for three weeks to supervise the making of our picture." But he soon discovered that the studio did not need him. When *Delicious* appeared in December 1931, it used only a small portion of the rhapsody; some songs had been dropped, and Ira gently noted:

> My brother and I had a pretty good time writing for the movies. . . . Of course working for the movie audience is a little different. But we managed to slip in a few of the things that theatre-goers like.

The worst comment made on the film appeared in *Outlook and Independent:* "George Gershwin is said to have written the music involved, but you'd never know it. . . . Civilization hasn't had such a setback since the Dark Ages."

The first Hollywood junket had not gone badly. George never ex-

163

First trip to Hollywood, George in the foreground, Artur Rodzinski in the background, on a day when a Rodzinski-conducted concert containing Gershwin works was discussed. GERSHWIN COLLECTION

pected that the movie would use all of his rhapsody; when he was frustrated in his desire to give more of himself than the movies knew how to use, he merely shrugged his shoulders and turned his thoughts to other enterprises. It was his first experience with writing music for a corporation instead of a handful of theatrical producers, his first encounter with an almost totally impersonal economic world. One of the compensations for his few months in California, however, was a healthy account at the Bank of America. Once he returned to New York, George kept a good portion of this money aside and used it to buy paintings.

George Kaufman and Morrie Ryskind, who had teamed up to write for the Marx Brothers, now were encouraged toward an even more successful co-authorship; before 1930 was out they had had the idea for what was to be their greatest musical satire, *Of Thee I Sing*. When the Gershwins returned to New York from Hollywood in the spring of 1931, Kaufman and Ryskind announced that they were headed for At-

George, Guy Bolton, and Ira in Hollywood to work on *Delicious*. GERSHWIN COLLECTION

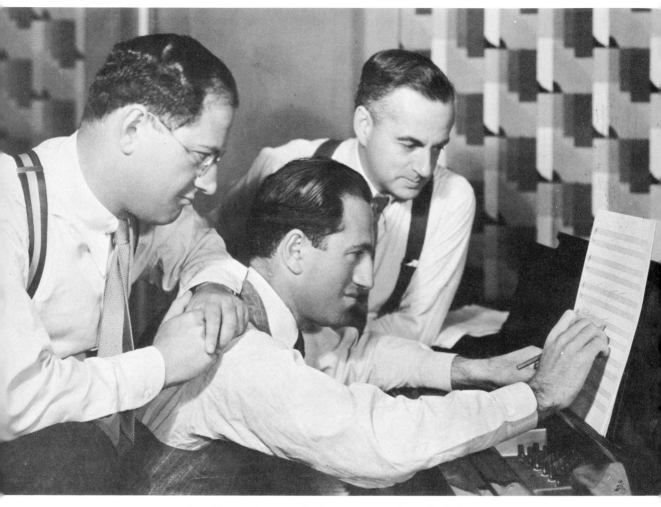

Ira, Guy Bolton, and George at work on *Delicious*. CULVER SERVICE

lantic City, where they expected to rough out the first act in sixteen days; as promised, they mailed their manuscript so that the Gershwins had it on the seventeenth day. While in Hollywood, George and Ira had worked up a couple of numbers. Now they had to use the book and make an integrated score. By December 8, when the show pulled into Boston's Majestic Theatre, matters were in fine shape.

Strike Up the Band had bubbled with patter songs, finalettos, recitatives, caroled couplets, and choral quatrains. Still, it was a show with many separate songs, and the Gershwins had collaborated in their usual fashion: first usually came the music, and then developed the words. *Of Thee I Sing*'s structure, however, required different materials. No more would songs be adjuncts to the plot; now they must be a good part

Ira's early draft for the lyric to "Of Thee I Sing," begun in Hollywood while the Gershwins were doing *Delicious*. COPYRIGHT 1931 BY NEW WORLD MUSIC CORPORATION. USED BY PERMISSION

William Gaxton, Lois Moran, George Murphy, and Victor Moore; *Of Thee I Sing*. CULVER SERVICE

The Music Box during the tenure of *Of Thee I Sing*. COURTESY WARNER BROTHERS

Victor Moore and William Gaxton as Vice-President Alexander Throttlebottom and President John P. Wintergreen in *Of Thee I Sing*. CULVER SERVICE

of the plot itself. Therefore, Ira began sketching out many of his lyrical notions and letting George devise musical settings for them.

"In the show there are no verse-and-chorus songs," Ira explained to one interviewer:

1930–
1932

> There is a sort of recitative running along and lots of finales and finalettos. It has meant easier work for both of us. It is hard to sit down and stretch out some single idea for thirty-two measures. That is what you do with the usual song. In this show you develop ideas, condensing pages of possible dialogue into a few lines of song. And George found it easier to write these measures, too, though he works much the same at anything he attempts.

Ira and George with George S. Kaufman (left) and Morrie Ryskind, the creators of *Strike Up the Band*, *Of Thee I Sing*, and *Let 'Em Eat Cake*.
GERSHWIN COLLECTION

George—happy—at the piano playing "I Got Rhythm" at the opening of the Manhattan Theatre, August 5, 1931.
GERSHWIN COLLECTION

Ira's customary modesty concealed the fact that it was largely he and his brother who turned the play into a comic opera, our first wholly integrated musical. George's music so superbly effaced itself and yet showed such distinctiveness that *Of Thee I Sing* emerged as the most inspired musical commentary on contemporary mores since Kurt Weill's *Die Dreigroschenoper*.

The plot of *Of Thee I Sing* scarcely needs retelling. The story of John P. Wintergreen who became President of the U.S.A. by campaigning upon a platform of LOVE (with secondary assertions of the importance of corn muffins) has become a national legend. Before *Of Thee I Sing* opened in Boston, however, some wondered if it would not become a miss rather than a myth. New York rehearsals had begun in November 1931, when the flame of the American economy sputtered so uncertainly that jokes about the government seemed somewhat like carrying a lighted candle into a storm. The Depression allowed one small theatrical luxury, though: there was so little demand for theatrical sets that for the last ten days of rehearsal the cast could run through the

Fritz Reiner, George, Deems Taylor, and Robert Russell Bennett in Lewisohn Stadium at a rehearsal for an all-American program. Reiner shared the podium with Bill Daly and Taylor. George was represented by the *Rhapsody in Blue*, Taylor by his *Through the Looking-Glass* suite, and Bennett by a *March for Two Pianos*, in which he and Oscar Levant played duo-piano. WIDE WORLD PHOTOS

George, Charles Purcell, and Oscar Straus. When Straus came to the U.S. to conduct a revival of *The Chocolate Soldier*, George had a party for him at the Riverside Drive penthouse. GERSHWIN COLLECTION

show with full scenery. At the New York dress rehearsal, just before the sets were struck and shipped to Boston, Kaufman regarded the affair with such moroseness that his interest could probably have been bought for a bargain price. Later, when the show revealed itself to be a hit, he was happier but still mystified.

One evening Kaufman was standing with George Gershwin at the back of the Music Box, watching the audience revel in their contrived lunacies. "What's the matter with them?" Kaufman complained. "Don't they know we're kidding love?" George replied that the show did no such thing: "You may think you're kidding love, but when John P.

171

Dr. Gregory Zilboorg,
George's analyst, as
sketched by George.
COURTESY VICTOR J.
HAMMER

Wintergreen faces impeachment to stand by the girl he married, that's championing love—and the audience knows it." Perhaps this was the plot strength that *Strike Up the Band* lacked and that no amount of satirical stage flourishes could disguise. "Don't knock love, my boy," Ira once told an impatient admirer. "Without it, I'd be out of business." Both Gershwins believed in a strong book; and an empathic couple, deeply in love, helped immeasurably.

From the first the Gershwins themselves seem to have had no doubts about *Of Thee I Sing*. On opening night in Boston the trumpets fluttered and a spotlight flared as George came down the aisle to lead the orchestra. ("Not Harlem hot, but Park Avenue hot!" conductor Charles Previn had admonished the musicians at the previous night's dress rehearsal.) Of the opening performance H. T. Parker of the Boston *Evening Transcript* deliberated: "It escapes errors of taste or excess; often, as with the Vice-President, no more than travesties national habit; shuns New York outside a single scene; rejects all things Broadwayish for the satisfactions of a wider field." Later, when he returned to see the minor revisions made during the Boston run, he complained that William Gaxton had evidently taken matters too much into his own hands. The almost Popean satire, where the victims were public types and not recognizable public figures, had been blunted as Gaxton began aping the mannerisms of Jimmy Walker. Parker was chagrined that Gaxton's part had also been padded with cheap gags: "to play up to the comedians and down to an inevitable part of the audience." Aesthetically this may have been a decline in standards, but New Yorkers did not seem to mind.

There is a story, perhaps apocryphal, that on opening night in New York Gaxton muttered to Victor "Throttlebottom" Moore backstage, "You don't suppose we'll be arrested, do you, Victor?" Mr. Moore quavered back, "I don't know. I hear Hoover and a lot of other people are pretty sensitive about the dignity of the high offices of President and Vice-President." But, as observed by the press on opening night, "Mr. Al Smith laughed himself red-faced, Mr. Jimmy Walker forgot the pitiful plight of poor, dear Cuba, Mr. Otto Kahn cried 'Bravo,'" and producer Sam Harris, who had given Kaufman a free hand with the entire production, no longer was apprehensive as he listened from his office upstairs.

Only the France-America Society took exception to the show. Passing a resolution that demanded that references to the French war debt be deleted, they also asked that the French envoy be made less of a burlesque. Unexpectedly they did not look askance at Diana Devereaux, the show's beautiful blossom, who was "the illegitimate daughter of an illegitimate son of an illegitimate nephew of Napoleon." Kaufman replied that he would gladly blue-pencil anything the Society disliked, provided that they gave him some lines equally funny.

"VOTE FOR PROSPERITY–AND SEE WHAT YOU GET," proclaimed a banner in the torchlight parade that opened the show. It seems almost to have been an ironic comment on George Gershwin's official recognition for scoring the hit. On May 2, 1932, the authors of the book and lyrics of *Of Thee I Sing* were awarded the Pulitzer Prize. Peculiarly, the man who gave so much to the show with his whimsical and satiric score was not even mentioned in this first award to an American musical comedy. The awarding committee construed "American play" to mean the drama of words; but it was a queer interpretation that could settle upon a musical and ignore the score. Alfred Knopf published the book and lyrics of the show, thereby making it the first American musical comedy to be so preserved between boards—and so popular a one that it went through seven printings before the year

ended. The omission of the music allows us to see the play in its rewarded state; it is still one of the most original musical comedy librettos
ever conceived, but it is not the brilliant tour de force that nightly
danced upon the stage of the Music Box.

When *Of Thee I Sing* won its Pulitzer Prize, Gilbert Gabriel said
that the show so revolutionized the concept of the musical comedy that
the "award was given in hope as well as in hooray." But Brooks Atkinson, who thought regretfully of *Reunion in Vienna, Mourning Becomes Electra,* and *The Animal Kingdom*—all contestants for the prize
that year—called the decision "more whim than judgment." Now that
we have the perspective of decades, it does not seem to have been a bad
choice after all.

In any collaboration it is always difficult to assign responsibility and
apportion praise. The Pulitzer Prize—by forgetting the music—has unintentionally proved how essential is George's score. And there is no
question about the excellence of Ira's lyrics. From the moment they
heard the opening rally couplet, "He's the man the people choose:
Loves the Irish and the Jews," the audience knew that lyrically they
were to be in for a different sort of evening.

> Who is the lucky girl to be?
> Who is to leave the bourgeoisie?

Copyright 1932 by New World Music Corporation. Used by Permission.

chorused the girls at the Atlantic City Beauty Contest, which was to pick a wife for the President of the U.S.A. The judges there later exclaimed:

> What a charming epiglottis,
> What a lovely coat of tan;
> Oh, the man who isn't hot is
> Not a man.

From curtain up to curtain down the show was a delight of lyrics and music.

No sooner had *Of Thee I Sing* begun its Boston tryout, however, than speculation arose about the talent that had presided over the book. The *Christian Science Monitor* so assumed the impeccability of Kaufman's taste that when it pointed out "various coarsenesses which are quite gratuitous and which belong to the tradition of a lower type of musical comedy," it flatly said: "Here, we think, we discern the hand of the assistant librettist. So long as there is the unmistakable Kaufman touch, all is well." Kaufman had staged the show; perhaps the brilliance of his direction had been responsible for this unsolicited extra praise. The *Monitor* reviewer may also have been unnecessarily influenced by the growing legend of *Strike Up the Band,* which lost so much of its keen-

When at the Sam Harris Office Ira received this certificate (plus a check for $333.33), he was also handed a subpoena; this made him one of the many (authors and management) connected with *Of Thee I Sing* to be sued for plagiarism. The charges, however, misfired, and the plaintiff had to pay them.

THE·TRUSTEES·OF·COLUMBIA·UNIVERSITY
IN·THE·CITY·OF·NEW·YORK
TO·ALL·PERSONS·TO·WHOM·THESE·PRESENTS·MAY·COME·GREETING
BE·IT·KNOWN·THAT
Ira Gershwin
HAS·BEEN·AWARDED
The Pulitzer Prize in Letters for "Of Thee I Sing," the original American play performed in New York during the year, best representing the educational value and power of the stage.
IN·ACCORDANCE·WITH·THE·PROVISIONS·OF·THE·STATUTES·OF·THE UNIVERSITY·GOVERNING·SUCH·AWARD
IN·WITNESS·WHEREOF·WE·HAVE·CAUSED·THIS·DIPLOMA·TO·BE·SIGNED BY·THE·PRESIDENT·OF·THE·UNIVERSITY·AND·OUR·CORPORATE·SEAL·TO·BE HERETO·AFFIXED·IN·THE·CITY·OF·NEW·YORK·ON·THE · FIRST DAY·OF · JUNE · IN·THE·YEAR·OF·OUR·LORD·ONE·THOUSAND·NINE HUNDRED·AND·THIRTY-TWO

PRESIDENT

ness when Ryskind redid the book for the commercially successful revival. However, when *Of Thee I Sing* received the Pulitzer Prize, Kaufman himself modestly disclaimed all responsibility for the show's excellence, saying that all four collaborators had been united in two desires: to write something "to which we might listen for ten minutes without being ashamed" and, of course, to make money.

In the spring of 1931, when the Gershwins were back at the Riverside Drive penthouses from Hollywood, George had begun to work up the sketches from the film's *Manhattan Rhapsody*. He was busily orchestrating it on March 14; on May 23 he had completed the entire work. The manuscript is generally clean, as if the writing came easily. On June 16 George wrote Goldberg that "the orchestral parts of my new Rhapsody have been copied. With the exception of two piano cadenzas it is ready to be played and I believe I shall buy myself an hour and a half's reading time next week, after which I shall let you know just how it sounds."

Goldberg was now deep in the writing of his biography of George, and regularly wrote asking questions. On June 30, interspersing answers with his own enthusiasm for the new work, George wrote: "And now for some good news—I hired fifty-five men last Friday to play the orchestration of the new Rhapsody, and the result was most gratifying. In many respects, such as orchestration and form, it is the best thing I've written. It is a bit longer than I expected, about fifteen and one-half minutes.

"The National Broadcasting Company, whose studio I used, are connected by wire with the Victor Recording Laboratories so the studio, as a great favor to me, had a record made of the rehearsal. I shall get it tomorrow. Good idea, eh?

"I am calling it just plain Second Rhapsody and, although the piano has quite a few solo parts, I may just make it one of the orchestral instruments, instead of solo."

Some paragraphs of this unusually long letter were devoted to observations of his mother, his childhood, but his pleasure over the *Second Rhapsody* intrudes again: "To go back to the Rhapsody for a moment," he proceeded to explain, "I wrote it mainly because I wanted to write a serious composition and found the opportunity in California. Nearly everybody comes back from California with a western tan and a pocket-

George and Jerome Kern in a broadcasting studio, June 1933. GERSHWIN
COLLECTION

First page of the *Second Rhapsody*, on which George altered the introduction by the piano from four bars to six. The title page reads: "2nd Rhapsody for Orchestra with piano." COPYRIGHT 1932 BY NEW WORLD MUSIC CORPORATION. USED BY PERMISSION

full of motion picture money. I decided to come back with both those things and a serious composition—if the climate would let me. I was under no obligation to the Fox Company to write this. But, you know, the old artistic soul must be appeased every so often.

"There is no program to the Rhapsody. As the part of the picture where it is to be played takes place in many streets of New York, I used a starting-point what I called 'a rivet theme' but, after that, I just wrote a piece of music without a program."

In the same letter George expressed his delight in the group of French paintings that had been added to his growing art collection. George's cousin, Henry Botkin, an accomplished artist who had coached George in his painting, was in Europe, where he scouted for oils he felt would interest George. George numbered many artists among his friends, including Maurice Sterne and Max Weber, who, like Botkin, encouraged George in his own work and in adding to his very important collection of modern art. Of them all George had a great fondness for the work of Rouault.

Possibly the influence of Rouault may be heard in the *Second Rhapsody*, for George frequently expressed the hope to be able to write music "the way Rouault paints." The *Second Rhapsody* is really a more interesting work than the first though it has not enjoyed the same popularity. Harmonically the *Second Rhapsody* is of a darker hue than any previous work—from its rather sinister opening rivet motif to the solemn slow theme (a close relative of the first rhapsody's famous song-like melody). The *Second Rhapsody* is austere Gershwin, technically complex and quite modern in sound. It is not derivative Gershwin, which makes it all the more valuable. Orchestrally, too, the skill that *An American in Paris* pointed toward reaches fruition in the *Second Rhapsody* with its brilliant effects and subtle thematic development.

Unlike most other "serious" Gershwin works the *Second Rhapsody* did not have a premiere hearing almost on being written. For a while Toscanini had seemed inclined toward giving it a first performance, or at least so George understood from the interventions of mutual friends close to the conductor. But George had given up the wooing and had concentrated, with Ira, on getting work done on the next show, *Of Thee I Sing*. Shortly after the New York opening George journeyed to Boston to premiere the *Second Rhapsody* with the Boston Symphony

Serge Koussevitzky and
George in Boston for the
premiere of the *Second
Rhapsody*, January 1932.

under Serge Koussevitzky, whose interest in contemporary scores
greatly exceeded his New York rival's.

George had decided to dedicate the *Second Rhapsody* to his friend
Max Dreyfus, then in London. Dreyfus cabled George:

AM TOUCHED BEYOND WORDS YOUR THOUGHTFULNESS IN DEDICATING
SECOND RHAPSODY TO ME IT IS ABOUT THE NICEST THING THAT
HAS HAPPENED TO ME AND DEEPLY APPRECIATED . . .

From Boston, where the *Second Rhapsody* was performed for the
first time on January 29, 1932, George explained something of its genesis: "I had seven weeks in California. The amount of music which the
picture required was small and quickly written. The parties and night
life of Hollywood did not interest me in the least. They bored me in
fact. Here was my chance to do some serious work. Seven weeks of
almost uninterrupted opportunity to write the best music I could possibly think of! What a chance."

180

The *Rhapsody* was well received in Boston, also in New York, where it got a first hearing on February 5. One reviewer, however, found the piece "Humdrum, with emphasis on the last syllable."

The death of Morris Gershwin on May 15 had taken the festivity out of Ira's Pulitzer Prize and altered George's plans for a European trip. He did take a brief vacation in Havana, where he became deeply interested in Cuban music and native instruments, which inspired his next orchestral work; to assure authenticity, he brought some of the instruments back to New York with him.

During July of 1932 he composed *Rumba*, working rapidly to be able to have the work ready for an all-Gershwin concert at the stadium in August. He finished the orchestration on the ninth and the concert took place on the sixteenth. George shared piano chores with Oscar Levant, the latter playing the *Concerto* with Bill Daly conducting. George played the two rhapsodies with Albert Coates conducting. Coates also led the *American* and the just-completed *Rumba*.

For the program George supplied a rather stilted commentary:

> In my composition I have endeavored to combine the Cuban rhythms with my own thematic material. The result is a symphonic ouverture which embodies the essence of the Cuban dance. It has three main parts.

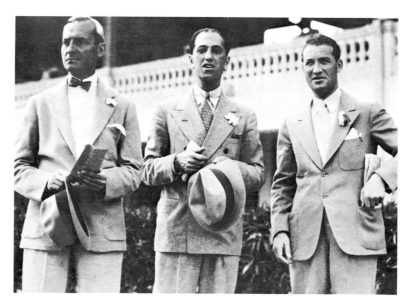

George in Havana with his friends, Ev Jacobs and Emil Mosbacher—at the track in February 1932. On this trip George was so taken with Cuban percussion instruments they brought about his writing *Rumba*, later called *Cuban Overture*.
GERSHWIN COLLECTION

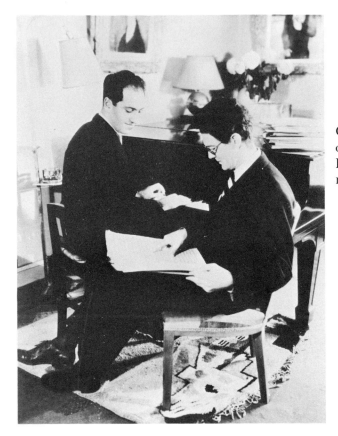

George and Bill Daly going
over a score in the
Riverside Drive penthouse.

The first part (Moderato e Molto Ritmato) is preceded by a (forte) introduction featuring some of the thematic material. Then comes a three part contrapuntal episode leading to a second theme. The first part finishes with a recurrence of the first theme combined with fragments of the second.

A solo clarinet cadenza leads to a middle part, which is in a plaintive mood. It is a gradually developing canon in a polytonal manner. This part concludes with a climax based on an ostinato of the theme in the canon, after which a sudden change in tempo brings us back to the rumba dance rhythms.

The finale is a development of the preceding material in a stretto-like manner. This leads us back once again to the main theme.

The conclusion of the work is a coda featuring the Cuban instruments of percussion.

George's purely analytical approach may have resulted from his recent studies with Joseph Schillinger, a theorist who had all but reduced the

Title page of the *Cuban Overture;* knowing exactly what effect he wanted, George was careful to show where he wished the Cuban instruments to be placed.

Ira, Lee, Ellin and Irving Berlin, and
George in Nassau, Bahamas, 1933.
GERSHWIN COLLECTION

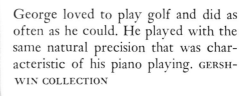

George loved to play golf and did as
often as he could. He played with the
same natural precision that was characteristic of his piano playing. GERSH-
WIN COLLECTION

composition of music to mathematics. The intricate mathematical relationships in music fascinated George, and he found, too, that his study with Schillinger helped him in some of the purely technical, almost mechanical aspects of composition. *Rumba*, with its canon and with its "climax based on an ostinato of the theme of the canon," is the sort of thing George and Schillinger might explore. So would a song like "Mine," with its contrapuntal construction. But George merely found the technical terminology for much that he had been doing intuitively.

By 1932, the year of *Rumba*, or, as it was soon to be renamed, *Cuban Overture*, and just before he was to begin work on his finest accomplishment, George was a well-read musicologist. He often would startle his friends with some obscure fact, in either the life of a composer or the history of music. He absorbed books on music history and theory. He also attended concerts and recitals, followed the doings of the League of Composers (though he was never a member), subscribed to the recondite publication edited by Henry Cowell, *New Music*. And he collected records that mirrored his tastes: an unwieldy album of the *Art of the Fugue*, much Stravinsky, including *Les Noces* and the *Symphony of Psalms*; among the Beethoven albums was the *Quartet in C Major, Op. 59, No. 3*; and Schubert's *C Major Quintet*, Brahms's *Piano Concerto No. 2 in B Flat*, and the Sibelius *Violin Concerto* were stacked next to Berg's *Lyric Suite* and the Schoenberg *String Quartets*. Interspersed were popular records, not all Gershwin.

The last show George and Ira did for Aarons and Freedley turned out to be a disaster that separated the producing partners. The title, *Pardon My English*, was only too appropriate, for it turned out to be a dialect show that hardly did justice to Ira's crisp lyrics. Nor did the assorted dialects of Lyda Roberti, Jack Pearl, and George Givot (Jack Buchanan, who would have added the British contribution to the international mélange, quit the show in Boston) contribute to the intelligibility of song or plot; but the plot was not their fault—and that is where the fault lay. After opening at the Majestic on January 20 the show floundered through forty-six performances.

For *Pardon My English* George and Ira had come up with a distinguished score, but most of it has entered that province belonging to musical comedy connoisseurs. For example, there is the conversational ballad, in which Ira matched George's sophistication, "Isn't It a Pity?", and another, "The Lorelei," with a particularly distinctive verse; there

1930–
1932

Kreuger: Billions of dollars were lost us
Billions of dollars it cost us
Because this viper double crossed us!

Supreme Court: This dirty viper double crossed us

Wintergreen: Hinky dinky parlay vous
(To Thrott.)   Things look pretty black for you.
Wintergreen: Order in the court! Proceed

Kreuger: The score was 8 to 8
And we were going great
    And what did he do ?
      What did I do ?
Thrott.: (wistfully)
Kreuger: What did you do!

                In inning number nine
He showed he had no spine
    And what did he do ?
Thrott.:   What did I do ?
 Sup. Ct/   What did you do!

K.   The others were at bat
And suddenly like that
    What did he do
      What did I do ?
All: WHAT DID HE DO

Kreuger: He called a foul a fair!
It was a foul, I swear!

Supreme Court: He knew the ball was foul
He knew it by our howl
Kr.:   and that's what he did
         That's what he did
All: That's what he did!

Su. Ct/   Deny it if you can
You hypocritical man
   You son of a gun
   You gave the run
To the player from Japan

Kr.   And so we lost the game
Our fortune and our fair name
   This son of a gun
   Gave them the run
And he's the one to blame

S.Ct.:   Hinky dinky parlay vous
Things look pretty black for you.

Wint.   You've heard them say you were remiss
Now what have you got to say to this ?

Throt.:   I say the man's a traitor indescribable
K: I say they gave him money and he's bribable
Disgracing all of us who feel we're Aryan
We want to do away with this barbarian
The Army wants to handle this barbarian

A page from the libretto of *Let 'Em Eat Cake*, with George's doodles in the margins and Ira's revisions in his own typescript. COURTESY NEW WORLD MUSIC CORPORATION

Tony, George's
terrier, was often
in the news either
by getting lost or
stolen, but somehow
always returned.
The photo was
taken by George.
COURTESY ARTHUR
GERSHWIN

are as well several rare, and delightful, Gershwin waltzes. Ira had some
fun concocting the lyrics for a song, unfortunately never used, the
witty "Freud and Jung and Adler." However, though the brothers
knew that their contribution to the show was of good quality, it was no
consolation in view of the show's premature closing.

By now George was seriously thinking of tackling opera. Still he
found no time for it until he was able to clear away the work on *Let
'Em Eat Cake*, the sequel to *Of Thee I Sing*. But, like *Pardon My
English* earlier in the year, *Let 'Em Eat Cake* did not go.

Two flops in a year were more than enough for the Gershwins.
George was eager to get away from the conventional musical. The
announcement came that the Theatre Guild would produce a Gersh-
win-scored *Porgy* and, although George had been in communication
with Heyward for over a year when this was published on November 3,
1933, he had not yet begun to compose any of the music.

Portrait, 1933. PHOTO BY CARL VAN VECHTEN

1933-1935

Opera, for some reason known best to those who keep a dying, perhaps dead, art form artificially alive, is thought of as being on a higher and, of course, more "serious" level than musical comedy.

Actually, in its nineteenth-century form, opera is inimical to the American scene: opera from its own golden age is florid, bombastic, overcharged with emotion, musically excessive, and likely as not weighted down with librettos just as silly as the most gossamer book of the typical musical of the Twenties.

Perhaps there was some kind of wisdom, though somewhat misguided, in the choice by early self-consciously "American" composers who attempted what was felt to be authentic American operas by drafting the American Indian as the subject. The result was a total destruction of the indigenous Indian musical material (if it was drawn upon at all) by subjecting it to Western concepts of scale and harmony, elements that did not enter into Indian music at all. And, further, the romanticizing of the Red Man made for maudlin story material; even Victor Herbert attempted such an excursion in his unsuccessful *Natoma*.

George was not for the Indian to furnish him an operatic theme, but he was intrigued by the idea of doing a real opera. He and Ira had seen too many of their most interesting efforts go down with the show. Opera was somehow enduring, and George was certain that in *Porgy* he had the right subject for a full-scale opera: Heyward had treated the Negro with dignity and intelligence, as well as understanding (no little feat at the time). Also, song was a natural expression of emotional outlet for the Gullah Negro of Charleston, where Heyward had done his searching for true, undistorted local color.

Though the actual composition of the sole Gershwin opera belongs to some twenty months spanning 1934 and 1935, the drawn-out process of its creation—to go back a little—began two years before.

After George concluded his tour with the Boston Symphony, performing the *Second Rhapsody*—with *Of Thee I Sing* running to capacity at the Music Box, and with work about to begin on *Pardon My English*—he wrote again to Heyward:

GEORGE GERSHWIN
33 RIVERSIDE DRIVE
NEW YORK, NEW YORK

March 29 - 1932

My dear Mr. Heyward:

I am about to go abroad in a little over a week, and in
    thinking of ideas for new compositions, I came back
    to one that I had several years ago - namely, PORGY -
    and the thought of setting it to music. It is still
    the most outstanding play that I know, about the
    colored people.

I should like very much to talk with you before I leave
    for Europe, and the only way that I imagine that
    would be possible would be by telephone. So if
    you will be good enough to either telephone me
    collect at TRafalgar 7-0727 - or send me your
    telephone number by telegram, I will be glad to call
    you.

Is there any chance of your being abroad in the next
    couple of months?

I hope this letter finds you and your wife in the best
    of health, and hoping to hear from you soon, I am

                            Sincerely yours,

George Gershwin

DuBose Heyward
Dawn Hill
Hendersonville, North Carolina

Heyward, who was beginning to feel the impact of the Depression, was happy to hear again from George, not only because it would give him an opportunity to work and earn an income but also to collaborate with the Gershwins. He immediately replied to George's letter, informing him that the *Porgy* operatic rights were "free and clear."

Heyward was then a little disappointed when George told him, on May 20, 1932: "Of course there is no possibility of the operatic version's being written before January 1933 [when *Pardon My English* was scheduled to open]. I shall be around here most of the summer and will read the book several times to see what ideas I can evolve as to how it should be done. Any notions I get I shall forward to you. I think it would be wise for us to meet—either here or where you are—several times, before any real start is made."

Thus the summer went by, and then it was George's turn for a jolt. Heyward had heard from his agent in New York that Al Jolson was interested in doing *Porgy* as a musical. Early in September, Heyward wrote George, "I cannot see brother Jolson as Porgy, but I have heard that he was casting about for something more artistic than his usual Sonny Boy line, and what his real potentialities are, I have very little idea.

"Of course, this does not shake me in my desire to work with you on the story, only it reminds me that I evidently have an asset in Porgy, and in these trying times this has to be considered. Therefore, before I turn this down flat, I think we should execute the customary agreement with your producer, with whom, I presume, you have already been discussing the matter. With this attended to I will withdraw from sale the picture rights, which are at present on the market. It seems to me that this is very important for both of us, as certainly neither of us would wish to put our time on it without this protection.

"Will you please at the earliest possible moment wire me whether your associates are prepared to enter into a definite agreement at this time, so that I may know how to handle the Jolson matter. I will then leave promptly for New York so that we may get that settled, and also have our first conference on the rewriting of the book."

Assuring George that he was not trying to force a decision upon him, Heyward suggested a compromise, "Would it be possible to use Jolson, and arrange some sort of agreement with him, or is that too preposterous?"

George found it "very interesting that Al Jolson would like to play the part of Porgy, but I really don't know how he would be in it. Of course he is a very big star, who certainly knows how to put over a song, and it might mean more to you financially if he should do it—provided the rest of the production were well done. The sort of thing I had in mind for *Porgy* is a much more serious thing than Jolson could ever do.

"Of course I would not attempt to write music to your play until I had all the themes and musical devices worked out for such an undertaking. It would be more a labor of love than anything else.

"If you can see your way to making some ready money from Jolson's version I don't know that it would hurt a later version done by an all-colored cast."

As for the all-important producer who might solve Heyward's "Jolson matter," George concluded with an admission, "I have not planned with any producers yet as I should like to write the work first and then see who would be the best one to do it." He did try to reassure Heyward by mentioning that Herman Shumlin, producer of the hit *Grand Hotel*, was very much interested in the idea.

Heyward's literary agents were becoming even more concerned than the author. On October 14, 1932, George received a phone call from Heyward's agent, who was by then being practically harassed by the anxious Jolson. His eagerness was understandable, for the *Show Boat* team, Jerome Kern and Oscar Hammerstein II, was planning to furnish the songs. If this were to materialize, the musical *Porgy* would be closer to George's conception than he originally thought the Jolson version could have been, though George was unaware of it.

George spoke to the agent, and then wrote to Heyward that "if Jolson wanted to do the play and that it meant some money for you I saw no objection to it in view of the fact that Jolson couldn't do an operatic version of it anyway. His version would undoubtedly be the play as you wrote it with the addition of perhaps a few songs.

"I really don't think that Jolson would consider doing an operatic version as I am quite sure he would consider that out of his line. I have taken this attitude because I wouldn't want to stand in the way of your making some money with your property at the present time, and also because I don't believe that it would hurt a serious operatic version in any way."

Three days later Heyward informed George that he had learned "of circumstances that have put me in a fairly tight spot financially," a New York bank holding much of his savings had been closed by the Depression, and he was forced to release *Porgy* to Jolson. "Of course what I would like to be able to afford would be to wait indefinitely for your operatic version, and to work with you myself without the least thought of the commercial angle.

"It is not my idea to work in any way upon a possible Jolson musical, but merely to sell the story. Later I shall hope to work with you as we outlined in our recent conversation."

George's understanding of Heyward's problems, plus the fact that he knew that he would not get to the work for some time whatever his claim on it, prompted Heyward to write on October 17, 1932: "Please let me tell you that I think your attitude in this matter simply splendid. It makes me all the more eager to work with you some day, some time, before we wake up and find ourselves in our dotage."

Thoughts of a possible opera went then into discard; work on *Pardon My English* kept the Gershwins involved. At about mid-point in their struggles George took a little time out to conduct the Musicians' Symphony Orchestra on November 1 at the Metropolitan Opera House. George played the piano parts of the *Concerto* and a suite of songs that had been prepared for the previous summer's first all-Gershwin concert at Lewisohn Stadium. George conducted *An American in Paris* (he had little actual instruction in this; he practiced by conducting before the phonograph) and the *Cuban Overture*.

Bill Daly served as conductor for the first two selections. His familiarity with the scores (he had arranged and orchestrated, with George,

Bill Daly, friend and trusted interpreter, to whom George dedicated the *Preludes*. PHOTO BY GEORGE GERSHWIN

the song suite) instigated a diatribe by one of the members of the orchestra, Allan Langley, that was then published in Nathan's *American Spectator* under the title "The Gershwin Myth."

For the January 15, 1933, issue of the New York *Times* Bill composed a fine rebuttal that was at the same time a tribute to George. He began by noting that "Langley definitely tried to convey to the reader the idea that Gershwin is not the orchestrator, and probably not the author, of the works attributed to him. I am signally honored by being mentioned as a probable 'ghost writer,' as attest the following:

> As for *An American in Paris*, the genial Daly was constantly in rehearsal attendance, both as repetiteur and advisor, and any member of the orchestra could testify that he knew more about the score than Gershwin. The point is that no previous claimant to honors in symphonic composition has ever presented so much argument and so much controversy as to whether his work was his own or not.

"I thank Mr. Langley for the compliment," the much-aroused Bill Daly continued, "but I neither wrote nor orchestrated the *American*. My only contribution consisted of a few suggestions about reinforcing the score here and there, and I'm not sure that Gershwin, probably with good reason, accepted them. But, then, Gershwin receives many such suggestions from his many friends to whom he always plays his various compositions, light or symphonic, while they are in the process of being written. Possibly Mr. Langley feels that we all get together (and we'd have to meet in the Yankee Stadium) and write Mr. Gershwin's music for him.

"I would only be too happy to be known as the composer of *An American in Paris*, or of any of the Gershwin works, or as the orchestrator of them. But, alas! I am by trade a conductor (and because Gershwin thinks I am a good one, especially for his music, maybe Mr. Langley has been thrown off the scent). It is true that I orchestrate many Gershwin numbers for the theater; but so does Russell Bennett. And I have reduced some of his symphonic works for smaller orchestra for use on the radio. And it is true that we are close friends—to my great profit—and that I use that relationship to criticize. But this is far from the role that Mr. Langley suggests.

"In fine, the fact is that I have never written one note of any of his compositions, or so much as orchestrated one whole bar of his symphonic works.

"Mr. Langley's asseverations are of importance only through the fact that they are now published and are sent abroad in the world to influence those who have no means of checking up on the facts, and to give comfort to those who want to think that Gershwin is a myth.

"I suppose I should really resent the fact that Langley attributes Gershwin's work to me, since Langley finds all of it so bad. But fortunately for my amour propre, I have heard some of Langley's compositions. He really should stay away from ink and stick to his viola."

George was too much involved with the problems connected with *Pardon My English* to get into the argument; he put aside the idea of writing an opera until the Jolson situation cleared up. In addition, he and Ira set to work on *Let 'Em Eat Cake*, and there was the radio contract in the offing. Also the almost legendary penthouse apartment on Riverside Drive was given up in favor of a spacious duplex at 132 East 72nd Street, where George now lived alone. Leonore and Ira, however, lived directly across the street at 125. What with working on the operetta and with setting up the new apartment George gave little thought to the opera, though in all this time—that is, since he had more or less bowed out of the *Porgy* picture the year before—negotiations actually continued on the opera project.

In the fall of 1933 Aimee Semple McPherson-Hutton made her Broadway debut at the Capitol Theatre. As one newspaper syndicate reported, "She simply was trying to quiet the turbulent waters of economics and pessimism, just as the stormy waters were quieted in Bible times." Kaufman and Ryskind, George and Ira Gershwin also had something to say about what was happening to the world, but they did not plan for themselves so startling a change of pace. Like proverbial shoemakers they stuck to their last success and plotted a sequel to *Of Thee I Sing*.

Let 'Em Eat Cake opened at Boston's Shubert Theatre October 2, 1933, moved on to New York's Imperial on October 21, and—alas—after an early enthusiastic box office, died with its ninetieth performance. Knopf also published the book and lyrics, but the score remains comparatively unknown. Its unhappy fate is particularly regretted when we realize that *Let 'Em Eat Cake* was the most sophisticated and fully developed of the Gershwin political musicals.

A corner of the living room. The bust (left) is by Noguchi, the caricature by film director John Huston, the lithograph by George Bellows (a Gershwin favorite). GERSHWIN COLLECTION

The dining room and part of the living room, 33 Riverside Drive. GERSHWIN COLLECTION

The view from the dining room onto the terrace. From the terrace the Gershwins could see Manhattan to great advantage, over the Hudson to New Jersey, and north up the river for miles. To the right of the window hangs a favorite Modigliani. GERSHWIN COLLECTION

The bookcase where George kept a few books but many scores of the music he liked to study. The center painting is by Thomas Hart Benton. GERSHWIN COLLECTION

George's piano in the Riverside Drive apartment. Derain's portrait of Kisling is to the left, Chagall's *Rabbi* to the right. GERSHWIN COLLECTION

The athletic and celebrity corner of the penthouse. Included in the collection of autographs on the wall are a letter from Stravinsky, and photos of Alban Berg, Irving Berlin, George, Duke of Kent, and Jack Dempsey. GERSHWIN COLLECTION

The bedroom in George's Riverside Drive apartment. The screen is an interpretation of *An American in Paris*, painted by Henry Botkin. GERSHWIN COLLECTION

Once more a torchlight parade opened the production. Unfortunately one of the banners proclaimed: "THE SAME PROMISES AS LAST TIME." This was the difficulty the show could not escape. What sequel is ever equal? seems to have been the thought of many even before they got to the theater. Indeed, the ready-made hatchets brought by the Socialites to the benefit opening so upset Sam Harris, the show's producer and a gentleman famous for his tact and word, that he told *Variety* that first nights of his shows would henceforth be for "critics plus a paying audience, the receipts going to charity." Among the show's official reviewers only Percy Hammond flatly asserted that *Let 'Em Eat Cake* was "a funnier, prettier and crueller conspiracy against Washington, D.C.," than had been *Of Thee I Sing*. Gilbert Gabriel, the Gershwins' old admirer, wrote, "I think we might all say in accents kindly and even congratulatory that, yes, it was another noble anomaly, another more or less success, but don't—for God's sake, don't—let it happen a third time."

While *Of Thee I Sing* had satirized a presumably present situation, *Let 'Em Eat Cake* was conceived as a nightmarish projection of America's future: John P. Wintergreen and his cohorts, who got into office through the beauty contests and connivances of *Of Thee I Sing*, have been pushed out of Washington by the presidential election of John P. Tweedledee. Ill-trained to be anything except decorative, the ex-bureaucrats converge on Union Square, where the Wintergreens (using the savings of Alexander Throttlebottom) go into the business of making "Maryblue" shirts.

Business is so bad during the national Depression that Wintergreen plots a Blue Shirt revolution—primarily to drum up sales. The movement catches on, an army is formed, Tweedledee is pushed out of office, and Wintergreen now has to make good his promise to the revolutionary troops: to collect the foreign war debts for them. When representatives of nine nations refuse to pay, a ball game is scheduled between them and the Justices of the Supreme Court—winner take all. Alexander Throttlebottom is made umpire, and when he rules in favor of the League of Nations he is hauled before an American Tribunal and sentenced to be guillotined. The Army takes over the government and Wintergreen is next for decapitation. Throttlebottom has his head in the machine, ready for the knife, when Mary appears with a style show that halts the proceedings. Wintergreen restores the republic and returns to the shirt business. And who at last becomes President of the U.S.A.?— Alexander Throttlebottom.

By the time the show opened, there flared revolution in Cuba, and U.S. headlines blared: "TOO CLOSE FOR COMFORT!" and "NO SIGNS OF REVOLUTION HERE!" Still, the situation implicit in *Let 'Em Eat Cake* had become, many feared, a reality. In the vigor of its attacks, in the still-marked advance upon contemporary musical comedy, and in its imaginative outspokenness the show was closer to the original *Strike Up the Band* than to the first account of John P. Wintergreen and the vicissitudes of his presidency. There is so intense a vision of fascist America that its creators were obviously aroused by the seriousness of their intent. (Before the Boston opening one interviewer noted that "Irritation mounting almost to homicidal mania, but caught and held under control by main strength, is the keynote of Mr. Kaufman in the flesh.") The playwrights offered no prescription for the national malady, but tried to return the production to the world of make-believe-that-we-were-only-teasing. The trouble was that even in pretense there was nothing positive. The show was negative in tone from start to finish; its most characteristic cry was:

> Happiness will fill our cup,
> When it's "Down with ev'rything that's up!"

It was also visually a dour production: a second act entirely in blue. And the couple who in *Of Thee I Sing* had been deeply in love were now absorbed more in politics than in each other. Small wonder the show depressed everyone.

"Wintergreen for President" again opened the evening, but there could now be heard another strain, "Tweedledee for President," rising in counterpart to it. This cacophonous beginning immediately established the mood of the new Gershwin music. In the previous year George had whipped up two contrapuntal waltzes for the fiasco *Pardon My English;* though they never got beyond Boston, they had clearly indicated George's intent to put counterpoint and countermelody upon the Broadway stage. By the time of *Let 'Em Eat Cake* he could tell the press:

I've written most of the music for this show contrapuntally, and it is that very insistence on the sharpness of a form that gives my music the acid touch it has—which points the words of the lyrics, and is in keeping with the satire of the piece. At least, I feel that it is the counterpoint which helps me do what I am trying to do.

Most critics could not see what he was attempting with the score, and for a moment George seemed to have shot too far ahead of his admirers. "Mine" was the only love song, and this annoyed the same audience that two years earlier had delighted in the unusual music for *Of Thee I Sing.* Yet George did not waver in his conviction that *Let 'Em Eat Cake* was "the composer's claim to legitimacy."

Something of the new Gershwin attitude toward music was seen in "Blue, Blue, Blue," which came to the show via George's notebooks. Ira remembered this sweet balladic tune and suggested that it be the opening of the second act. George had greater ambition for the strain, feeling that it could be made into something particularly fine on its own. Characteristically, however, he deferred to the needs of the show and gave it to Ira, who contrived:

> Blue, blue, blue—
> Not pink or purple or yellow,
> Not brown like Mr. Othello,
> But blue, blue, blue!
>
> The U.S.A. is a Blue S.A.
> It's a dream come true.

Copyright 1933 by New World Music Corporation. Used by Permission.

The unexpected melodic letdown in the final bars perfectly suited Ira's purposes: he could mortise the song into the play and also contrast the melodic sweetness with words that too seemed sweet but had frightening implications. Once again the lyricist was making the fullest possible use of his material.

Other than the sympathetic character of Victor Moore's Throttlebottom the only acclaimed contribution to *Let 'Em Eat Cake* was the lyrics. Once again Ira had contrived recitatives, quatrains, and patter songs. But instead of writing the words first he had improvised "lead lines" and introductory remarks. He let George, who was evolving com-

George's line drawing of Ira. COURTESY IRA GERSHWIN

plicated contrapuntal structures, build songs that he would then fill with words. George felt that he had succeeded in writing humorous music; the critics disagreed. They also took umbrage at a Kaufman and a Ryskind who could near the end of the book with a guillotine upon the stage and a possible victim in the beloved Alexander Throttlebottom. But all acknowledged that if the others had lost their sense of humor Ira had kept his.

In Ira's lyrics there is always a benevolent quality, as though even in evil lurks some virtue that needs cultivation. In a world where innuendo passed as sophistication, antagonism as liberalism, and a wisecrack as wisdom, it was not surprising that Ring Lardner—the Twenties' greatest satirist—should observe of Ira's accomplishments: "You can count on the fingers of one thumb the present-day writers of song words who could wear becomingly the mantle of W. S. Gilbert, or even the squirrel neckpiece of Ira Gershwin."

Five days after *Let 'Em Eat Cake* opened, a contract was signed with the Theatre Guild for a musical version of *Porgy*. On November 3, with all legal questions answered, the Guild announced the fact to the press. Jolson, Kern, and Hammerstein had withdrawn their claim to the work. Now George and Heyward had the clearance they needed; and George, especially, had all his musical assignments out of the way.

Heyward, of course, had never actually abandoned the project. He began early to adapt the play for eventual musical handling. He did this by marking passages in the script, one of which:

> *Hush, lil' baby, don' yo' cry*
> *Hush, lil' baby, don' yo' cry*
> *Fadder an' mudder born to die.*

Copyright 1925 by George H. Doran

he questioningly marked "Lyric?" in his bold script. This passage, which is also in the novel, became "Summertime." Heyward's inspiration was the beautiful southern folk spiritual-lullaby "All My Trials." The final "Summertime" is completely different—and the melody is not related to the original folk tune.

By November 12 Heyward was ready: "I enclose two copies of the first scene which I have worked over for you to start on.

"I have cut everything possible, and marked a couple of possible fur-

Visiting the Heywards in Charleston. PHOTO BY PAUL MUELLER. GERSHWIN COLLECTION

ther cuts in pencil on ms. As a matter of fact, this is now a very brief scene considering that it carries all of the exposition necessary for the play."

Heyward did not subscribe entirely to the idea of adhering to straight opera form, including recitative. This was the sole major point the collaborators disagreed over. "I have been thinking a lot about this job," Heyward continued, "and have a pretty definite feeling about the treatment which I submit for your consideration. I feel more and more that all dialog should be spoken. It is fast moving, and we will cut it to the bone, but this will give the opera speed and tempo. This will give you a chance to develop a new treatment, carrying the orchestration through the performance (as you suggested) but enriching it with pantomime and action on the stage, and with such music (singing) as grows out of the action. Also, in scenes like the fight, the whole thing can be treated as a unified composition drawing on lighting, orchestra, wailing of crowd, mass sounds of horror from people, etc., instead of singing. It can be lifted to a terrific climax. That fight was treated with a great deal of noise in the play. That is not my idea of best art in handling it.

"I am offering a new idea for opening of scene as you will see from the script. The play opened with a regular riot of color. This makes an entirely different opening, which I think is important. What I have

in mind is to let the scene, as I describe it, merge with the overture, almost in the sense of illustration, giving the added force of sight and
sound. I think it would be very effective to have the lights go out during overture, so that the curtain rises in darkness, then the first scene
will begin to come up as the music takes up the theme of jazz from the
dance hall piano." For this transitional, rather impressionistic effect
George composed his most modern (in sound) piano music, but the
passage was fated to be cut during the Boston tryout.

When Heyward's package arrived George was getting ready to appear with the Pittsburgh Symphony. He got around to writing a week
later, on November 25, 1933, in which he told Heyward, "Think you
have done a swell job, especially with the new lyrics." But he noted, in
answer to Heyward's suggestion of more spoken dialogue, "There may
be too much talk . . ."

George also admitted that "on account of many things I have to do at
present I haven't actually started composing," and went on to reassure
Heyward, "I want to do a great deal of thinking about the thing and the
gathering in of thematic material before the actual writing begins."

George was planning to leave on December 2 for Florida with his
friend Emil Mosbacher. On the way south he arranged for a stopover in
Charleston to meet with Heyward and expressed the hope of their finding time "to see the town and hear some spirituals and perhaps go to a
colored cafe or two if there are any."

At Mosbacher's in Florida, and during the short time with the Heywards in Charleston, George rested—as much as was possible for him—
in preparation for an extensive tour with an orchestra in what amounted
to one-night stands. To furnish himself with a new showpiece, George
worked up the "*I Got Rhythm*" *Variations*, which he dedicated to Ira.
Though the writing in the *Variations* is complex, much of it was composed away from the piano—some of it in Heyward's study in Charleston, some in Palm Beach.

On December 19 George was making his plans for returning to
New York, but with another stop in Charleston "at 1:30 the afternoon
of Jan. second." He would only stay overnight, yet George hoped
"we can hear some real singing as well as have a final discussion on
the first two scenes of the opera." They also looked around for a place
that George could rent once he was free of contractual obligations in
New York.

George and James Melton at George's practice keyboard during the tour that featured George playing, among other Gershwin compositions, the *"I Got Rhythm"* Variations. GERSHWIN COLLECTION

George with the Leo Reisman band, with which he toured in 1934. GERSH-
WIN COLLECTION

In Syracuse on the cross-country tour, January–February 1934. GERSHWIN COLLECTION

Not long after his return from the south George completed the *"I Got Rhythm" Variations* on January 6, 1934, just in time for the tour that was to begin in Boston on the fourteenth. With George were James Melton and the Leo Reisman Orchestra, conducted by Charles Previn. The tour covered points as various as Omaha, Detroit, and Toronto before concluding at the Academy of Music in Brooklyn on February 10, and George described it as "an arduous but exciting trip of 12,000 miles which took 28 days. The tour was a fine artistic success for me and would have been splendid financially if my foolish manager hadn't booked me into seven towns that were too small to support such an expensive organization as I carried. Nevertheless, it was a very worthwhile thing for me to have done and I have many pleasant memories of Cities I had not visited before."

207

There were, in fact, more than forty cities through which they passed during this tour, according to Paul Mueller, who had, thanks to Kay Swift, been hired by George as a kind of factotum. The tour had been planned around the tenth anniversary of the *Rhapsody in Blue*. Obviously it promised great expectations, for George had hired a special train for the more than fifty musicians, their instruments, and the other trappings necessary to such a venture (George, for example, carried no less than four bags plus his heavy practice keyboard which he entrusted to no one but Paul).

"I had three major functions," Paul recalls. The first was to look after the instruments and to see that they were carefully unloaded and delivered to the concert hall; the fact that the first violinist carried a priceless Stradivarius did not at all simplify Paul's life. His second function was to give George a daily massage to keep him in trim since he was away from his usual tennis court and golf course. The final function was to keep people away, especially women, who tended to overwhelm both George and Melton.

Paul Mueller recalls, with both amusement and apprehension, the "brazen women" en route who made his life so joyless. Many stops for the orchestra were sponsored by local music clubs or other culture groups, whose membership was largely made up of women, who made

Paul Mueller, who joined George ca. 1931 as an all-around aide and who remained with him until the end, in 1937. COURTESY KATHI MUELLER

a point of meeting the train upon arrival. In St. Paul, for example, a mob of women met them at the station. As Paul and James Melton had left the train before George, they led the way through the crowd with George trailing diffidently behind. Paul carried the practice keyboard. Soon he and Melton were surrounded. A woman threw her arms around Melton, kissed him, then turned to Paul, saying, "Welcome to St. Paul, Mr. Gershwin!" and planted a kiss on his cheek.

This was generally the tenor of the tour. In Kansas City the concert was held in the Armory and backstage Paul encountered a dowager who announced, "I'm looking for my niece, have you seen her?" No, he had not, but she was soon discovered in Melton's dressing room—and forcibly, but gently, evicted.

It was a hectic twenty-eight days. Traveling with half a hundred raffish musicians provided its moments too. With the tour losing money George was preoccupied and perhaps more serious than was his custom, which made him the target of their jibes. It was at Montreal, for example, as they were leaving Canada and re-entering the United States, that just as the Customs officials entered their car, someone (it was the third violinist, the company joker) shouted out, "Hey, George, you better hide those diamonds, those guys are getting on!"

The result was that, as George fretted, the Customs men held them up for more than an hour searching for the "diamonds." So it was with much relief that George eventually saw the lights of home again.

Waiting for him when he returned was a letter from Heyward and more of the expanding libretto. "I hope," Heyward wrote, "you will be eager to see some more of the script, so am sending the next two scenes . . . I have about completed the next scene also, but it is not yet typed, and I want to do a little more work on it.

"Act 2, scene 1 may seem a little long to you, but I have reduced it from 39 pages in the talking script to 18 for the opera, and it is strong on humor and action. Let me know how you feel about it and if you think it needs more lyrics.

"Act 2, scene 2 ought to be good," Heyward went on. "I have cut out the conventional Negro vaudeville stuff that was in the original play and incorporated material that is authentic and plenty 'hot' as well. I have discovered for the first time a type of secular dance that is done here that is straight from the African phallic dance, and that is undoubtedly a complete survival."

E. Y. "Yip" Harburg and Harold
Arlen, Ira's collaborators on *Life
Begins at 8:40*. ASCAP. COURTESY
E. Y. HARBURG

George composed his interpretation of the dance as "I Ain't Got No
Shame," which just precedes "It Ain't Necessarily So" in the second
scene of Act 2. It was cut before *Porgy and Bess* opened in New York.
Heyward suggested also another local touch in the way of a "native
band of harmonicas, combs, etc. It will make an extraordinary introduction to the primitive scene of passion between Crown and Bess."

The Theatre Guild was hoping for a production of the opera in the
fall of 1934, a hope in which Heyward joined them, but George could
not give any definite date for the production. It must have pleased Heyward, though, when George finally informed him, in the letter of February 26, 1934, "I have begun composing music for the First Act and
I am starting with the songs and spirituals first."

Almost two years had gone by since the letter to Heyward in 1932.
The first song composed was "Summertime," the first song in the opera.
Ira, who had been assisting with the editing of the book and lyrics, as
well as making suggestions, thought that the melody of "Summertime"
was lovely but that it was a mistake to begin the evening with a lullaby.
But George persisted and the song stood in its position. Ira's work up to
this point had been rather sporadic, as he was more actively involved
with Harold Arlen and E. Y. Harburg on *Life Begins at 8:40*.

210 "I really think you are doing a magnificent job with the new libretto,"

Ira's quick pencil sketch of Harold Arlen working on *Life Begins at 8:40*. Re the meeting that resulted in the titling of the show, Ira said, "We were at John Murray Anderson's for lunch. It was one of those English lunches where you started with a salad, and then there was something, and then there was nothing." COURTESY HAROLD ARLEN

12.10 A.M. 3/12/34.

HAROLD ARLEN AT WORK
By
Ira Gershwin

George told Heyward, "and hope I can match it musically." He also reported that he had seen an opera with an all-Negro cast. "I saw '4 Saints in 3 Acts,' an opera by Gertrude Stein and Virgil Thomson, with a colored cast. The libretto was entirely in Stein's manner, which means that it had the effect of a 5-year-old child prattling on. Musically, it sounded early 19th century, which was a happy inspiration and made the libretto bearable—in fact, quite entertaining. There may be one or two in the cast that would be useful to us."

Both Heyward and George were hoping that the other would make the long trip that would enable them to collaborate more closely. But George was forced to stay in New York for his weekly radio show until June 1, after which he planned to spend a month or two with Heyward, who preferred the milder climate and gentler atmosphere of Charleston. George's program, *Music by Gershwin*, served not only as a means of presenting his own music but also as an outlet for younger composers he respected: Harold Arlen, Oscar Levant, Morton Gould, Dana Suesse, Rube Bloom—and his brother, Arthur Gershwin, who had also begun to compose.

Heyward was a little disturbed over the radio's holding George in New York. He wrote on March 2, 1934, "I have been hearing you on the radio and the reception was so good it seemed as though you were in the room. In fact, the illusion was so perfect I could hardly keep from shouting at you 'Swell show, George, but what the hell is the news about PORGY!!!' "

Heyward, too, had been giving some attention to the American opera scene. The Stein-Thomson work did not concern him as much as a Howard Hanson opera with an early-American setting, *Merry Mount*, which had also been broadcast. "I was relieved," he commented. "From the advance ballyhoo I thought something revolutionary was coming that might steal our thunder, but it seemed to me to be pretty much the conventional thing.

"I am naturally disappointed that you have tied yourself up so long in New York. I believe that if you had gotten down for a reasonably long stay and gotten deep into the sources here you would have done a bigger job. I am not criticising your decision. I know well what an enormously advantageous arrangement the radio is, and I know, also, how this tour of yours and the broadcasts are rolling up publicity that will be good business for us when the show opens, only I am disappointed. There is so much here that you have not yet gotten hold of. Anyway, this can be offset to a great extent by my going on and working with you, and I shall do this, availing myself of your invitation, and stopping with you with pleasure. . . .

"As for the script from now on, I am sort of at a deadlock. The storm scene must stand about as is with very few cuts in dialog. Musically it must be done when we are together. It must carry itself on the big scene when Crown sings against the spiritual, and I can't do the lyrics until I get your ideas as to time."

Heyward brought up again the importance of a fall production, admitting that the pressing reason was one of finances. "I have been letting everything else go," he said, "counting on it for early fall. If it is going to be late, I will have to get something else, myself, to carry me over." To accomplish this, Heyward eventually accepted a Hollywood contract under which he wrote two outstanding screen plays, *The Emperor Jones* and *The Good Earth*.

And so the first great American opera was underwritten, so to speak, by Hollywood and the radio via a laxative (George's sponsor was Feenamint, which was a source of ribald amusement to his friends who were aware of his chronic constipation). Heyward's observation was subtle.

Reading the script of *Music by Gershwin*, George's radio program that served to introduce not only his music but the songs of younger composers.

and to the point, "the ends justified the means, and . . . they also served who only sat and waited."

With his letter Heyward had included the text for the third scene of Act 2. On March 8, 1934, George wrote: "I think it is a very interesting and touching scene, although a bit on the long side. However, I see one or two places that do not seem terribly important to the action which could be cut." George then proceeds to counsel Heyward on the art of showmanship: "You must be sure that the opera is not too long as I am a great believer in not giving people too much of a good thing. . . .

"I am working as much as I can on our opus and am finding it very interesting. I am skipping around—writing a bit here and a bit there. It doesn't go too fast but that doesn't worry me as I think it is all going to work out very well." Indirectly George was informing Heyward not to count upon a fall 1934 production and also not to fret over the musical content because of the little digging George had done into actual folk music.

George depended upon Heyward for guidance: "I would like to write the song that opens the 2nd Act, sung by Jake with the fish nets [this would be "It Take a Long Pull to Get There"], but I don't know the rhythm you had in mind—especially for the answers of the chorus, so I would appreciate it if you would put dots and dashes over the lyric and send it to me. . . . Ira and I have worked up some words to music in the very opening, in Jazzbo Brown's room while the people are dancing, and I finished it up with a sort of a chant."

Several days went by before George heard from Heyward again; the writer had been laid low by the flu. On March 19 he was well enough, after a siege of ten days, to send George his "rather vague idea for the rhythm" for the boat song. "If you will imagine yourself at an oar," he suggested to George, "and write music to conform to that rhythm that will give you a better idea than anything I can write."

Enclosed with Heyward's letter was Scene 4 of Act 2. "This scene will give you the greatest musical opportunity of the show. I bank heavily on it to top the big effect of Act 1, Scene 2. The scene builds rapidly to Crown's jazz song being done against the spiritual of the crowd [Heyward is referring to the Storm Scene, and Crown's mocking song, "A Red Headed Woman"]. I have made no effort to suggest words for these songs, because the music is the basic value. I should

think that it would be best for you to work out the two tunes and

An early pencil sketch of the opening of Scene 2, Act 1 of *Porgy and Bess*.

musical effects, then get Ira to work with you on the words as this is a job calling for the closest sort of collaboration."

Fine and sensitive poet though he was, Heyward realized that the actual setting of lyrics to music was a highly specialized job, and that Ira's working over of the lyrics prepared them for a more effective setting by George.

Heyward was planning to come to New York in mid-April, but before that, on March 27, he finished the first draft of the last act and sent it off immediately to George to give him time to assimilate it thoroughly before he arrived.

"Do not be alarmed about any inclination toward too much length," Heyward cautioned. "There are many places where we can cut in conference without disrupting the story. For instance: the opening episode

DuBose Heyward in the study of his Folly Beach home. COURTESY MRS. DUBOSE HEYWARD

in Act 3, Scene 2, with the detective and the women. This is swell comedy, and the audience loved it, but if necessary, it can be moved out entirely, and the detective can go right to Porgy."

The April conference went smoothly and final discussions on the handling of the opera were held. There was a spot in the first act that needed lightening and George, at the piano, improvised the sort of thing he had in mind: a jaunty rhythmic tune. It was so good that both Du-Bose and Ira insisted that the "example" be developed into the desired song. Ira suggested "I Got Plenty o' Nuttin'" as a title—and shortly after added the twist, "and nuttin's plenty for me." He and Heyward then joined in the working up of a dummy lyric, Ira contributing "I got no car, I got no mule, I got no misery," and Heyward some of the other lines. Heyward, who had up to this moment been writing the lyrics first

The Heyward cottage at Folly Beach, directly opposite the one rented by George and Henry Botkin. COURTESY MRS. DUBOSE HEYWARD

George and Henry Botkin at Folly Beach. PHOTO BY PAUL MUELLER. GERSHWIN COLLECTION

Henry Botkin's painting of the cottage at Folly Beach, South Carolina. COURTESY IRA GERSHWIN

to his songs, was eager to do the words of an already completed melody. So a "lead sheet" containing the dummy lyric that fitted the tune exactly according to rhythm and accentuation (though not always making sense) was taken back to Folly Beach, South Carolina, where he wrote up the lyric—using many of the original lines—then sent it back to the Gershwins, and Ira in turn made some revisions and then the song was ready to go into the opera.

George worked hard through May and on the twenty-third completed the first scene of the opera. As June approached, and with it a release from the radio chores he detested, he made plans to go south. The spot chosen was Folly Island, about ten miles from Charleston, where the Heywards made their summer home.

George and his cousin, Harry Botkin, were given a festive send-off at Pennsylvania Station when they left in mid-June for Folly Beach. Botkin, who was painting Negro subjects and was in search of material for his canvases, went along to paint and, of course, to provide the necessary companionship for George. Paul Mueller, George's all-around aide, preceded them by car, with the heavy baggage, and in order to be able to pick them up when they arrived at Charleston to drive them to Folly Island. With him George carried the Porgy manuscript and his painting materials. Ira remained behind to put the remaining final touches on *Life Begins at 8:40.*

Living conditions on Folly Island greatly contrasted with life in a 72nd Street duplex. George and Harry had rented a four-room beach cottage that was to serve as their headquarters and workshop for the next five weeks. It was a small frame structure (since blown down by a hurricane) with only the minimal conveniences. Water was brought in from Charleston in five-gallon crocks. George's room held a small iron bed (generally unmade), his clothing hung from convenient nails and hooks; a small washbasin and an upright piano, also brought in from Charleston, completed the room's furnishings. Harry's quarters, directly across the hallway from George's, were no more luxurious.

From the screened-in porch they could look over the beach to the Atlantic. On the beach they often watched giant turtles sleeping or burying eggs; and in the ocean they could see, besides the swimming turtles, porpoises, the fins of sharks. The latter settled any question of swimming for them. In the nearby swamps, bull alligators roared in counterpoint to George's playing. He had never been so close to primitive nature before, nor so far from civilization.

Harry wrote home about the wild-life: "Many, many eerie sand

George roughing it at Folly Beach, tanned, barefoot, and brimming with musical ideas.
PHOTO BY PAUL MUELLER

"My Studio—Folly Beach," George's water color showing where he worked and slept during the five weeks on Folly Island.
PHOTO BY G. D. HACKETT. COURTESY ARTHUR GERSHWIN

crabs looking very much like glass spiders, crawled around the cottage. They were the color of the beach sand; nature's way of camouflaging them. Droves of bugs and insects fly against the screens and the noisy crickets drove George to distraction, keeping him awake nights." Harry remembers that only when Paul went outside and struck the trees with a stick could George get some sleep.

Five days after their arrival George wrote to his mother his own impressions of life at Folly Beach: "The place down here looks like a battered, old South Sea Island. There was a storm 2 weeks ago which tore down a few houses along the beach & the place is so primitive they just let them stay that way. Imagine, there's not *one* telephone on the whole island—public or private. The nearest phone is about 10 miles away.

"Our first three days here were cool, the place being swept by an ocean breeze. Yesterday was the first hot day (it must have been 95 in town & brought the flys, gnats, mosquitos. There are so many swamps

Exterior of the Folly Beach cottage where George worked on *Porgy and Bess* and his cousin, Henry Botkin, painted. George even attempted to grow a beard, but was not happy with the result. In the photo he is standing on the steps. When Kay Swift visited some years later she learned that the cottage had been blown into the sea by a storm. PHOTO BY PAUL MUELLER, GERSHWIN COLLECTION

in the district that when a breeze comes in from the land there's nothing to do but scratch."

He also suggested to his mother—"I know you love your comforts" —not to make the trip to Folly Island. He mentioned, too, that he was glad he hadn't brought Tony (his dog) because of the heat and that he and Harry wore nothing but bathing suits all day.

There were, of course, excursions to the mainland for sight-seeing trips, shopping, and "Gershwin evenings" in the homes of Charleston's aristocracy. This helped to make up to some extent for the lack of excitement and activity that George had become accustomed to in New York.

The Heywards joined George and Harry. The group traveled to James Island nearby, with its population of Gullah Negroes, who were cut off from the mainland, and where older traditions and songs were preserved. One of the customs was the practice of what was called "shouting," a combination of singing and the beating an extraordinarily complex rhythmic pattern with the hands and feet. Heyward recalled with as much pride as surprise the time that they had attended a church meeting where George joined in the shouting and stole the show from the champion shouter, to the delight of the congregation.

Another time, as they were about to enter a church, George stopped Heyward. "Listen," he suggested to his collaborator.

Heyward, who had heard prayer-meeting singing so often, more or less took it all for granted, but George's manner caused him to listen closely and analytically from the musical standpoint. The congregation was distinctly but unevenly broken into groups, each singing a different melodic line, all then blending into an almost incomprehensible but powerful prayer. George adapted the idea for the remarkable six-voice prayer that opens and closes Scene 4 of the second act.

Ideas were coming in exciting profusion. Harry noted that George composed rapidly, as quickly as someone might type a letter. George, however, envied Harry, feeling that he was really having all the fun in painting. George, of course, couldn't resist taking time out to paint. He was elated. One day, heady from the flow of work, he stopped Dorothy Heyward as she was about to leave for a trip to town. He was eager to play something for her. Because she was in a hurry she tried to postpone the session, but he persisted, "Listen to the greatest music composed in America!" he declared.

If he envied Harry's painting, he envied his cousin's beard even more. At a party in Charleston he had noticed that Harry had received more attention than he had, a fact George attributed to the goatee. He then decided that he would grow a beard also, but gave up after a few days, not impressed with the results.

A news release of July 7, 1934, described him as "Bare and black above the waist, habitually wearing only a two-inch beard and a pair of once white linen knickers." George also made some statements about the work on *Porgy*, touched with his customary naïve candor: "The production will be a serious attempt to put into operatic form a purely American theme. If I am successful it will resemble a combination of the drama and romance of *Carmen* and the beauty of *Meistersinger*, if you can imagine that.

"I believe it will be something never done before. *Green Pastures?* This will be infinitely more sophisticated. I am trying to get a sensational dramatic effect. I hope to accomplish this by having the few whites in the production speak their lines while the Negroes, in answering, will sing."

In comparing the races George found the white man "more unemotional, dull, and drab." It was Heyward who felt that for George the trip to Folly Island, and especially his visits to the "experience" services, was more of a home-coming than an excursion. When George played on the island, people gathered around the cottage to listen, keeping time as they did.

In August, George and Harry returned to New York; George's radio contract called for him to begin work again in October. He devoted all of his free time to *Porgy;* in September 1934 he all but completed the orchestration of the second scene of Act 1. He was skipping around, composing the songs, and then working on orchestrating from the vocal score.

With the planning for the broadcasts out of the way, and excepting the weekly rehearsals, George gave more and more time to the opera. On November 5, 1934, he wrote to Heyward, saying that he "would like to set a tentative date for rehearsals. Second, I would like to have auditions started during January or February so that those people we choose for the parts can be learning the music and save us so much time . . .

"I had a long talk with Ernst Lubitsch when he was here at the apartment the other evening after I played him a few bits of the opera. He gave me some interesting slants, such as having the scenery just a bit off realism with very free use of lighting to enhance dramatic events. These ideas of Lubitsch's coincide with my feelings—how about yours?"

He reported on the progress of composition. "Ira has written the lyrics for Porgy and Bess' first duet and I really think this bit of melody will be most effective."

The duet was "Bess, You Is My Woman Now." When he finished, he was anxious to get the reaction of his "genial friend," Dr. Albert Sirmay, his editor at Chappell's, the publisher, and an old friend and adviser. As George played, Sirmay, touched, began to cry. George looked up from the keyboard. "Doc," he asked, "are you laughing?" Sirmay assured him that the opposite was true. George was curious as to what the song contained that so affected his friend. Sirmay explained that the music was so lovely and so fitting that he was emotionally moved.

George picked up the phone on the piano and called Ira in his apartment across the street.

"Ira, come right over."

Ira's reply was the conventional one: "Why?" To Ira so spontaneous a move was not attractive.

George explained cryptically, "Because something is happening here."

Ira wanted to know what could be so important as to require him to become involved with two elevator rides and a walk across 72nd Street.

Giving up, George explained, "I just played the duet for the Doc, and Ira, he's crying!" Though greatly pleased to have been able to arouse so the emotions of a man he admired (and who admired him even more), George could never stop teasing Sirmay about the incident, even up to opening night, when George announced that he had to check to see "if we got the Doc crying."

In his report to Heyward he continued, "Incidentally, I start and finish the storm scene with six different prayers sung simultaneously. This has somewhat the effect we heard in Hendersonville as we stood outside the Holy Rollers Church."

By December of 1934 concrete plans for eventual production were being made. The Theatre Guild was seeking a director and had just about made up their minds to engage Rouben Mamoulian, who had directed the original play. George was more excited about more personal developments: "Theresa Helburn came up for lunch the other day with

Sam Behrman to hear some of the Porgy music and I must say they were most enthusiastic and excited. Also, I played some of the music for Deems Taylor whose judgment I respect highly, and he was so enthusiastic that I blush to mention it.

"Here is an exciting piece of news: I heard about a man singer who teaches music in Washington and arranged to have him come and sing for me on Sunday several weeks ago. In my opinion he is the closest to a colored Lawrence Tibbett I have ever heard. He is about six feet tall and very well proportioned with a rich booming voice. He would make a superb Crown and, I think, just as good a Porgy. He is coming to sing for me again during Christmas week. I shall ask the Guild to take an option on his services."

The singer was Todd Duncan, who portrayed Porgy. On January 24, 1935, George wrote to Duncan, who by then had been signed, that "I am leaving for Florida this weekend where I begin the task of orchestrating the opera. I just finished a trio in the last scene for Porgy, Serena, and Maria which I think will interest you very much."

The trio section of "Oh, Where's My Bess?", one of the high points in the opera, was cut before *Porgy and Bess* opened in New York.

Once settled in Emil Mosbacher's Palm Beach house, George set to "the task of orchestrating the opera" in earnest. The full vocal score was finished, but the orchestration was barely touched. George reported his progress to Ira in New York:

① Monday

Hello Ira,

How are you big brother? It seems funny writing to you + not being in a foreign country. Palm Beach is once more itself after a few days of cold weather. I'm sitting in the patio of the charming house Emil has rented, writing to you after orchestrating for a few hours this morning. Expect to finish scoring Scene II Act I this week. It goes slowly, there being

2.

millions of notes to write.

DuBose, whom I saw in Charleston was very pleased with your lyrics + thought it would be agreeable to him to split the lyric royalties with you. He is coming north for a few weeks around the first of April.

Wrote Mamoulian of taking 25% of the opera + told him how it would be split, namely, 4 thousand for me, 4 thousand for Emil + 2 thousand for you. Just received his answer in which he says he'd rather not have any outside money in the property meaning of course Emil's interest. that 10 thousand represents 25% based on a 40 thousand dollar production. the cost may go higher in which case I think if we took 15% between us it would not be risking too much & yet we'd have a good interest in the undertaking. What do you think?

Spoke to mom on the phone last night. She seems quite well. I think I'll run down to

Miami to dine with her some night this week.

Flash! Mrs. Dodge Sloan is naming a horse after me. By Sir Galahad out of Melodia.

Flash! I needed a 4 to break 80 yesterday. OH I forgot to mention - a 4 on a par 5 hole.

Write, big boy & let know what goes on. One of those old fashioned newsy letters of which you are undisputed king. Send my love to Lee & Arthur. Hope you are well & happy.   George

Back in New York, George became involved with auditions, and other decisions and assignments. It was decided that Alexander Smallens, who had conducted *Four Saints in Three Acts*, which George had seen, and who was a noted champion of new music, would conduct the opera. At a Town Hall Stravinsky concert George had run into a friend, Alexander Steinert, who had had a great deal of experience, most of it gained in European operas, and asked him to coach the singers. Assisting him was J. Rosamond Johnson, who also would play Lawyer Frazier in the opera.

In Hollywood, Mamoulian accepted the bid to direct the undertaking; a decision he made even before hearing any of the music. Anne Wiggins Brown filled the role of Bess by writing a letter to George requesting an audition. George's choice for the role of Sportin' Life was John W. Bubbles, of the vaudeville team Buck and Bubbles.

Rehearsals were set for sometime in August and George was now writing feverishly against that date. The work piled up; assisting in the boresome job of copying were the two faithfuls, Kay Swift and Dr. Sirmay. Copying of the orchestral score was sent out and then had to be checked carefully against George's many-volumed manuscript.

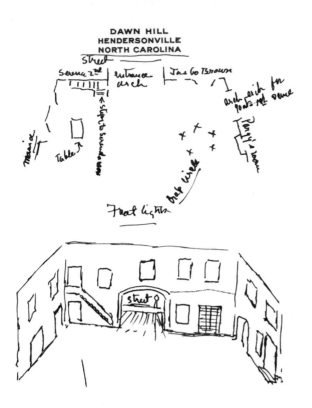

DuBose Heyward's sketch for the stage setting for *Porgy and Bess* which he included in the script sent to George. COURTESY DR. ALBERT SIRMAY, FROM THE COLLECTION OF THE LIBRARY OF CONGRESS

The chronology of the opera's completion manifests the speed at which George worked: The first scene of Act 3 is inscribed "July 22, 1935 (Finished)," the second scene is dated "Aug. 4, 1935," and the end of the manuscript is signed in full and marked "Finished August 23, 1935."

Three days later rehearsals began. George, however, was still working on the opera's music, for there was still the opening music to do. Actual work, not counting the inevitable changes that go with rehearsals, on *Porgy and Bess* was concluded in September (probably the second) 1935, about three weeks before George's thirty-seventh birthday, which preceded the Boston opening by four days. In all, about eleven months were spent in composition and another nine orchestrating. Still George, true to form, made the deadline just in time.

Rehearsals began officially on August 26. The job of fitting the pieces together fell to Mamoulian, who not only had the problem of making sense of seeming chaos, but also of whipping the cast into shape, instilling discipline, and in general making an entity of the several elements.

226

George, Heyward, and Steinert had an additional problem, that of coaching educated, sophisticated Negroes to sing in approximation of authentic dialect.

George was proud of his choice of Bubbles as Sportin' Life, but Bubbles found working with real script—and especially with a libretto—not to his tastes. He also, since he could not read music, changed the melodies and rhythms from performance to performance, to the dismay of Smallens and to the consternation of other members of the cast who missed cues, and he added to the already-confused rehearsals. George was so certain that Bubbles would work out that he stood in the way of his being fired. George was vindicated eventually by one of the classic performances of the American stage.

Before the cast was to entrain for the Boston opening, a performance was held at Carnegie Hall. Without the distraction of movement or

In Palm Beach, Florida, orchestrating *Porgy and Bess*, February 1935. GERSHWIN COLLECTION

Kay Swift, who assisted in preparing *Porgy and Bess* for the printers and often played two-piano duets with George. To her George dedicated his *Songbook*.

PHOTO BY ALBERT PETERSEN.

COURTESY KATHARINE KAUFMAN

Dr. Albert Sirmay, George's "genial good friend" and musical editor, who helped in preparing Gershwin music for publication. COURTESY CHAPPELL & COMPANY, INC.

scenery this performance has been remembered as the most memorable of the opera ever heard. Also, it was complete, as George wrote it, running to over four hours.

The week in Boston before the opening meant the paring down of the music and the tightening of action. The piano music went out, so did "The Buzzard Song," and the trio in "Where's My Bess?" George, Smallens, and Mamoulian walked in Boston Common late into the night discussing the cuts before they were actually made. George's instinctive showmanship overruled his creator's pride in the work as he wrote it.

On opening night, September 30, 1935, the enthusiasm of George's friends seemed to infect the rest of the audience, who applauded the final curtain with un-Bostonian vivacity. Serge Koussevitzky, making one of his rare appearances at the theater, recognized in *Porgy and Bess* "a great advance in American opera." Even the morning's papers were positive in their appraisals. In *The Transcript* Moses Smith observed that, "Gershwin must now be accepted as a serious composer." *The Christian Science Monitor* recognized the opera as "Gershwin's most important contribution to music."

On October 10, 1935, *Porgy and Bess* opened in New York, appropriately at the Alvin Theatre. In the audience was the usual glittering Gershwin crowd from the oddly assorted worlds of music, Broadway, finance, literature, as well as the Lower East Side and the Bronx, represented by proud relatives.

Alexander Steinert, one-time voice coach for the Russian Opera Singers. He was chosen by George to coach the singers in *Porgy and Bess.*

Putting the last note to *Porgy and Bess*, August 1935. GERSHWIN COLLECTION

When the curtain went down the audience reacted as the one in Boston had. The authors were called on the stage to thunderous applause. Later there was a party at Condé Nast's sumptuous Park Avenue apartment, with Paul Whiteman's band to play and the *Porgy and Bess* cast to sing highlights from the opera. George was presented with a handsome silver tray covered with facsimile signatures of his many friends and colleagues.

But the critics next morning, particularly the music critics, did not find much to praise in *Porgy and Bess*. To begin with, they were thrown into customary confusion by the fusion of musical comedy and grand opera, which George himself preferred calling a "folk opera." Leonard Liebling was one of the few to recognize it as "the first authentic American opera," but Winthrop Sargeant found in it "no advance in American operatic composition." George was disappointed in Olin Downes's review in the *Times*, in which the critic felt that George had failed to "utilize all the resources of the operatic composer" (whatever that meant) and confessed that the opera-operetta-Broadway treatment disturbed him.

George and Rouben Mamoulian at a rehearsal of *Porgy and Bess*. WIDE WORLD PHOTOS

In Boston for the tryout of *Porgy and Bess*, October 1935. COURTESY ROBERT
BREEN

232

George, though not happy with such dismissals, was not inclined to defend himself publicly. Wisely he chose to let time do that, but it might have been enlightening had the critics been able to look into one of the notebooks he used during the *Porgy* period. While composing he dipped into what he called "the icebox," a large notebook, for several musical ideas for the opera. On one of its pages he had jotted down what may be the nearest we have of his musical credo, as if he wished to be reminded while he worked of certain precepts to shape that work. His precise meaning is not known for he did not discuss these reminders with Kay Swift, who was using the same notebook (he from the front and she from the back), but the notations are provocative:

Melodic
Nothing neutral
Utter simplicity
Directness

These were undoubtedly the guiding principles (actually applicable to all his work), not some predefined concept of what opera was supposed to be.

In *Porgy and Bess* George created a living picture of a people; he depicted their emotions in music—in every instance in music fitting to the mood and character. This is opera; as for "all the resources," he utilized song, dance, orchestral passages, recitative with uncommon mastery. He also created the first true American opera, based upon folklike though original themes, in a believable American setting. This is evident, not only in the songs, but in the writing for the orchestra. In terms of what he set out to do, *Porgy and Bess* is one of George's most successful accomplishments. Why this went unrecognized in 1935 by the critics is difficult to explain (especially since so many of them have later almost completely reversed their opinions). George himself never lost faith in the opera even though it was soon obvious, before the run was far along, that it would not prove to be a popular box-office success. After a short stay at the Alvin of only 124 performances an attempt was made to prolong the life of *Porgy and Bess* by scheduling a tour that began in Philadelphia on January 27, 1936. After visiting, briefly, Pittsburgh and Chicago, it closed in Washington, D.C., on March 21.

The entire investment of $70,000 was lost; whatever royalties George

Performance shot—
Porgy and Bess. PHOTO
BY GEORGE GERSHWIN

Opening-night curtain call at the Alvin Theatre. George, DuBose Heyward, and Rouben Mamoulian in stage center with the cast around them: Georgette Harvey (Maria), Ruby Elzy (Serena), Todd Duncan (Porgy), Anne Brown (Bess—partly hidden by George), Warren Coleman (Crown), and Edward Matthews (Jake). COURTESY WARREN COLEMAN

John W. Bubbles as Sportin'
Life. PHOTO BY CARL VAN
VECHTEN

Ruby Elzy as Serena, who sang
"My Man's Gone Now." PHOTO
BY GEORGE GERSHWIN

Eva Jessye, choral director for
Porgy and Bess. COURTESY EVA
JESSYE

had earned went toward the payment of the copyist's fees. The Heywards had planned to buy a house with their expected *Porgy and Bess* royalties, but this plan was set aside. Ira realized $2000 from *Porgy and Bess*, but was doing much better with his and Vernon Duke's *Ziegfeld Follies*, which had opened on January 30.

George tried to rest after the strenuous months he had put into *Porgy and Bess* by taking a short vacation in Mexico. He decided to extract a suite for orchestra from the opera, thereby preserving some of the themes and assuring performances of the music in conjunction with his appearances around the country.

His collection of paintings, which had grown considerably under the guidance and searching of Botkin, gave him some solace. So did an exhibition at the Society of Independent Artists on April 21, at which he exhibited a couple of his own canvases. But the fact caused no noticeable stir and Harry cautioned George to wait till he could give a one-man show, for he was improving all the time, and people would come to see the painting of Gershwin the artist, and not some paintings by Gershwin the composer.

Attending the opening of Cole Porter's *Jubilee*, October 12, 1935, two nights after the opening of *Porgy and Bess*. In *Jubilee* Eva Standing did a skit burlesquing Elsa Maxwell. According to Isaac Goldberg, "it was Eva Standing who held out as the great novelty of her Greek bacchanale the fact that Gershwin had promised not to play." CULVER SERVICE

Working on Ruby Elzy's portrait. GERSHWIN COLLECTION

George and his cousin, the artist Henry Botkin, discussing painting, their favorite mutual topic. Botkin assisted George in assembling an outstanding collection of modern art, including works by Picasso, Modigliani, Siqueiros, Rouault and Chagall, among others. Perhaps the most famous painting in the Gershwin Collection, Picasso's *Absinthe Drinker*, is to the left. Directly behind Botkin is his own painting, "Ten Miles from Charleston," made while he and George stayed at Folly Beach. COURTESY HENRY BOTKIN

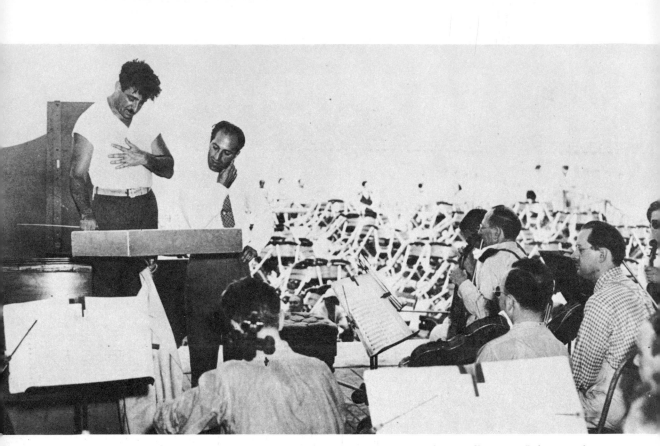

Preparing for the Gershwin concert at Lewisohn Stadium on July 9 and 10. Alexander Smallens and George in discussion. UNITED PRESS PHOTO

On July 9 and 10 George appeared at Lewisohn Stadium for a Gershwin concert. Alexander Smallens conducted, George played the *Rhapsody* and *Concerto*, and Anne Brown, Todd Duncan, Ruby Elzy, and the Eva Jessye Choir sang selections from George's labor of love.

It was already set that George and Ira would leave for Hollywood in a month; on these two consecutive hot nights New York heard Gershwin play Gershwin for the last time.

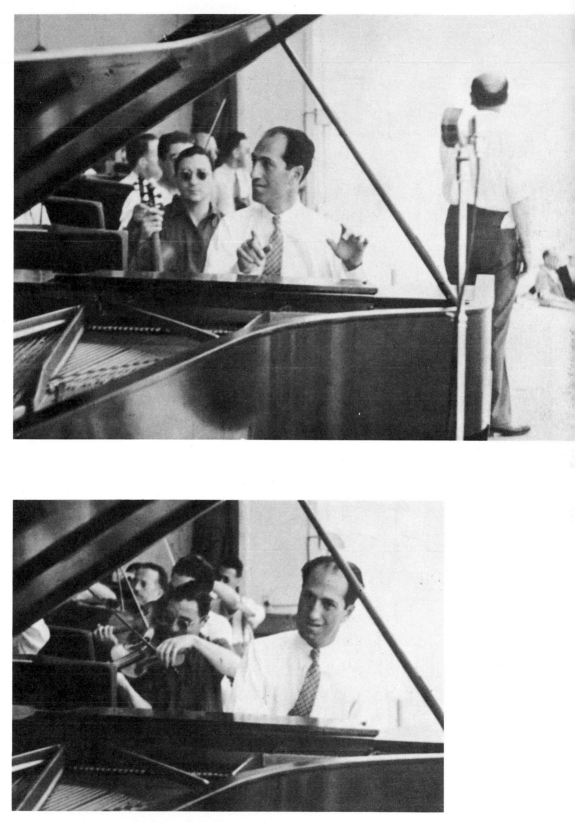

George at the piano during rehearsal. EUROPEAN

In the apartment on East 72nd Street. GERSHWIN COLLECTION

1936-1937

Late in the summer of 1936, before they had consigned their furniture, books, and paintings to storage and abandoned their 72nd Street apartments, the Gershwins gave a farewell party in George's place. Although they had committed themselves to a Hollywood assignment to begin that August, they expected this to be solely an eastern evening; but they reckoned without the eager efficiency of the studio, whose messenger broke in upon the gathering to deliver the preliminary script. The brothers dutifully retired to glance at it—but they quickly emerged, George complaining: "Gosh, but I wish I was back in New York!"

The second trip to Hollywood, which began auspiciously in the fall of 1936 and ended abruptly in July 1937 with the death of George Gershwin, is a period that too easily postures a fashionable, almost classical attitude: the fall of the hero, the death of the artist. Ever since that Sunday morning when the intense flame that was George's life finally consumed itself, many have speculated that it was Hollywood that destroyed him. If one subscribes to this notion, however, he must accept two other assumptions—neither of which is valid. First, he must look upon George's theatrical experience as comparatively an easy one that unaccustomed him to criticism. (The difficulties the Gershwins had with Ziegfeld, when they had to sue for their money; the ordeal of *Funny Face*, when it went so badly in its road tryouts that Alex Aarons accused George and Ira of not trying to write a hit score; and the tribulations of *Pardon My English*, which was so sorry a production that Morrie Ryskind was unwilling to let his name be associated with the show—all these must be forgotten.)

The Hollywood myth also asks that we believe George Gershwin was a shy man of such sensitivity that criticism could mortally wound him. Of all creative geniuses George Gershwin was one of the least personally sensitive; instead, he was so youthfully brash, so confident in his work, that he seems never to have succumbed to doubts or imagined insults. All his life he and Ira were so professional in their attitude toward their work that, if a producer or star disliked a song, they preferred writing another rather than arguing or being song salesmen. George's early death is not a symbolic statement of his sensitivity; nor was its geographical location in any way responsible. The brain tumor that destroyed him was for the world a tragedy of incalculable proportion, but it had no relationship to his life other than putting an end to it.

The beginning of 1936 had found both brothers uncommonly weary: Ira physically exhausted, and George bored to distraction. Worn down from working so long on the often-postponed *Ziegfeld Follies of 1936* (music by Vernon Duke), Ira left with Leonore and with Vincente Minnelli for Trinidad shortly after the show opened its successful Winter Garden run on January 30. Meanwhile, George floundered in the wake of creative excitement churned up the previous October by the opening of *Porgy and Bess*.

On December 17, 1935, returning from a Caribbean holiday with Edward Warburg, then director of the American Ballet of the Metropolitan, George found himself being serenaded at pierside by the *Porgy and Bess* cast. But attention did not calm his restiveness. He had sailed to Mexico in search of Indian music and had not found any; he had been frustrated also in his hope that Mexican melodies would inspire him as the Cuban trip earlier had led to the *Cuban Overture*. The result of all this was a flat pronouncement: "I am going to interest myself in politics, and it is true that in Mexico I talked a great deal with Diego Rivera, and

George, the Leica fan, photographing at Kay Swift's in 1936. The fascinated child was Kay's daughter, Andrea.
GERSHWIN COLLECTION

Photo by candlelight. George was fascinated, as a candid camera fan, by various lighting situations, and the use of candlelight from below was an especial favorite technique for a time. It was not terribly flattering to adults, but children came off fairly well. In this shot he has caught Kay Swift's daughters, Andrea and Kay, in a happy mood. COURTESY MRS. ROBERT A. LEVIN

with his radical friends, who discussed at length their doctrines and their intentions." It was a singularly naïve remark from a man who was famous for being apolitical. Significantly he concluded, "I'm going to try to develop my brains more in music to match my emotional development." (George had always publicly subscribed to the conventional explanation for the artistic talent: "To my mind all artists are a combination of two elements—the heart and the brain. Some composers overdo one of the elements in their work. Tschaikowsky—although he was a good technician—was apt to stress the heart too much in his music; Berlioz was all mind. Now Bach was a glorious example of the unity of the two.") George's Mexican letters had revealed an anxiety to get back to New York and to work; he was now looking for something to do, and the pierside politico immediately forgot the Mexican radicals.

While Ira vacationed in search of that "Island in the West Indies" so accurately charted in the *Follies*, George's drive for work impelled him to write a song—any song—to be at it again. Feeling that he could not even wait until Ira returned, he began a collaboration with Albert Stillman; their "King of Swing" was published by the newly formed Gershwin Publishing Company but never amounted to much. (Buck and Bubbles introduced the number at the Radio City Music Hall on May 28, 1936. Fritz Kreisler's musical, *The King Steps Out*, with Grace Moore and Franchot Tone, was the screen attraction; and the stage revue—"With Entire Musical Score by George Gershwin"—was called "Swing Is King.")

A more significant creative attempt by George had been the *Suite from "Porgy and Bess,"* a five-part reworking of the operatic score: I. Catfish Row, II. Porgy Sings, III. Fugue, IV. Hurricane, V. Good Morning, Brother. This series of extracts, which is not to be confused with the widely known and frequently recorded *Porgy and Bess* synthesis of Robert Russell Bennett, was given its world premiere at Philadelphia on January 21, 1936, under the baton of Alexander Smallens. After it was recorded nearly thirty years later, Ira retitled it "Catfish Row." (On the same program George himself played the *Concerto in F*.) About this same time George began telling New York friends that he wanted to get started on a symphony. Fearful of contemplated changes in the copyright laws that might jeopardize the incomes of writers and composers, George appeared with a group on February 25 before the House Patents Committee in Washington to defend existing

Luigi Pirandello, Rouben
Mamoulian, and George in
New York in the spring of
1936. GERSHWIN COLLECTION

Leopold Godowsky, pianist,
composer, and Frankie's
father-in-law. PHOTO BY
GEORGE GERSHWIN

David Siqueiros, the Mexican
artist. PHOTO BY GEORGE
GERSHWIN

George and his mother, 1936. COURTESY ARTHUR GERSHWIN

Ira and his mother, 1936. GERSHWIN COLLECTION

legislation. By this time *Porgy and Bess* had gone on tour: an aesthetic triumph, a financial disappointment. Warren Munsell of the Theatre Guild warned George well in advance that there would be no way to prevent the show's closing on March 21 in Washington.

So, in the spring of 1936 the Gershwins began contemplating a return to Hollywood. At first George and Ira talked a bit about doing their own screenplay as well as the music and lyrics. They considered basing a Fred Astaire film on an episode of some years earlier when George had vacationed with Eddie Knopf at Grove Park Inn in Asheville, North Carolina; the two had never quite forgotten the enforced sepulchral silence of that hotel with its gargantuan fireplaces and squeakless guests. Ira's recently proved facility with sketches (he had collaborated with David Freedman on the fifteen-minute first-act finale of the *Follies*) convinced George that, if Freedman would work with them, they could dash off an entire film in the Clarence Budington Kelland tradition. When Freedman took a job in California to write for Eddie Cantor, however, these ideas were discarded.

On February 17 Sam Howard of the Phil Berg-Bert Allenberg Agency wrote George about a Hollywood contract; George answered that he and Ira wanted $100,000 plus a percentage—in brief, an improvement on the 1930 Hollywood agreement. But the man who in 1930 had gone to the Coast with, in his own phrase, "a hit under the belt"—he was thinking of *Girl Crazy*—found himself in 1936 trying to make the trip after a flop opera—and the movie-makers seemed less enthusiastic. (Significantly, Ira's *Follies* was a hit, but Hollywood at that time still believed that the Gershwins meant, in Isaac Goldberg's phrase, "Principally George; and incidentally, Ira.") The Howard inquiry began the written negotiations for a Hollywood year that George later classified as "just being commercial." In his favor was a studio production rush toward musicals, which, in the scramble, *might* make the industry forgive George his opera.

In early April, George and Ira gave Arthur Lyons, then one of Hollywood's biggest agents, a one-month option "to submit the names of George and Ira Gershwin for a motion picture contract with a major studio." Within two weeks Lyons had turned up several proposals: he conferred with Pandro S. Berman at RKO about *Strike Up the Band* as a musical either for Fred Astaire or Harold Lloyd. He worked up enthusiasm too at Universal for this as a Harold Lloyd property. "BERMAN

247

Josephine Baker in the *Ziegfeld Follies*, the 1936 version. Scott Fitzgerald loved her "chocolate arabesques." CULVER SERVICE

ALSO ENTHUSIASTIC ABOUT DAMSEL IN DISTRESS," the P. G. Wodehouse novel. On May 14 another telegram came from Lyons saying that Pan Berman

> ANXIOUS TO MAKE DEAL WITH YOU FOR NEXT ASTAIRE ROGERS
> PICTURE NAMELY WATCH YOUR STEP AN ORIGINAL WHICH I
> TOLD YOU AND IRA ABOUT SATURDAY STOP BERMAN AND STUDIO
> EXECUTIVES ARGUING ABOUT PRICE LEEWAY FOR SCORE AND
> LYRICS STOP SEEMS TOP STUDIO WILL ALLOW IS SIXTY
> THOUSAND DOLLARS BERMAN KNOWS WE WANT MORE AND IN
> VIEW OF HIS ANXIETY TO GET YOU IS PUTTING UP STRONG
> ARGUMENT WITH HIS EXECUTIVES.

Lyon's option expired without a contract being signed. When Alex S. Kempner asked for an option, he became the first agent to admit that the studios were somewhat apprehensive about inviting the Gershwins to Hollywood: there was "an ill-founded belief that George Gershwin would only be interested in writing so-called 'high brow' material and would not be willing to write the LADY BE GOOD type of material." Once again, the trouble was *Porgy and Bess*.

Option or no, Lyons wired George and Ira on June 10 that Berman had offered $60,000 for twenty weeks' work:

> BOTH FRED ASTAIRE AND GINGER ROGERS DELIGHTED WITH
> POSSIBILITY OF YOUR DOING THIS. . . . AFTER YOU TALK
> WITH BERMAN YOU WILL BE CONVINCED THAT THIS IS THE
> RIGHT SETUP FOR YOU AND THAT THIS IS THE TYPE OF
> PICTURE YOU HAVE BEEN LOOKING FOR.

Rudy Vallee, Irving Berlin, George, and Gene Buck of ASCAP, appearing before a congressional committee in Washington, D.C., on a copyright-revision hearing, February 1936. UNITED PRESS PHOTO

Emily Paley of whom George once wrote, "A warm day in June could take lessons from you." PHOTO BY GEORGE GERSHWIN

Arthur Gershwin.

The brothers tried holding out for $75,000 for twenty, or $60,000 for sixteen, weeks.

Archie Selwyn, the brother of Edgar Selwyn, wired them the following day that he could get the Gershwins a Hollywood assignment for either a Cantor or a Crosby picture. The same difficulty reappeared, however: "THEY ARE AFRAID YOU WILL ONLY DO HIGHBROW SONGS SO WIRE ME ON THIS SCORE SO I CAN REASSURE THEM." George stalled for ten days, then telegraphed Selwyn he would be interested if the RKO negotiations collapsed. He concluded with his commercial manifesto: "INCIDENTALLY RUMORS ABOUT HIGHBROW MUSIC RIDICULOUS STOP AM OUT TO WRITE HITS."

Stories circulated that RKO was drawing up a contract, and on June 23 Irving Berlin (who had fashioned a jaunty *Top Hat* for Astaire and Rogers) prematurely congratulated George: "There is no setup in Hollywood that can compare with doing an Astaire picture, and I know you will be very happy with it." The next day Berman wired the brothers to come to terms: "I THINK YOU ARE LETTING A FEW THOUSAND DOLLARS KEEP YOU FROM HAVING LOT OF FUN AND WHEN YOU FIGURE THE GOVERNMENT GETS EIGHTY PERCENT OF IT DO YOU THINK ITS NICE TO MAKE ME SUFFER THIS WAY." Berman, who had had Berlin, Porter, and Kern working for him, determined now to have the Gershwins. The Gershwins gave in, and on June 26 they closed the deal: one picture at $55,000 for sixteen weeks, with an option for a second picture, sixteen weeks at $70,000. In mid-July Archie Selwyn informed George: "Sam Goldwyn is definitely interested in you either before or after you do the Astaire show." Before they left New York, therefore, the Gershwins were almost assured a year's work on the Coast.

During the first half of 1936 George had continued his concertizing. At programs in St. Louis, Washington, Boston, and Chicago he introduced his *Suite from "Porgy and Bess,"* and appeared as soloist in the *Concerto in F* and the *Rhapsody in Blue*. While the RKO contract was being negotiated, George was also invited to appear with the San Francisco Symphony as soloist during their 1937 season in their "new $6,000,000 opera house." An English impresario wanted to schedule a European tour for George in the winter of 1937–38. And Ravinia was so pleased with George's July 25 concert they asked if they could not commission a Gershwin work for 1937. At such moments "being highbrow" seemed to have favorable repercussions after all.

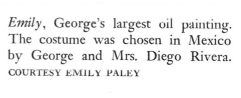

Emily, George's largest oil painting. The costume was chosen in Mexico by George and Mrs. Diego Rivera. COURTESY EMILY PALEY

Mabel Schirmer, a very special friend of the Gershwins, and one of those in the Siqueiros Concert Hall portrait. It was Mabel's remark that "Deep down inside of all the Gershwins— George, Ira, Frankie—there's a motor, always going, always running." PHOTO BY GEORGE GERSHWIN

Lou Paley. PHOTO BY GEORGE GERSHWIN

Irving Caesar.
PHOTO BY GEORGE
GERSHWIN

On August 10 the Gershwins flew from Newark, New Jersey, to Glendale, California. Bill Daly, who saw them off, observed that "Ira seemed somewhat disappointed that the aeroplane wasn't bigger: maybe he'd been looking at pictures of the China Clipper." George, Ira, and Lee made of a suite in the Beverly Wilshire Hotel their temporary residence and atelier, and there the brothers immediately set to work on an Astaire song called "Hi-Ho!" Since the script of *Shall We Dance* was still only the outline of ideas, the Gershwins imagined that this unusually long, programmatic song could be incorporated into the plot. The studio liked it enormously; Mark Sandrich, director of the picture, exclaimed, "This is real $4.40 stuff." But it took a lot of footage to establish its mood, and when the producer found that he must spend 44,000 De-

When George went to Mexico, he thought about having his portrait painted by Rivera, but he returned to New York with this pencil sketch signed by the model. COURTESY ARTHUR GERSHWIN

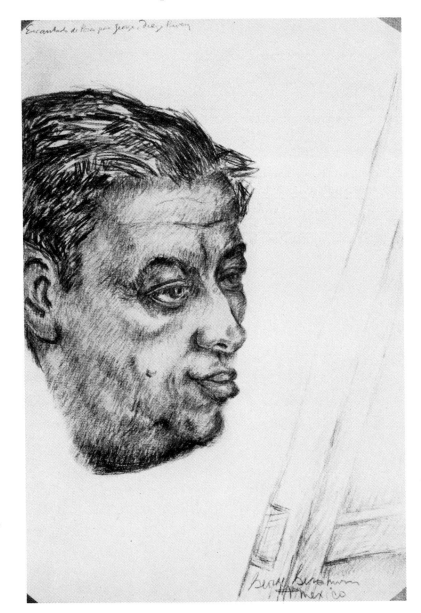

pression-year dollars to stage it, he cut it from the agenda. "Hi-Ho!" remained in manuscript until 1968, when it was published to commemorate the exhibition, *GERSHWIN: George the Music/Ira the Words*, at the Museum of the City of New York. Earlier—a dozen or more years after its inception—the song had been heard in the out-of-town tryouts of S. N. Behrman's *Let Me Hear the Melody*, his undeservedly short-lived play based on recollections of Scott Fitzgerald and George Gershwin. In 1968 "Hi-Ho!" was recorded by Tony Bennett in an arrangement that ignored George's conceptual harmonies and the remarkable left-hand commentary; and that ho-hum version got "Hi-Ho!" nowhere. Before George and Ira completed "Hi-Ho!" however, Vincente Minnelli interrupted them to do "By Strauss" for his New York revue, *The Show Is On*.

On the evening of August 18 George and Ira attended a night ASCAP meeting, Gene Buck presiding. The session discussed the recent copyright hearings in Washington and also the contract binding the Warner Brothers music holdings to ASCAP. It was an ideal introduction of the Gershwins to the abundant talent at work in Hollywood: Arthur Freed, Nacio Herb Brown, Harold Arlen, Yip Harburg, Vincent Youmans, Harry Warren (then probably the most successful of the film composers), Bert Kalmar, Harry Ruby, Buddy DeSylva, among others—all old friends of the Gershwins. Also on the Coast were Irving Berlin, Jerome Kern, and Sigmund Romberg; and back and forth a great deal was Cole Porter.

A typical George Gershwin autograph, this one from a girl's autograph book. GG's trademark was the self-caricature and the collector also received a few bars from her favorite Gershwin song. COURTESY MRS. ROBERT A. LEVIN

On August 22 the Gershwins leased a large Spanish residence at 1019 North Roxbury Drive, Beverly Hills. George wrote his secretary in New York:

> We have gone practically crazy trying to find a house in which to live and work. . . . However, the day before yesterday we found one that will serve beautifully. The furniture leaves a little to be desired, but it has a swimming pool and tennis court.

For the resumption of a communal life such as they had not known since their earlier visit to California, they settled on a house that was spacious enough to contain three so distinct personalities; and it epitomized the restfulness of California—for $800 a month.

Architecturally the house was like Miles Calman's in "Crazy Sundays": it "was built for great emotional moments—there was an air of listening, as if the far silences of its vistas hid an audience." A large crepe myrtle flowered beneath Leonore's window; and orange and lemon trees gave their warm fragrance to the rear lawn. The swimming pool and tennis court become the symbols of a party world that in New York they had characterized with penthouses and ping-pong tables; and in this house, just two blocks north of Sunset Boulevard, they rebuilt a California version of life on 103rd Street. Sunday brunches outdoors became a tradition; Lillian Hellman, Rouben Mamoulian, Vincente Minnelli, Elizabeth Allan, Dashiell Hammett, Gilbert Gabriel, Oscar Levant —these would be among the guests who chattered vivaciously for George's home movie camera. Getting settled out west so excited George that he began thinking of having part of his art collection shipped to him. And after two months in the land of stylish motors he sold his old Buick and bought a Cord.

On August 27 he reported to his publisher, Max Dreyfus: "Ira and I sang a few songs for Pandro Berman and Mark Sandrich the other day and the boys seemed delighted with our stuff. It makes us happy to know that we are working with people who speak our language." He also ran through the songs for Fred Astaire, often as they were being written, and always to Astaire's delight. They so reciprocated an understanding and appreciation of each other's work that the score was tailored to Astaire's impeccability. The melody of "Slap That Bass," for example, was inspired by Astaire's dancing, and the lyric by Ira's awareness of

George, in New York, following the "failure" of *Porgy and Bess* and just prior to leaving for California. Many who knew him consider this the best, most true, photo taken of him at the time. PRINT BY G. D. HACKETT, GERSHWIN COLLECTION

In Newark, boarding a plane for Hollywood, August 1936. CULVER SERVICE

Astaire's brittle enunciation, which would give especial charm even to "in which case"—the language ordinarily of contingencies and contracts.

George's thoughts were not wholly in Hollywood, however; he brooded over Dreyfus's inability to arrange a London tour for *Porgy and Bess:* "I have a feeling that it might prove to be a sensation all

Arriving in California to work on *Stepping Toes,* eventually called *Shall We Dance.* CULVER SERVICE

On the *Shall We Dance* set. Seated are Fred Astaire, Ginger Rogers, and George. Standing: Hermes Pan, the dance director; Mark Sandrich, the director; Ira, and Nathaniel Shilkret, musical director. GERSHWIN COLLECTION

Fred Astaire and George play four-hand piano while Ira watches. *Shall We Dance*. COURTESY ARTHUR GERSHWIN

Ginger Rogers in a sequence
from *Shall We Dance*.
CULVER SERVICE

Mark Sandrich and George
watch Rogers and Astaire
do a scene for *Shall We
Dance*. GERSHWIN COLLECTION

E. Y. "Yip" Harburg in
Beverly Hills. GERSHWIN
COLLECTION

through Europe." By the first week in September, his bubbling enthusiasm for Hollywood had somewhat cooled. "The script isn't finished yet for our picture so we can't really work as hard as we would like to," he intimated to Albert Sirmay in New York. He and Ira had also seen a preview of *Swing Time*, another in the series of fine Astaire-Rogers films, and they were impressed and somewhat concerned by the high standard that was inevitably expected of their own score. (*Shall We Dance* was to be this team's *seventh* film musical.)

At least two distinguished Gershwin songs were soon to be well out of the way, however. "Let's Call the Whole Thing Off," which is one of the finest Gershwin songs with its convoluted logic and intricate rhythms, had been mapped out even before the brothers boarded the plane for the Coast. Once in California they had little trouble either with "They All Laughed," which remains the only song they wrote at their studio at RKO (which was Lily Pons's old dressing room and, therefore, rather snug).

Paul Mueller, by this time, had packed eight hundred pounds of general personal things into George's Buick, including Tony, the dog, and headed westward. Besides the usual mechanical troubles with the car, Paul had his hands full with Tony, who became very sick and had to be

Gerda Mueller, in the pool at 1019 North Roxbury Drive, with Tony, newly arrived from New York. COURTESY PAUL MUELLER

George, Harold Arlen, and Lawrence Tibbett around the Roxbury Drive pool. PHOTO BY JOHN MCGOWAN

Harold Arlen and Ira in sporting attire on the tennis court at the Gershwins' Beverly Hills home. Arnold Schoenberg often came to play with George on this court. PHOTO BY GEORGE GERSHWIN

Jerome Kern. PHOTO BY
GEORGE GERSHWIN

Oscar Levant. PHOTO BY LEONORE GERSHWIN

left behind with a veterinarian en route (and showed up six weeks later
in the bloom of health and ready to challenge every other canine in
Beverly Hills).

Soon after he had rejoined the Gershwins Paul was perturbed to
see George had recently acquired a strange electrical gadget—"it looked
like a football helmet with steel bands that were clamped around his
head." George, perhaps because he was in Hollywood, had become
more conscious than ever of his receding hairline. The new device, he
had been convinced, would electronically produce miracles. Inside the
"helmet" were various electrodes which sent shocks into the scalp; at
the same time the entire thing vibrated, apparently massaging George's
head. But what disturbed Paul most of all was the tight band around
his head which he was certain was cutting off the blood supply.

Disturbed, Paul gave George a speech about cutting off the blood to
the brain. "You are doing yourself harm," he argued.

"You don't know what you're talking about," George replied and continued with his strange treatment for baldness. Within less than a year Paul would wonder about that machine again.

George now wrote Emil Mosbacher that if the studio used "the songs that we have already written, then we're way ahead of the script writers." He conceded that not all of the Gershwins similarly reared with impatience: "Ira, of course, loves it out here. He can relax much more out here than in the East—and you know how Ira loves his relaxation." Forced himself to lead a quieter creative life, George went to Arrowhead for a weekend. "A more beautiful place and climate I have never seen nor felt. I had a grand time." He instructed his secretary to send out fifteen of his favorite paintings; two days later, on September 10, he wrote her to pack his own paints and painting box as well. Meanwhile both Gershwins formed a permanent identity with southern California when they gave "Strike Up the Band" to the local university for its school song. (Ira supplied new words to convert it to "Strike Up the Band for U.C.L.A.")

September 18: "We are giving a big party Saturday night for Moss Hart's new teeth, he having had all sorts of things done to his teeth with porcelain. We expect about seventy-five people." Already the Gershwins were immersed in Hollywood's party world; of the innumerable affairs they attended, perhaps the most memorable was the March 6, 1937, roller-rink party given by Ginger Rogers and Alfred Vanderbilt; it temporarily revolutionized Hollywood society with its calculated informality and exclusive (but lengthy) blue-chip guest list.

At Ginger Rogers's roller-skating party, with June Lang.
GERSHWIN COLLECTION

Later in September, George was still writing New York, "There's nothing much new except that we are still enjoying the sun and tennis, but really have not gotten down to serious work yet as the script is pretty slow in being finished," On September 30 he noted: "Ira and I are still waiting for the script. . . ." Yet these difficulties did not efface the justified triumph of California life: "Ira and I seem to be able to work pretty well out here, when we get down to it."

At the end of September, Warren Munsell of the Theatre Guild confirmed George's suspicion that any European tour of the opera would fail unless the cast cut their salaries—which they would not do. So Munsell urged him to consider selling the property to the films. More important, he asked if George didn't think he "ought to begin to work on . . . [a new operetta] now so that we will have it for next fall at the

With Lynn Riggs discussing
their proposed *The Lights of
Lamy*. GERSHWIN COLLECTION

latest?" One week later he replied that he had recently met Lynn Riggs,
who had promised to think of an idea for an opera. George added that
the Astaire-Rogers film went in easy stages and called it "the best assignment in Hollywood."

Finding himself often unoccupied, he wrote Schillinger for advice
about continuing in California his musical training. Schillinger replied
with customary condescension:

> If I were you, I would study with Schoenberg *and* with Toch.
> Why not find out what the well reputed composers have to say on
> the subject. I think it would be a good idea to work with Schoen-
> berg on 4 part fugues and to let Toch supervise your prospective
> symphonic composition.

The most important musical friendship George formed on his western
trip was with Arnold Schoenberg, then head of the Music Department
at U.C.L.A. In January there was a Schoenberg Festival at the school;
George was one of the sponsors of the private recordings by the Kolisch
Quartet of Schoenberg's string quartets. He also contributed to the payment for the provocative photographs of Schoenberg by Edward Weston, from one of which George was to make his large oil portrait of
the "pantonal" composer. And when George was not discussing music

264

Igor Stravinsky. George's record collection reflected a great admiration for Stravinsky's music; so did a framed reproduction of a Picasso drawing and some manuscript pages of Stravinsky's autobiography that George prized. COURTESY BOOSEY AND HAWKES

Arnold Schoenberg, the arch-modernist, and George, who called himself (with unusual accuracy) a "modern romantic," became great friends during the last Hollywood months. PHOTO BY EDWARD WESTON. COURTESY BRETT WESTON

265

with Schoenberg, he was playing tennis with him on the court at 1019. During these months George also saw a little of Stravinsky; in March he received inscribed copies (with a caricature portrait) of the composer's autobiography and of Merle Armitage's *Strawinsky*. There is a legend that on this or some similar occasion George asked Stravinsky how much he would charge to give lessons to him; when Stravinsky found out how much George made each year, he is supposed to have asked in astonishment if he could not take lessons from Gershwin. All very pleasant, but all untrue.

On October 24 George reported being "on the last lap of our score."

> Ira and I have written a song called "They Can't Take That Away from Me" which I think has distinct potentialities of going places. . . .

Disenchantment with the Goldwyn Coast had not set in, as it would later; he was happy with their songs and, characteristically, loved to play them for an admiring audience. Harold Arlen remembers those days with warmth and a chuckle. "He would drop by, ring the bell and dash for the piano, play. *Then* he'd say hello." One of the songs he was anxious to demonstrate on one of these visits was "They Can't Take That Away from Me." As he played it through a second time, Anya Arlen improvised a little eight-bar counterpoint. "He loved it," Arlen recalls, "and every time he played it he asked Annie—in her little voice —to sing." This occurred quite often in the latter days of 1936 and early 1937. Once George even brought Rose Gershwin to the Arlens for a typical musical visit. He was pleased with how things were going.

George hoped that his own newly formed publishing company would handle the score to *Shall We Dance*. Even though it was a commercial year for him on the Coast, he insisted that the Gershwin Publishing Company have as its catalogue program "a combination of production and good popular music." Popular alone, he added, would not interest him. (Nothing came of his attempts to make Gershwin Publishing an active publishing house, for his death ended all enthusiasm for the venture.) By November 13 he and Ira were "working on the last song for the Astaire picture and hope to have it finished, along with a ballet, in about a week. . . . We haven't a title for the picture as yet, but we are all struggling hard to find just the right phrase." Originally known as

Watch Your Step, the movie had subsequently been labeled *Stepping Toes* (with variants being *Stepping Stones* and *Stepping High*). The final title, *Shall We Dance*, was proposed by Vincente Minnelli; in the spring of 1937 the Gershwins composed the song "Shall We Dance," to plug the film and to fulfill a hope of Pan Berman's. The previous Astaire-Rogers film had had "6 Big Hits," and he felt that *Shall We Dance* should equal it. Ira in particular was somewhat amused by Berman's notion that every Gershwin film song inevitably would be a hit.

On December 3 George reported to New York:

> The Astaire picture is practically finished and so far everybody is happy. The studio, realizing Gershwin can be a low-brow, has just taken up their option on our contract for the next Astaire movie which, incidentally, will be minus Rogers. Fred has wanted to go it alone for a long time and he'll get his chance in the next picture.

In mid-March of 1937 *Variety* was to circulate the wondrous news that Astaire would not be going it alone after all: his co-star would be Carole

Poolside living in Beverly Hills; though seated on Anya Arlen's lap, George plays hard to get. COURTESY HAROLD ARLEN

George, Doris Warner, Dorothy Fields, Jerome Kern, and Ira at the Cocoanut Grove, the occasion being a party given by Maureen O'Sullivan.
UNITED PRESS PHOTO

Lombard—at a salary of $200,000 (Astaire was to get $250,000.) Back in those days of tinsel and awes Miss Lombard reigned so supremely over Hollywood that, when her pet dog expired, the news was of such magnitude that an obituary notice (with prescribed heavy black border) appeared in *Variety*. But Miss Lombard did not appear in *A Damsel in Distress* after all, and the part fell to Joan Fontaine. Still, one cannot help wondering what Miss Lombard would have done for the picture.

George's December 3 letter continued:

> Hollywood has taken on quite a new color since our last visit six years ago. There are many people in the business today who talk the language of smart showmen and it is therefore much more agreeable working out here. We have many friends here from the East, so the social life has also improved greatly. All the writingmen and tunesmiths get together in a way that is practically impossible in the East. I've seen a great deal of Irving Berlin and Jerome Kern at poker parties and dinners and the feeling around is very "gemutlich."

268   So he jauntily rationalized life "just being commercial."

For an interview in the Los Angeles *Evening News* he also put a pleasant face on matters; the paper emphasized that

> one thing he won't bother to write is the background music. He suggests the theme for staff writers at RKO, but refuses to be bothered with work which "hacks" can do. . . . Anyone can orchestrate, he seems to think. . . .
>
> He doesn't work very much with the script, because the studio, he says, doesn't like the music to be all of one tone, contrary to the plan followed by a stage production. Just so long as it keeps to the general atmosphere, it satisfies film producers.

George's publicly known enthusiasm for work suggests that he shrugged off many tasks only because the studio would not trust them to him, seldom before having encountered so varied a talent that wished to give so much of itself. And we know how anxious he was to get a script for the film.

George and Irving Berlin, a time exposure. PHOTO BY GEORGE GERSHWIN. ASCAP

In Seattle for a concert,
December 1936. GERSHWIN
COLLECTION

At work on his painting
of Arnold Schoenberg.
December 1936. CULVER
SERVICE

With Mrs. Sidney Fish, a
friend of the New York
party days, and hostess to
the Gershwins at Carmel.
GERSHWIN COLLECTION

As the work on *Shall We Dance* concluded, George late in November started preparing for a series of winter concerts. (His natural pianistic ability was such that he seldom needed much practice before he was ready to perform; it was anything from a flashy arpeggio, made just before he left the house, to an hour or so of Czerny.) When he arrived in Seattle on December 14 for his first appearance, he was suffering from a cold, but he played as scheduled the following day and again conducted the *Suite from "Porgy and Bess."* He returned to Beverly Hills for the holidays with his family, his mother, sister, and brother-in-law having come out from the east for a visit. During this brief vacation he temporarily resumed his painting, quickly producing oil portraits of Jerome Kern and Arnold Schoenberg—the latter, George's last completed oil.

On January 8 George and Ira left for Carmel, where, on January 11, the *Monterey Peninsula Herald* trumpeted:

> Monterey Peninsula today became (temporarily) the world's musical motion picture capital. . . . George Gershwin is here. Ira Gershwin is here. Pandro Berman is here. George Stevens is here. P. Wolfson is here. Plus numerous secretaries, first, second and third assistants, and a large staff of supernumeraries. . . . For today's conference has to do with Fred [Astaire]'s next picture.

All met at the hacienda of Mr. and Mrs. Sidney Fish, old friends of the Gershwins. Between conferences George and Ira called on Robinson Jeffers, an acknowledged admirer of Ira's "It Ain't Necessarily So."

In San Francisco, where George performed under Pierre Monteux, he told the press that he would like to be known as the "insomnia composer." "I'd like my music to keep people—all kinds of people—awake when they should be sleeping. I'd like my compositions to be so vital that I'd be required by law to dispense sedatives with each score sold."

To the press he also announced that he wanted to do another opera. "When I find a story that pleases me I shall compose a cowboy opera. Indians, however, are taboo." It was not an unusual remark for him; late in 1929 he had admonished Isaac Goldberg about such "native" subjects for an opera: "Don't talk Indians to me, either . . . for the Indian is as much a foreigner to a contemporary American as is a Russian."

Jan 4, 1937.

PALO CORONA RANCH
CARMEL P.O.
MONTEREY COUNTY
CALIFORNIA

Dear Emily,

First, I'll start by giving my sincerest good wishes to Lou. You will come later on. Then I will tell you how much I miss you both + how nice it will be when you get out to visit us. Then I will tell you, that I am at the above ranch for the week end staying with my friends Sidney + Olga Fish,

2

on my way to San Francisco where I have three concerts next week with the S.F. symphony with Pierre Monteux conducting. After which I shall tell you about the group that is coming up from L.A. to hear me play + see the sights + new bridge. They are, Mother, Ira + Lee, Jerome Kern, wife + daughter, Dorothy Fields + brother Herbie + sweetheart Felix Young + several others. We plan to have much fun.

3

PALO CORONA RANCH
CARMEL P.O.
MONTEREY COUNTY
CALIFORNIA

then I must inform you about two concerts that have just been arranged in Los Angeles with Klemperer conducting an 'All Gershwin' programe on Feb. 10 + 11th. We shall have Todd Duncan come out for these + sing some of "Porgy" music. I wish you could come. Not to sing — just to be here.

The Astaire picture is being "shot" + is most

4

interesting to watch as I have never really seen a picture made before. It fascinates me to see the amazing things they do with sound recording, for instance. And lighting. And cutting. And so forth.

I understand Eddie Robinson is back with a multitude of masterpieces which I cannot wait to see. When I see them I shall write you as I do not suppose you viewed them in New York.

A typical letter from George to Emily Paley. COURTESY EMILY PALEY

George did not reveal in San Francisco that he was considering three separate possibilities for a fall Broadway show: Warren Munsell had written him in early November that the Theatre Guild had been asked to do a Center Theatre show, and they hoped that George would work with Robert E. Sherwood on "a cavalcade of American history," which would have a Rip Van Winkle prologue. This would be followed by a succession of scenes of historical moments, in each of which Rip awoke. Munsell admitted that "this is old hat in a sense, but . . ."

George liked Munsell's idea; yet there was a complication: Moss Hart had already asked him to do a Center Theatre show—however, with Sam Harris and Max Gordon as possible producers. Could the Guild get together with Hart, George wondered? The show that Hart and George Kaufman suggested to the Gershwins was also somewhat old hat—a musical about writing a musical. But it was to be unique in that the Gershwins, Hart, and Kaufman would appear and play themselves. Ira soon disengaged himself from this aspect of the project; the others settled for his being only an off-stage voice. This idea for a musical developed so quickly during the Hollywood year that,

5–

PALO CORONA RANCH
CARMEL P.O.
MONTEREY COUNTY
CALIFORNIA

Recently my masseur suggested a hike in the hills. I acquiesced + have become a victim to its vigorous charm. For the past week, every day, hot or cold, we walked back in the hills + really Em, I feel as tho I have discovered something wonderful. It is so refreshing & invigorating. Better than golf, because it eliminates the aggravation that in-evitably comes with that Pastime.

6

there's not much more to write about now except my hopes + wishes for your health + happiness + your mother's quick entry into a successful hotel, with nice landlords, + love to Lou + you.

Yours,

George

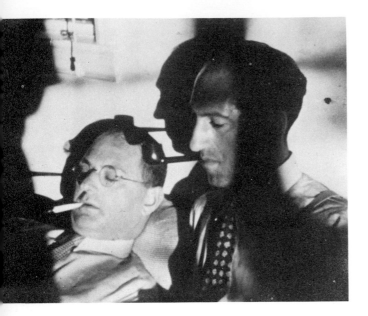

Still from a motion picture film by Harold Arlen of Ira and George at work in George's workroom at 1019 North Roxbury Drive. In this room, Arlen recalls, "George had his piano and also his art materials for painting." COURTESY HAROLD ARLEN

even while the Gershwins were in San Francisco, they were on the phone with their potential collaborators, and ideas raced up and down the Coast. Eventually, after the death of George Gershwin, these notions culminated in *I'd Rather Be Right*, with music by Rodgers and Hart and a portrayal of Franklin Roosevelt by George M. Cohan. The only idea the two shows ultimately shared was that it should be about living personages.

The third and, to George, most enticing idea concerned an opera, with a book by Lynn Riggs. Riggs had come up from Santa Fe on November 17, bringing with him a plot that he immediately wrote up in Hollywood and called *The Lights of Lamy*. It was the story of a young Mexican who lives almost within sight of Lamy, New Mexico, and who goes there to find a crack continental express stalled by floods. The train overflows with cross-sectional America—everything from movie stars to small-town merchants and revivalists. There is a clash between the Mexican and American cultures, between the young Mexican and the American seducer of his sweetheart. There was to be tragedy but also a quasi-optimistic ending, such as in *Porgy and Bess*. (When Riggs, in February 1936, first wired George about an opera, he urged the composer to come to Santa Fe, where "THIS COUNTRY HAS SEEN

274 THE DEEPEST AND WIDEST RANGE OF WHAT AMERICA IS ABOUT.") George

refused to commit himself even to Riggs, however, without first getting in touch with DuBose Heyward; on January 26 he wrote his old collaborator, "How about planning another opera or operetta for the future? . . . I am very anxious to start thinking about a serious musicale."

From San Francisco, George went across the bay to Berkeley, where he gave a concert at the University of California on Sunday, January 17. Three days later he was in Detroit, where he performed so successfully that the director of the Detroit Concert Society wrote him that she wanted him to return for the 1937–38 season, her "only 'repeat'." The cycle of concerts quickly tired George, and he looked forward to the final ones in February.

February began with conferences on the new Astaire picture, *A Damsel in Distress*. On February 6 George acknowledged his election to the Royal Academy of Santa Cecilia, Rome—Italy's highest award to a foreign composer. On February 9 he was invited to premiere his next original composition at the Biennale Festival in September. And on February 10 and 11 he made his final concert appearances when he was soloist at an all-Gershwin concert at the Los Angeles Philharmonic. George had wanted Fritz Reiner to conduct, but Reiner was in Oslo; Otto Klemperer canceled his own appearance when he found that the budget would allow only two rehearsals. So Alexander Smallens, conductor of *Porgy and Bess*, took the podium. George wrote DuBose Heyward that he hoped the concert "might whip up some enthusiasm for picture possibilities on the part of the studios who, as you know, are keen about it, but slightly afraid on account of the color question." As a further precaution to make the program a success, George brought Todd Duncan west and scheduled so many supplementary rehearsals at his own expense that George's customary fee fell from $2000 to $670. The concert was a sensation. But in playing the *Concerto in F* he fumbled through some chords; the mistake, while apparently unnoticed by the audience, troubled him considerably. It was the first indication of a failing co-ordination. He had a complete physical checkup toward the end of February and passed it without difficulty.

The story of the rest of the spring is of George's consuming desire to get on with the work and get it done. "The California sunshine may be partly responsible. Certainly the climate, the swimming pools, the tennis courts and the hiking trails are distracting," he complained ironically. "They're so delightful that they make Hollywood—for me—rather a difficult place in which to concentrate upon work." The ever-present guests at 1019 had also begun to bother him; so he took to Aileen Pringle's Santa Monica home as a morning retreat where he could write in quiet. Near the end of his life he finally moved out of 1019 and into Yip Harburg's Beverly Hills home, where he could at last have silence. By the spring George's personal life had also taken a new turn when, after casual friendships with Hollywood starlets and stars like Simone Simon and Elizabeth Allan, he became seriously interested in Paulette Goddard and saw a great deal of her, both in Beverly Hills and Palm Springs.

By mid-March negotiations were under way with Merle Armitage for a Los Angeles revival of *Porgy and Bess*. Late the following month George was to receive the David Bispham Memorial Medal from the American Opera Society in Chicago—further recognition that his opera had not failed.

That spring George began thinking of selling his life story to the movies. In mid-April he wrote his first biographer, Isaac Goldberg, that "it doesn't seem more than eight minutes—or maybe it's eight years—I can't tell" since he had come west. He was not depressed, however, and insisted, "This picture business is more interesting than 'Once in a Lifetime' would lead you to believe. There is a real excitement about the opening of a film that compares favorably with a Broadway opening of a show." He was looking forward to the premiere of *Shall We Dance* at the Pantages on April 26.

On May 12 he again wrote Goldberg:

> We have been away from there [New York] for nine months already (just time to give birth to something or other) and the end is not yet in sight as we started this week on the "Goldwyn Follies," a super, super, stupendous, colossal, moving picture extravaganza which the "Great Goldwyn" is producing. Ira and I should be taking a vacation by this time, having just finished eight songs for the second Astaire picture "Damsel in Distress," but unfortunately Goldwyn cannot put off a half million dollars worth of principal salaries while the Gershwins bask in the sunshine of Arrowhead Springs.

Goldberg had written George appreciatively of *Shall We Dance*, which had received fine notices although *Variety* had had reservations

Simone Simon, with George in Beverly Hills. GERSHWIN COLLECTION

At Palm Springs,
with Paulette Goddard.
GERSHWIN COLLECTION

Los Angeles, February 1937. CULVER SERVICE

Conducting the rehearsal for the Los Angeles Philharmonic, February 1937.
GERSHWIN COLLECTION

about the score: "Lyrics are more interesting than the melodies, which are not fashioned for popular acceptance in the hum-and-whistle category." Goldberg praised not only the excellent songs but the incidental "Walking the Dog" music, a little sound-track piece that George had deliberately scored for salon orchestra—a therapeutic contrast with Hollywood's traditionally lush arrangements.

When George came to discuss *Shall We Dance*, his letter to Goldberg took on a different tone. Despite his enthusiasm and the fact that he had been a frequent visitor to the set, he clearly had been unprepared for what the movies were doing with his score:

> The picture does not take advantage of the songs as well as it should. They literally throw one or two songs away without any kind of a plug. This is mainly due to the structure of the story which does not include any other singers than Fred and Ginger and the amount of singing one can stand of these two is quite limited. In our next picture "Damsel in Distress" we have protected ourselves in that we have a Madrigal group of singers and have written two English type ballads for background music so the audience will get a chance to hear some singing besides the crooning of the stars. . . .
>
> On account of the "Goldwyn Follies" Ira and I have had to postpone the Kaufman-Hart opus until next year.

This is the clearest résumé George made of his feelings toward the end of his Hollywood year. Characteristically, Ira (who has always regarded Hollywood with almost paternal understanding) attributed any fault in the *Shall We Dance* music to the Gershwins. In December 1937 he explained: "George and I were pretty proud of 'Shall We Dance.' We thought it a smart score. It had a lot of hits. But all the songs were smart, a little sophisticated. Maybe that was a mistake, to put so many smart songs in one picture." It is not, of course, uncommon to criticize as George did Hollywood's use of material. Even the legendary Wodehousian gentleness collapsed before the treatment given Plum's *Damsel in Distress*. In his book, *Performing Flea*, Wodehouse noted that when the studio first bought the script

> they gave it to one of the R.K.O. writers to adapt, and he turned out a script all about crooks—no resemblance to the novel. Then it struck them that it might be a good thing to stick to the

story, so they chucked away the other script and called me in. I think it is going to make a good picture. But what uncongenial work picture-writing is. Somebody's got to do it, I suppose, but this is the last time they'll get me.

This disaffection was not due to the director of the picture, George Stevens; both the Gershwins and Wodehouse agreed that he was among Hollywood's best. Some of the feeling of the time was caught in Moss Hart's parody:

> A foggy day at RKO
> Had me down and had me low.
> I viewed the morning with alarm:
> Even Pan Berman had lost his charm.
> How long, I wondered, could these men last?
> But the age of miracles hadn't passed.
> For suddenly Mr. Giannini was there,
> And through foggy RKO
> The sun was shining everywhere.

Although the momentum to which he had geared himself in order to get through a year of so much work now slowed perceptibly, George drove himself on with his film songs. "I work when the spirit moves me and that is generally when I know I've a job that must be done soon," he said. He had been trying to do a ballet in Hollywood for some time and never quite managed it. Now he intended creating a full-scale one, "The Swing Symphony," for the *Goldwyn Follies*. He and Ira hurried on anxiously to leave six weeks of their contract for George to compose this work for Balanchine and his American ballet.

Back in New York, Eddie Warburg so appreciated news of George's initial attempt in this genre that in early June he urged the brothers to think about creating a ballet for his New York company. Nor was this the only means for George to profit away from Hollywood: on July 6 a cable came from Paris, asking his conditions for doing ten or fifteen European concerts late that year. By the time this cable arrived, however, George had been seriously ill for two weeks, Ira had had his brother and himself taken off contract, and the future for George Gershwin had already long gone by.

One of the last semi-
formal photographs of
George taken in the spring
of 1937 by Rex Hardy, Jr.
GERSHWIN COLLECTION

Even before George's fatal illness canceled all his plans, he himself
had changed them several times in those eleven months. Hollywood and
its sunny climate, which had temporarily so beguiled him that he
thought of making Beverly Hills his permanent home, gradually broke
its own enchantment. Ira, however, permanently succumbed to this tem-
perate climate and this geographical remoteness that protected him from
the business pressures of New York. George missed the quicker tempo
of the east, the competition and briskness of its people.

At the end of the spring the brothers compromised upon a new collaboration: Ira would buy a home in Beverly Hills and would also construct a studio-cottage that George, on short trips west, could use. George's immediate plans were to carry him abroad, where he would concertize, write that contemplated symphony, buy some paintings. First of all, he planned a string quartet: in Hollywood his newly formed friendship with Arnold Schoenberg had inspired him to develop themes for a Gershwin quartet. He determined to hole himself up in a Beverly Hills canyon and write before he left California—probably in late summer, after the Goldwyn assignment. The next-to-last page in George's Hollywood "Tune Book" contains this entry:

> *"Suite*
> comments
> working class
> Idle rich
> intolerance
> children
> Fear
> Nature"

Was this contemplated suite to have been the final reflection of his Hollywood experience?

George seldom admitted to his family or friends the darker feelings about life in California. But there was one person to whom he told a different story all that Hollywood year, a person who had been a friend from the very beginning. That was Mabel Schirmer. Ever since he met her around 1915–16 at the Paleys' apartment on Seventh Avenue he had responded to her humor, her wit, and her compassionate directness; and in the Siqueiros Concert Hall portrait, he made certain that she sat in the front row, next to Siqueiros himself. It takes a peculiar talent to accept the darker side of life, to perceive ingredients of tragedy in humor; and this ability Mabel has always had with unmalicious candor. George didn't like to speak badly of anyone; nor did he appreciate a person like Oscar Levant, who rose by felling others. But George was not self-deceived; he went into analysis because there were problems that plagued him, and there were very few with whom he could discuss freely that deeper level of his life. Mabel Schirmer, who had herself gone through analysis, was equipped to understand in a very special way.

George first wrote Mabel from California on September 1, 1936, saying that the Gershwins had at last found a "nice spacious, cheery house." There was even a fine Steinway. "The furnishings aren't all to our taste but then—you can't have everything, can you?" Mabel's reply "was like a tonic—you know, even tonics are needed out here in God's country." George had just seen *Swing Time;* and though he praised the film publicly, he confided to Mabel: "I don't think Kern has written any outstanding song hits . . . Of course, he never really was ideal for Astaire." On October 28 he brought up the weather (a refrain in all west to east correspondence): "Hollywood is a place of great extremes—when it rains, it pours—when it's cloudy, it's cloudy the whole day—and then the sun shines, well, you know all about that . . . I miss New York and the things it has to offer quite a good deal, and will probably miss it more as time goes on." On December 3 he worried that one of her letters to him had been lost in the mail and he reminded her "There's nothing like the phony glamour of Hollywood to bring out the need for one's real friends so, dear Mabel, quickly take your pen in hand . . ." He was thinking of flying back to New York for two weeks at Christmas, but now even that kind of junket depressed him. Shortly after New Year's he wrote her, "Perhaps dear Mabel this is our year. A year that will see both of us finding that elusive something that seems to bring happiness . . . The pendulum swings back, so I've heard, and it's about due to swing us back to a more satisfying state." Although the visit of his mother and Frankie and Leo to California had made life something "Like old times," it wasn't the old George: "The family is quite amazed at my ability to stay at home quietly for many evenings with no urge to go to parties & live the gay life. I am getting to be a home body—and loving it." But he concluded wistfully, "Remember, this is our year for happiness . . ."

Only concertizing seemed to revive the George that all had thought unvarying. En route from San Francisco to the Detroit engagement, he postcarded Mabel, "tired, but happy." And the day before the first of his two February concerts in Los Angeles he wrote her, "they tell me that they've seen nothing like the excitement for a concert in years. My friend, Arthur Lyons, is taking a room at the Trocadero and has invited 250 people to come in after the concert. He's going to great trouble to decorate the room and there will be two orchestras—one American and one Russian. I wish I could send a magic carpet for you,

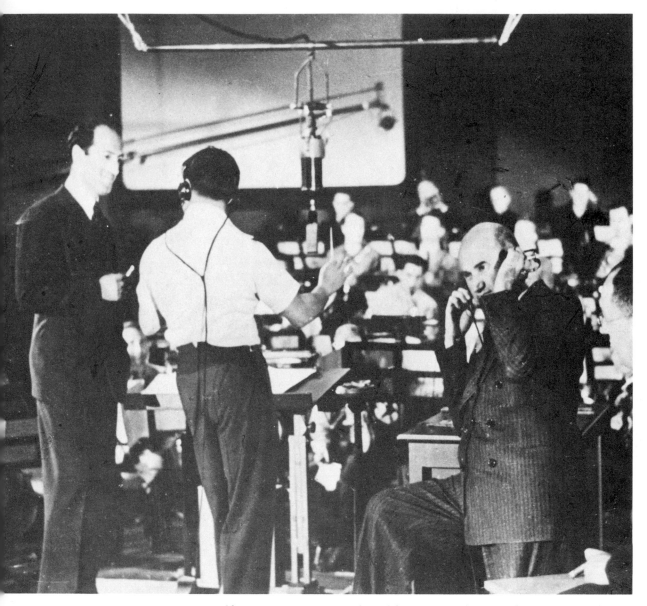

George, Alfred Newman, Samuel Goldwyn, listening to playbacks on the sound stage of *The Goldwyn Follies*. CULVER SERVICE

Emily and Lou . . ." As always, he wanted to share his happiest moments with the Paleys.

On March 19 George told Mabel that *Shall We Dance* was about finished. "Someone once said that when time hurries by, you are happy. If that is true we've been in Heaven." But by mid-May he confessed that "Ira and I have had to literally drag ourselves to work the last few days as we have just finished the second Astaire score and have to start right in on the 'Goldwyn Follies.' Even the Gershwins can't take that kind of routine." He reminded her of Ira's lyric: "Could you use me— for I certainly could use you." The correspondence with Mabel Schirmer thus puts all the Hollywood year, almost from its inception, into a steadily darkening spectrum. George was very good at keeping up a public front—even to Ira. But there needed to be at least one who could be told how unsatisfactory it had so often been—someone who would understand with compassionate reality. And that someone was Mabel Schirmer.

How much of George's anxiety to leave Hollywood derived from the brain tumor that, unknown to himself, was destroying him, and how much from his own rational judgment of the movie capital and its systems we shall never know. Fred Astaire has said, "George was a completely open-minded genius. He was thrilled by the development of show business, and he never groused about Hollywood." But George's letters and interviews revealed that he sensed what Scott Fitzgerald meant by his remark, "The climate wears you down." Lee remembers: "I never heard any of the Gershwins gossip or say they didn't like someone. George never made any remark like that at all, never said anything against anyone until the last month before his death—and that's pretty wonderful, when you think of it."

George was never deluded about Hollywood: it was a place that paid well and he went there because he wanted money. He felt no missionary impulse to elevate the level of film entertainment; and he probably would have agreed with John Dos Passos that, "Whether we like it or not it is in that great bargain sale of five and ten cent lusts and dreams that the new bottom level of our culture is being created," though he would not have phrased matters so sharply. If George had an especial complaint against the society of the film-makers it was that in a land of so many overvalued celebrities he himself was not so appreciated an individual as he had been in New York. And to the end of his life, his driving compulsion—almost an obsession—to work and have his work understood, made him demand that even an evening of entertainment, as long as Gershwin himself was present, must be partly a Gershwin evening.

There was also the fact that, having worked on three movies in quick succession, George felt that he had temporarily exhausted all their possibilities. Four years after George's death, Ira allowed that George grew dissatisfied with Hollywood partly because he

> felt that the music in pictures—although the songs could become big national hits on the air—wasn't so much. That is, he wasn't so much a part of the songs as he would be in New York. . . . There in New York George had always been consulted as to how the numbers should be done. . . . Here it seemed the moment your contract was ended . . . you were through. Then everything was left to the studio, to do whatever they wanted.

The studios assumed that their contracts gave them unchallengeable custody of these tunes. It did not matter how beautiful the pieces, how perfectly formed, how ethereally lovely. Once they had left 1019 North Roxbury Drive and journeyed across town to be locked up on the RKO lot, they were not supposed ever again to be wholly George and Ira's. Time has a way of defending the artist, however—even the well-paid one. Though few of us today may haunt the movie museums to see the brittle celluloid flare again with *Shall We Dance* and *A Damsel in Distress*, we all recognize that their scores have vitality elsewhere. They belong to the Gershwins, these songs that are among their finest.

It was during this period, late in the spring of 1937, though he appeared to be bronzed and in general good health, that he became increasingly restless, easily irritated, strangely despondent; he was so unlike himself. His friends, aware of the well-known preoccupation with his health, decided he was undoubtedly suffering from a nervous reaction to Hollywood's star-struck, unchallenging pace and that the phase would eventually pass. Even a visit to a doctor revealed nothing.

"All he needs is a psychoanalyst," was one summary observation, and most agreed. At the time, particularly in Hollywood, the analyst was as fashionable as mah jong had been during the Twenties. There was a nearly primitive tribal belief that the analyst could cure all such ills as one contracted in Hollywood.

In June, however, while working on the songs for the Goldwyn film, George began awakening early in the morning complaining of headaches and momentary dizziness; at times he seemed befuddled and physically depleted. Some of this—but certainly not all—might have been attributable to his resentment of Goldwyn's demands for "hit songs you can whistle," as if such could be manufactured to order. Especially galling was a summons into The Presence (himself buffered by a covey of yes men) to demonstrate the completed songs like any novice song writer. When Goldwyn heard the bridge to "I Was Doing All Right," he perked up. (He had not been happy with the other songs.) Maybe that eight-bar bridge should be repeated, he suggested. Ira was rather amused by this revelation of Goldwyn's aesthetic side, but George was furious. Later he bitterly told S. N. Behrman, "I had to live for this, that Sam Goldwyn should say to me: 'Why don't you write hits like Irving Berlin?'"

But there had been indications long before June that something other than a disaffection with Hollywood and its mores was afflicting George. The first intimation had occurred in February when he was appearing in Los Angeles with the Philharmonic. During rehearsals, while he was conducting the orchestra in a *Porgy and Bess* segment, he suddenly began to sway and appeared about to fall off the podium. Paul Mueller, seated in the first row, quickly leaped up and caught him.

"I'm all right, Paul," George assured him. "I think I just lost my balance for a minute." He continued with the rehearsal and the incident was forgotten. But at the evening performance George experienced a brief sudden blackout and fumbled a few notes in the *Concerto in F*. At the same time he was aware of a strange smell, "like burning rubber." These two episodes worried him, but a physical not long after revealed nothing and he dismissed them. But then in April came another moment of giddiness, the strange odor, and then they were gone. Considering the findings of the examination in late February, there seemed to be no cause for alarm.

So it was not until June, when he suffered blinding headaches and when uncharacteristic irritability and gross fatigue became evident, that it was obvious that something was gravely wrong. Even then it was difficult for anyone to believe that there was any physiological basis for George's complaints and atypical behavior.

He felt abandoned, friendless, and told Paul once that despite everything he had, he really had no friend in the world. Leonore Gershwin recalled: "I well remember what George once said when he complained he was lonely. I asked, '*When* are you lonely, George?' 'When I'm shaving,' he replied. 'But [naming a particularly aggressive hanger-on] is always with you—even then.' 'Yes, I know, but that isn't enough.'"

He became obsessed with the idea of marriage and settling down—he even proposed to several young women, though in general he found most in Hollywood "surprisingly selfish, stupid & career conscious." It was Paulette Goddard, despite the rumor that she was married to Charles Chaplin, who had captivated him and he was determined to make her Mrs. George Gershwin. He began to talk about sending for his furniture, in storage in New York, and of buying a house in Beverly Hills. Paul was disturbed by this and cautioned George about leaping into marriage. Harold Arlen also advised him to dismiss such ideas, but the counsel only upset George and brought out his hostility.

Early in June, then, George consulted Dr. Ernst Simmel, an analyst, who ultimately disagreed with George's own self-diagnosis—overwork —and advised him to see a physician. On June 9, 1937, George kept an appointment with Dr. Gabriel Segall, who examined him without finding any physical abnormalities. What with the spells of vertigo and headaches persisting, Segall decided to bring in a neurologist, Dr. Eugene Ziskind, for consultation. Except for finding that the function of one nasal passage was impaired (as a boy he had been kicked in the nose by a horse), all other probings indicated nothing. Even so, Segall and Ziskind arranged to place him in Cedars of Lebanon hospital for more extensive tests.

As later reconstructed by Dr. Noah Fabricant in his study of the case, "In the period between June 23 and June 26, X rays of the skull and blood studies revealed little of diagnostic import . . . Lumbar puncture [spinal tap] for the purpose of examining the spinal fluid was vehemently rejected by Gershwin. He was anxious to leave the hospital to continue his work . . ." This test, of course, would have disclosed the presence of a tumor in the brain.

George returned to Roxbury Drive and appeared to have improved; he slept better and mentioned the headaches less frequently. But the remission did not last: there were signs of a loss of co-ordination, he spilled water and food, he dropped things, he stumbled on the stairs— his playing of the piano was poor. Considering the various negative

Working at 1019 North Roxbury Drive on *A Damsel in Distress*, spring of
1937. PHOTO BY REX HARDY, JR. GERSHWIN COLLECTION

findings of the comprehensive medical examinations there was still the chance that George's illness was psychological, though many by this time had serious doubts.

Anya and Harold Arlen with E. Y. Harburg dropped by the house early in July to say goodbyes; Arlen and Harburg were to work on a new show in New York. They were appalled by George's appearance. "Just two weeks before," Arlen recalls, "he looked so vital. Pale? He looked strange." George appeared to be weak, listless, as he said, "Do you have to go? All my friends are leaving me."

Harburg offered George the use of his cottage just a few blocks away; obviously it would be wise to get George away from Roxbury Drive. So George, Paul, and a male nurse to look after George when Paul was out moved into the Harburg cottage on July 4. It devolved upon Paul to shuttle between the two houses.

This was not to be the solution, though George continued to work intermittently, rested, and now and then attempted to play the piano. But his life had taken on a nightmare quality in this strange, desolate house: the parties over, the piano silent, the laughter gone. One starlet sent him flowers enclosing a note she must have imagined was amusing: "Get well soon," she had written, "or these will be growing on top of you."

George was not always rational. Even before the move there were times when he might suddenly and inexplicably lose his temper, or he would remain in his room with the shades drawn (the bright sunlight was, of course, painful during the headache periods). And once when Paul was driving him to an appointment with Dr. Simmel (whom George was certain was doing him no good), George managed to open the door on the driver's side and tried to push Paul out of the speeding car. Somehow Paul managed to maintain control of the Cord and struggled back behind the wheel and slammed the door shut. Shaken, he pulled off the highway and stopped.

"What are you trying to do, kill us?" he demanded. "What have I ever done to you? Why did you do that?"

George, his face bathed in perspiration, put his hands to his head and could only reply, "I don't know."

Another incident, hauntingly sad, occurred after the move. A box of chocolates had been sent to George by someone of whom he was not very fond. He opened the box, gathered the candy up in his hands,

Ira on the Goldwyn lot.
CULVER SERVICE

kneaded it into a viscous mass and rubbed the mixture over his body. "I then had to give him a bath," Paul remembered sorrowfully.

Not long after—on Friday, July 9, one month to the day since George had gone to Dr. Segall—came a sudden and definite worsening of George's condition. In the morning he had spent a little time at the piano and later, in the afternoon around five, drowsy, he thought he'd take a nap. He soon fell into deep sleep that intensified into coma. He was never to awaken from this sleep.

He was immediately rushed to the hospital where he was examined by a neurosurgeon, Dr. Carl Rand. Now all the evidence was explicit: reflexes were gone and there were other symptoms pointing toward what some had suspected—a brain tumor, though its precise location and extent were unknown. The decision was for prompt surgery if at all possible by one of the outstanding neurosurgeons in the country, Dr. Walter Dandy of Johns Hopkins in Baltimore.

This touched off a frantic search for Dandy, who could not be reached at the hospital, his office, or his home; he was, in fact, vacationing aboard a yacht somewhere on Chesapeake Bay. Out of desperation, George Pallay, one of George's friends, called the White House for help in the search. That afternoon (it was now Saturday, the tenth, the second day of George's coma) two Navy destroyers were dispatched to find the yacht.

Like something out of the movies for which George had been writing,

Jerome Cowan, Vera Zorina, and Phil Baker in *The Goldwyn Follies*.
CULVER SERVICE

the yacht was dramatically located and soon Dandy, with motorcycle escort, was speeded to Cumberland, Maryland. From there he was able to consult with the physicians on the West Coast, who asked him to fly out to perform the delicate operation. At the same time, Emil Mosbacher, another friend of George's, was arranging for a private plane to be ready at Newark Airport for Dandy's flight west. Agreeing to attempt the operation, Dandy boarded yet another plane at Cumberland for the flight to Newark.

While these intricate arrangements were being made in the east, an alternate plan was set in motion in the west. Another noted neurosurgeon was found, though also not without difficulty. He was Dr. Howard Naffziger of the University of California Medical School at Berkeley. Like Dandy, Naffziger happened to be vacationing at the time—in his case, at Lake Tahoe, beyond the reach of a telephone. But he too was eventually found and Paul Mueller was sent up to bring him to Los Angeles. As their plane flew southward the doctor questioned Paul to ascertain certain facts even before he arrived; in turn, Paul asked questions also. The fact that they both spoke German made conversation easier and informal.

What might bring on the sudden appearance of a brain tumor? Paul wanted to know. Dr. Naffziger suggested several possibilities; a child, he explained, might suffer a head injury leading to the formation of a blood clot in the brain around which tissue would grow. As an adult the person might never ever suffer from this, might even live a complete normal lifetime without incident. But some form of disturbance, or aggravation, could readily unleash a precipitate manifestation. This was offered as conjecture, a generalization, and not a medical opinion. Still, as they flew through the darkness, Paul could not help but think back to that strange gadget George had used in the attempt to save his hair.

It was the evening of July 10 when they arrived at Cedars of Lebanon Hospital; Dr. Dandy was at that same moment at Newark Airport awaiting final word before taking off for California. Upon examining George, Naffziger found his condition so bad that he suggested immediate surgery. There was no point in Dandy's proceeding on— time had all but run out. Dandy concurred and remained in Newark, but remained in touch with the operating theater on an open phone line.

George was quickly wheeled into the operating room for preliminary exploration to locate the exact site of the tumor. This procedure required an hour and a half, after which two additional hours were spent in the X-ray room. "Energetic surgical intervention," in the medical phrase, was immediately begun and continued for nearly five hours by the team of doctors. It was found that George suffered from a cystic

Ira and Vernon Duke at work on "Spring Again," for *The Goldwyn Follies.* GERSHWIN COLLECTION

degeneration of a tumor in the right temporal lobe. It was obviously hopeless.

Dandy later observed that "although the tumor in a large part might have been extirpated and he would have recovered for a little while, it would have recurred very quickly since the whole thing fulminated so suddenly at the onset. I think the outcome is much the best for himself, for a man as brilliant as he with recurring tumor would have been terrible; it would have been slow death."

It was morning, a dank, gray morning. Distraught, anguished, exhausted, family and friends straggled out of the hospital for their homes, some of them believing that George had survived a long, serious operation. He had, of course, but a few were aware that there would be no recovery. Leonore, who was driven back to Roxbury Drive by Pallay—they had been preceded by Ira driven by Paul—learned the truth from Pallay. She did not have the heart to tell Ira.

When Max Dreyfus called that morning Ira was unaware of the fact that George never regained consciousness and was already gone. He reassured their old publisher "there's nothing to worry about." On a rainy Sunday—July 11, 1937—at ten thirty-five in the morning, the brilliant flame that had been the life of George Gershwin, aged only thirty-eight, flickered out.

"It was Sunday—not a day, but rather a gap between two other days," Scott Fitzgerald wrote of Hollywood's Day of Rest. "Behind . . . lay sets and sequences, the long waits under the crane that swung the microphone, the hundred miles a day by automobiles to and fro across a county, the struggles of rival ingenuities in the conference rooms, the ceaseless compromise, the clash and strain of many personalities fighting for their lives." Behind, in the chaos of Hollywood, lay, however, the artistic forms that once again the Gershwins had achieved in the reality of commercial life.

On the day of George's funeral in New York the film studios in California halted at ten o'clock for a moment of mourning silence. It was their final honor to this man who filled our world with sound and song and gave our lives a tempo. The silent moment past, the cameras rolled again, the world moves on; yet rising all around us are the songs of the Gershwins. Each year since 1937 we hear them more delightedly and gratefully than ever before—ever discovering in them a resilient charm, a durable brilliance, a permanent beauty.

George playing at an RKO-Radio Pictures convention on June 16, 1937—this candid snapshot is the last photograph taken of him. GERSHWIN COLLECTION

THE PASTIMES AND PRESENT
TIMES OF IRA GERSHWIN

In 1935 Kurt Weill had attended one of George's 72nd Street parties. It
may not have been the first meeting of the composers, but it was their
first frank conversational exchange. George said that he had always liked
the score of *Die Dreigroschenoper;* his one reservation was the *squitcha-
dicka* voice of the leading lady. Unfortunately, standing next to Kurt
was his wife, Lotte Lenya, the lady whose "screechy voice" may have
bothered George but enchanted a continent. It was this same evening
that Ira first met Kurt. Weill had recently come to America, but he was
already aware of Ira's accomplishments and he immediately expressed
the hope that they might someday work together. Ira—who feels that all
collaborations are marriages of uncertain durability, stabilized even
temporarily only with finesse—was somewhat taken aback by so direct
an invitation from a stranger. Five years later, however, he did begin his
fortunate collaboration with Weill, a joining together of two talents
that was to have delightful results.

Lady in the Dark opened at New York's Alvin Theatre on January
23, 1941. It was Ira's first major work after the death of George Gershwin in July 1937. In the intervening years he had written a few songs
with Harry Warren and Jerome Kern, but although these had been liked
by several producers, nothing happened to them until 1968 when some
of the Kern collaborations were published: "Once There Were Two of
Us" and its sequel, "Now That We Are One," and "No Question in My
Heart." He had also published one song with Vernon Duke to complete
the contractual agreement for the *Goldwyn Follies*, the picture whose

intent to have an all-Gershwin score had been blocked by the death of George.

Early in 1940 Moss Hart approached Ira about doing the lyrics to a show that then was titled, *I Am Listening,* and for which Kurt Weill had already agreed to supply the music. For a number of years Hart had collaborated with George Kaufman; now he announced that he was going to go it alone. "What does he mean, 'go it alone'?" Kurt was once heard to ask. "Now he's got *two* collaborators."

Kurt's discipline had trained him for the Continental experimental theater; he had had such little experience with American musical comedy that he sometimes reached back in rhythm numbers to the ragtime style of "Waiting for the Robert E. Lee." His own pianism was so singular that when Leopold Godowsky, Sr., heard Kurt play at one of George's parties, he turned quizzically to Ira: "*This* is a composer?" Kurt was a shrewd showman, however, and a man of impeccable taste; and he willingly accepted Ira's occasional suggestions, born from greater experience on Broadway. Kurt was one of the few theater composers

Kurt Weill and Lotte Lenya. COURTESY COLUMBIA RECORDS

who also orchestrated his works himself. And there are those who feel that shutting himself up in New City for months at a time, while he put the colors in the pit, gave him his greatest pleasure. Certainly his theatrical orchestrations remain among the most impressive of our time; yet his scores are not inferior to them.

Lady in the Dark was a new type of musical play, with its plot about psychoanalysis and its use of music and lyrics to depict the patient's dreams and dramatize his unconscious. In 1941 to Broadway it may have seemed profound. Today, with psychoanalysis so fully exploited a subject, the drama seems overly simple. The songs, music and lyrics, however, have not lost their strength. Consider the verse to "One Life to Live":

> There are many minds in circulation
> Believing in reincarnation.
>   In me you see
>   One who doesn't agree.
> Challenging possible affronts,
>   I believe I'll only live once
> And I want to make the most of it:
> If there's a party I want to be the host of it;
> If there's a haunted house I want to be the ghost of it;
> If I'm in town I want to be the toast of it.

Copyright © 1941 by Chappell & Co., Inc., New York, N.Y.

In the following five years Kurt and Ira collaborated on one other show and one film, each being done with definite style. *Where Do We Go from Here?*, their only movie co-authorship, was a 1945 wartime extravaganza with a genie plot (script by Morrie Ryskind) in which Fred MacMurray was catapulted to various moments in American history and allowed to perform in some bizarre way; the highlight of the picture was a twelve-minute *opéra bouffe*, "The Nina, the Pinta, the Santa Maria." It was the longest non-dancing musical sequence ever written for a film, and the critics were ecstatic about its multiple rhythms and recitatives. The final Gershwin-Weill collaboration was *The Firebrand of Florence*, in which the lyrics were such an integral part of the book that Ira shared billing for the libretto. This operetta concerned the life and loves of Cellini and was based upon Edwin Justin

Mayer's *The Firebrand*, which had been a hit in 1924. But this musical version did not go far commercially, and disappeared from the Alvin Theatre after only forty-three performances. Connoisseurs of the musical theater, however, regard it as an advance upon *The Chocolate Soldier* tradition of mock operetta—a genre which, alas, seems to have gone into eclipse.

After *Lady in the Dark* Ira had poor luck on Broadway. As evident, the subsequent work with Kurt had not gone well financially. So, in 1946 he undertook a new collaboration: Arthur Schwartz provided the music, and George Kaufman and Nunnally Johnson the book, for *Park Avenue*, a witty show about Manhattan's wealthy divorce set. It seemed an innocuous subject, but when it opened on November 4, 1946, critics complained that it was a "one joke" show; to complicate matters further, those for whom it was designed did not seem amused when their follies were paraded before them on the stage of the Shubert Theatre. That so distinguished a group of collaborators could have so misevaluated a group they knew intimately is one of the lingering mysteries about this production.

Park Avenue was the last of Ira's original Broadway musicals; it gives small comfort to know that he received the notices for the show. All the critics agreed that he had been up to his original tricks—concealing the "bad taste" in the plot beneath wit, good humor, and that winningly naïve attitude toward life that had made his friends earlier elect him Vice-President of the Sweet Fellows Society. Once again Ira was looking upon people as being better than they are, and their foibles as really not very important. Even Nevada won his endorsement:

> 'Neath the desert moonlight,
> Heavy hearts are soon light
> For tomorrow they're free—
> When the birds sing "Wake up,
> What a day to break up!
> Git along, get your decree!"
> No state, no state like Sweet Nevada!
> You just go out on horseback
> And gallop with divorce back.
> There's no state like Nevada for me!

Max Dreyfus and Ira around
the time of the writing of
Park Avenue. GERSHWIN
COLLECTION

For this show Ira concocted his first calypso, "The Land of Opportunitee," and a fine satire on the mother-in-law theme, "My Son-in-Law."
Arthur Schwartz was roughly handled by the critics; since his music is
perfectly wedded to the acclaimed lyrics, however, one wonders why
the praise accorded the lyricist could not have been extended to the composer as well.

What superficially might seem an easier task was laid out for Ira in
1951, when preparations were made to revive *Of Thee I Sing* and he
was asked to update the lyrics. But it was a challenge; the passing of
years compelled him to take the paraphrased Hoover hilarity, "Posterity Is Just around the Corner," and recast it to the less appealing "The
President Is Going to Be a Daddy." In other songs, where topical allusions needed freshening, he worked to somewhat more satisfactory results. The "Who Cares?" couplet, with its allusions to Yonkers' bank
failures, now became

> Who cares how history rates me,
> Long as your kiss intoxicates me?

And references to the moratorium and "how near we are to beer" were
put aside. Kaufman complimented Ira upon the revisions, but the revival,

which failed to bring back beloved Victor Moore in the role of Alexander Throttlebottom, did not win the public. The first act got as many laughs as it ever did; but the second, where the threat of war with France was supposed to mean something, seemed unimportant to a country that had just passed through its second World War.

Through the 1940s Ira put his mind also to a number of movies; indeed, their certain financial returns were an inducement when any Broadway venture was a risk. In 1943 Samuel Goldwyn undertook a film sympathetic to the Russian guerrilla; and Washington looked with favor upon this attention to one of our allies. Lillian Hellman whipped up the script and Ira was drafted for the lyrics. Since Goldwyn could not get either Prokofiev or Shostakovich for the score, he commissioned Aaron Copland. *North Star* was not a success—except in Russia, where there was much interest in the U.S. conception of the high living standards of the Soviet citizenry.

The following year Ira more than redeemed himself with the memorable *Cover Girl*, music by Jerome Kern. At the beginning of the work on the picture Arthur Schwartz (producer for the film) wired his writers "TOTE DAT BARGE—LIFT DAT TUNE." And indeed the hit of the film was a lovely and old-fashioned kind of Kern tune, the melodic "Long Ago and Far Away," which became the biggest commercial hit Ira ever had in any one year. Significantly, the lyric gave him trouble. (He felt that it was akin to the words of another well-paying song that had always made him nervous: "Love Walked In." Ira's complaint about these two ballads? "Neither says anything new, and 'Love Walked In' seems a bit pompous.")

In the following decade four other films sang to Ira's lyrics: *The Barkleys of Broadway* (1949) with music by Harry Warren; *Give a Girl a Break* (1953), music by Burton Lane; and *A Star Is Born* and *The Country Girl*, both released in 1954 with melodious scores by Harold Arlen. In all of these pictures there were distinctively Gershwin songs: "Shoes with Wings on" and "My One and Only Highland Fling," "In Our United State," and "The Man That Got Away." Appropriately, three of these four pictures have become movie classics: *The Barkleys* reunited Fred Astaire and Ginger Rogers in a memorable tribute to their films of the Thirties; *A Star Is Born* brought Judy Garland back to the screen in a film that has become her memorial; and *The Coun-*

Jerome Kern times, while Ira sings, the patter to "Sure Thing" for *Cover Girl*. COURTESY IRA GERSHWIN

Oscar Levant, producer Jesse Lasky, Ira, Leonore, and Robert Alda (who portrayed George Gershwin) on the set of *Rhapsody in Blue*. GERSHWIN COLLECTION

try Girl won Grace Kelly an Academy Award. But no work with others, no matter how congenial or successful, could bring to Ira the aesthetic thrill he had found in collaborating with his brother.

There are many accounts of the end of George's life, those last sad weeks in Beverly Hills. Some of the records are published, some are still given in confidential conversation. Some are accusatory, some self-serving; all are stained with melancholy, despair, and anger. The witnesses do not agree about all that happened in those days immediately after George's death, but on one point all concur: Leonore, by an extraordinary act of will, assumed command, forbade public tears—even at 1019

306

Leonore, Oscar Levant, Ira, and Arthur Freed watch a screening of *An American in Paris*. GERSHWIN COLLECTION

North Roxbury—and turned the spotlight upon Ira. He was the remaining Gershwin: insofar as Ira was a visible presence, then so far would Gershwin live.

It was not a role for which life had prepared Ira. He had always been one to put himself just beyond the spotlight, in that most intense darkness where the viewer's eye, blinded by incandescence, cannot see or focus—but where he, on the edge of light, could watch all with protected clarity. Ira had always made his being felt through his lyrics, through the rhetorical assumption of personality. But now, in Lee's phrase, "he must take his place"—and that meant being bodily evident. Nothing could change Ira's basic personality; but he was no longer to

307

Judy Garland, with
Jack Harmon (left)
and Don McCabe in
the "Gotta Have
Me Go with You"
sequence from *A
Star Is Born.* GERSH-
WIN COLLECTION

Bing Crosby as a fading musical comedy star in a scene from *The Country
Girl;* the song is "The Land around Us." GERSHWIN COLLECTION

be allowed to live like the Wizard of Oz and manifest himself solely through his creations.

When George died, there died too that galvanic charge that electrified a generation's melodic line. From whatever mysterious source that energy had drawn its strength, Ira always believed it could be found only in his brother and his brother's work. Lee could reaffirm Ira's identity and, like the character in Sybille Bedford's *A Legacy*, a book she admired, thicken the upholstery of life, allowing Ira to reflect, "I'm a man with a great many brakes—and, on the other hand, a good many pillows to fall back on." Indeed, it is as hostess *extraordinaire* that Lee appears in so many accounts of the period. But this is a misunderstanding of her character—akin to describing a piano by the grain of its wood: the description does not strike the important note. Virgil Thomson aptly called her a "colporteur of news"; and to Ira, who always fancies life vicariously, she has brought the world in microcosm: its energy and animosity, its violences and its rewards. She has helped immeasurably to make the name Gershwin, like the diamonds she prizes, an absolute in a world of shifting values.

One of George's strangest caricatures is of his sister-in-law, Lee, done in 1931 for the Goldberg biography. The jaw is angular, the lips are pursed, the eyes are closed—the caricature is blind to her beauty, her charm, her personal vulnerability. But George was aware of her belief that the truth could be many things and her wisdom to know that it could never be an ally. In her life, *façon de parler* has always provided *modus vivendi*—a fact that Truman Capote, in his own caricature of her in *The Muses Are Heard*, failed to observe. And when, after George's death, she became a creative force, this occasionally meant assuming even the mask of Rose: insistent authority, energy at its most direct and fundamental. "The name Gershwin means far more to Lee than it ever did to me," Ira has said.

But she also restricts her influence, and she has never interfered with Ira's work—seldom ever offering an opinion of it. Nor has she ever underestimated George's value. "If I hadn't been Ira's wife, I wouldn't have been in George's crowd at all. He moved too fast for me to keep up." She recognizes that George was a centrifugal force, a world revolved around him, whereas she is an individual energetically focused upon life, its modernity and continually unfolding riches and inventions. A favorite word with her is "stylish," emphasizing her wish to be alive to life in its evolving manifestations. For her, this always means going forward and not turning ever to yesterday for the excitation of feeling. Thus she knew she could never give Ira what he said he always needed, a push toward voluntary creation. (As Ira once admitted, "You know, I always avoided George when I could, because he would ask me what I was doing, tell me to get busy, and all that.") George called that breathless leap into the creative void *chutzpa*: that beguiling directness filled with laughter, that self-assurance in uncertainty which more limited souls recognize and cherish as the evidence of genius. Lee could not give Ira that creative energy—what human could? But much, so much, of what Ira later did accomplish is owed to the stimulation of her ungoverned brilliance and the fascination of her unpredictability; from one moment to the next Ira has never known what to expect from her.

"I always felt that if George hadn't been my brother and pushed me into lyric writing, I'd have been contented to be a bookkeeper," Ira once said. The irony is that, through death, George did what he had spent his life frustrating: making Ira into a bookkeeper. While George lived, Ira managed his brother's accounts and, until there was a secretary, wrote his checks and tallied his accounts. But after George's death, Ira became immersed in Gershwin finances. George died intestate; his mother, Rose, became his sole beneficiary. When she died in 1948 Ira became an heir, as well as one of four trustees, to that complicated estate. All these years since, he has concerned himself not only with his own finances but those affecting the considerable income which George's royalties and interests produce. "As long as I've ASCAP, I won't have to pass cap," he has been heard to mutter. Unfortunately, such security has not encouraged Ira's muse. Nor do high taxes easily entice the bookkeeper away from his accounts for the possible revenues from writing new songs.

All of us inevitably lead a portion of life in speculation and reflection. Ira, more than most. There has been the public image, the man who reluctantly "takes his place"; there has been a public/private man who still works through the material that George has left behind and of it has created a new kind of reality for himself and for his audience; and there is the private man, undoubtedly the most interesting of all. To know Ira Gershwin of these final years, one must attend to all these images that merge to form his identity.

George's drawing
of Leonore. GERSHWIN
COLLECTION

310

Lee and Ira, summer of 1959. PHOTO BY SAM SHAW, COURTESY IRA GERSHWIN

From very early, Ira has had an extraordinary memory of matters Gershwin and, despite his assertive modesty, a historical anticipation that the Gershwins were to be of more than their own time. When Isaac Goldberg, the musically inclined Harvard professor who had written on Gilbert and Sullivan and on *Tin Pan Alley*, was commissioned in 1929 to do a series of articles about George Gershwin (a series that, enlarged and put into a book, became the first biography of the composer), he engaged John McCauley, a New York researcher, to do most of the legwork. "Were it not for his brother Ira I doubt if I would have gotten

311

Ira Gershwin, Gent., in a
courtly moment at the
Pre-Commencement
Reception in his honor in
the Art Gallery,
University of Maryland.
UNIVERSITY OF MARYLAND

as much as I did," McCauley wrote Goldberg. "G.G. is willing enough
to talk but Ira has the best memory and gives you stuff with not so much
as a preliminary ahem. I had him while G.G. was called to the phone
ever so often." Ira has never abandoned the role then assumed. When
letters come, asking information, he carefully answers them as best he
can—usually is his careful, schoolboy, backhand handwriting. And as the
years bring more and more official attention for George—the marking
of his birthplace in Brooklyn, the naming of schools in Brooklyn and
Chicago and Stony Brook, the charting of a street in Hull, England, the
issuing of a gold commemorative medal in Switzerland, the naming
of prizes, the formation of scholarly collections at the Library of Congress, the Museum of the City of New York—Ira has quietly played
his role, always co-operating when there is honor to be paid George.

He has been less interested in awards given himself; but, in 1966,
when the University of Maryland awarded him a D.F.A. (it was not, as
he was quick to point out, an appointment as Division Freight Agent),
he made one of his infrequent public appearances when he went to College Park to receive it. Lee was particularly pleased at this honor paid
Ira, saying it meant more to her than his Pulitzer had. "I know what she
means," confessed Ira. "When you're young and get an award, it doesn't
mean much. But when you're seventy and get one—then it really does
mean something." That same trip east he visited the Library of Congress,
where a luncheon honored this man who has done so much to build the

Ira greets the terrapin
symbol of the University.
UNIVERSITY OF MARYLAND

Prof. Homer Ulrich, head of the Department of Music, conferring the
honorary Doctor of Fine Arts degree; Dr. Wilson H. Elkins, President
of the University of Maryland, offers
congratulations. UNIVERSITY OF MARY-
LAND

Dr. Gershwin being tendered
further congratulations by
Leonore. PHOTO BY L. D. STEWART

Gershwin archive there. (For over twenty years Ira has been annotating the manuscripts and memorabilia of his brother and giving them to our national library.)

Since 1967 he has also been forming an archive at the Museum of the City of New York. It was to honor these gifts—to view those made and to preview those promised—that in May 1968 the Theatre and Music Collection of the Museum of the City of New York opened their grand retrospective, *GERSHWIN: George the Music/Ira the Words*. Almost the entire second floor of the museum displayed Gershwiniana: manuscripts (many borrowed from the Library of Congress) and published music, paintings, sculpture, photographs, set designs and costumes, programs and posters, furniture, jewelry, books, and, of course, George's piano and baton—all set against backgrounds in shades of Gershwin blue. Mayor John Lindsay proclaimed "Gershwin Week in New York"; Larry Rivers designed the show's poster; the museum issued a catalogue of the exhibition, and there was also issued "Hi-Ho!" in a special limited edition, signed by Ira and augmented with one of George's check signatures. Sam Pearce, the curator of the Theatre and Music Collection, brilliantly designed the show and, with the aid of Melvin Parks and the curatorial staff, co-ordinated all these events and contributions so that the museum, for a summer in New York, re-created the Gershwin era.

Studying one of the panels in the Museum of the City of New York, the one devoted to the development and revisions of a lyric. At one point, bemused, Ira was overheard saying, "This Gershwin sure uses up a lot of paper." PHOTO BY MANNY GREENHAUS, MUSEUM OF THE CITY OF NEW YORK

Official presentation of the scroll bearing the proclamation of "Gershwin Week" in New York at the Museum of the City of New York. (Left to right:) Ira Gershwin; Leonore Gershwin; Louis S. Auchincloss, president of the museum; Mrs. Edwin Hilson, member of the museum's Board of Trustees, making the presentation on behalf of Mayor John Lindsay; Ralph R. Miller, director of the museum; Sam Pearce, curator of the museum and designer of the Gershwin exhibition; L. Arnold Weissberger, noted theatrical attorney and chairman of the museum's Friends of the Theatre and Music Collection. PHOTO BY MANNY GREENHAUS, COURTESY MUSEUM OF THE CITY OF NEW YORK

Leaving Russia after the premiere of *Porgy and Bess:* Harold Arlen, with Ira, who is trying to sell caviar to Horace Sutton. COURTESY HORACE SUTTON

On February 28, 1973, in commemoration of the seventy-fifth anniversary of George's birth, the U. S. Postal Service issued a special stamp in his honor—an official, and national, recognition his international reputation had earned him.

The less nostalgic have not had to depend upon awards and exhibitions, however, to sense the viability of the Gershwins. These many years have seen revivals of Gershwin songs and scores as well as new productions with Gershwin music. George had not been dead a year before plans were begun for a film biography. In 1941 Warner Bros. bought the rights, and a procession of screenwriters worked on the project: Robert Rossen, Clifford Odets, Sonya Levien, Howard Koch, and Elliot Paul. The assignment of Odets had especially been puzzling to Ira: " 'But Clifford, why you?'—my question implying that he was far more interested generally in plays about the class struggle, etc. He replied, 'What do you mean? George's life is the story of my life, of Moss Hart's life'—and he mentioned two or three others whose lives didn't seem to have much musical relevance either." Eventually in 1945 Jesse Lasky released his *Rhapsody in Blue*, an inaccurate and highly romantic conception of George's life; but it was prepared at a time when the world (just emerging from World War II) needed escape, romance, and music; and this film circled and recircled the globe. It still plays frequently on television, though it is now often titled *The Story of George Gershwin*. The honestly imaginative film *An American in Paris* won its Academy Award in 1951 and that film, done with Ira's assistance, remains a movie classic. And *Porgy and Bess* has become a legend of its own.

There have been several revivals of the opera but none so far-ranging and spectacular as that production by Blevins Davis and Robert Breen which opened in Dallas in 1952. It toured the world, played La Scala, penetrated what had seemed an impregnable Iron Curtain (Truman Capote's novel non-fiction, *The Muses Are Heard*, purports to depict some aspects of the tour to the U.S.S.R.), and undoubtedly generated the enthusiasm which led to Samuel Goldwyn's decision to buy and film the opera. Rouben Mamoulian had been given the directorial assignment but was "released" by Goldwyn three weeks before shooting commenced. Otto Preminger whipped the cast through their parts, but even Preminger's behavior occasionally seemed disloyal. ("The man's a regular Arnold Bennett," complained Goldwyn.) Preminger's interpretation of the "It Ain't Necessarily So" sequence particularly displeased the producer. "I want it sung like John L. Barrymore!" said Goldwyn. There was no inattention paid to credits: Samuel Goldwyn presents a Samuel Goldwyn Production produced by Samuel Goldwyn. And though Goldwyn himself called it *Bess and Porgy*, others dubbed the film *Sam, Porgy and Bess*. After the film's New York opening, Goldwyn thought he had had the last word: "The word to mouth is wonderful," he announced. But the mouthing, by Dorothy Dandridge and Sidney Poitier, to a song-track sung (but scarcely acknowledged) by Adele Addison and Robert McFerrin, convinced few. The opera was embalmed in artificiality and robbed of life. And that was what the real opera *Porgy and Bess* was about and is: life.

In the decades since 1937, several Gershwin songs have been published, songs that either had been heard in a New York production ("The Real American Folk Song" from *Ladies First* and "Dear Little Girl" from *Oh, Kay!*) or dropped on the road ("The Harlem River Chanty" from *Tip-Toes*) or written for, but never put in, a film ("Hi-Ho!" from *Shall We Dance* and "Just Another Rhumba" from *The Goldwyn Follies*). Also, some small orchestral and piano works have been brought out: "Promenade" (which is the "Walking the Dog" music from *Shall We Dance*), "Lullaby" (the early string quartet), and *Pardon My English*'s contrapuntal "Two Waltzes in C" (which Ira once wanted released as a "Wordless Operetta Suite": "His Waltz," "Her Waltz," and "Their Waltz"). The Gershwin archives contain many more works, and undoubtedly they will gradually make their way into print.

A more demanding undertaking for Ira has been the creation of new songs from George's manuscripts and notebooks. The first of such enterprises was "Dawn of a New Day," which Ira prepared, with Kay Swift's help, for the New York World's Fair in 1939. The song's verse music came from the refrain of "Come, Come, Come to Jesus," a song that George and Ira had written for an abortive show with Ben Hecht and Billy Rose ca. 1930. The refrain of "Dawn of a New Day" blended two other Gershwin themes, "as George would have done," said Ira. In 1946, for William Perlberg and George Seaton's film *The Shocking Miss Pilgrim*, Ira—again, with Kay Swift's invaluable assistance—constructed an entire score from the Gershwin archives, the first such posthumous score for a Hollywood musical. And in 1963 Ira drew

George's drawing
of Kay Swift.
COURTESY KAY SWIFT

upon those manuscripts and his own memories for the latest of these endeavors to give a chance to even the occasional and uncompleted melodies that George had left.

There were inevitable problems with a posthumous score: what producer would be willing to chance it? (If a special type of number were suddenly required, what guarantee that the composer's trunk of posthumous manuscripts would disclose it?) What accommodations could George's manuscripts make and legitimately remain authentic? Ira's predominant virtues in the enterprise are his wholehearted respect for George's music and an uncanny memory of phrases and figures. Ira can no longer read music in any traditional sense, and he cannot play the piano. When he was a boy his Aunt Kate had gotten him as far as page thirty-two of Beyer; that enabled him to perform "Pink Lady" at Christadora House for the boys to dance around together. "Sometimes I'd play 'The Fairy Waltz,' though that was really a duet I played with Kate." Yet he could ever look at a musical theme, even in manuscript, and identify it. (Once he came across a place card for Max Dreyfus with some bars of music scribbled on it by George. He thought a moment and then correctly identified "In Cupid's Garden," a tune nowadays restricted to bringing on circus elephants.)

When others play for Ira—no matter how awkward the rhythm or how hesitant the reading—he invariably and instantly recognizes any deviation from George's melodic line and harmonies. Ira's vision is geological, seeing a score like a cross section of the earth; and he remembers each rise and fall, no matter how minute. But he has small interest in the color and mood derived from key. Thus the geological picture is accurate only relatively; the absolute elevation has been forgotten. Ira has always chosen his musical key to bring the song within his singing range; and he has little interest in the loss from modulation or transposition. Perhaps he is right not to worry about such matters, for the music editors invariably alter the keys before publication, lowering a song's range. But those who have heard George's melodies in their created key may pardonably find all other readings diminished.

Ira's involvement with *Kiss Me, Stupid*, a film that derided fidelity and marriage, began, ironically, at an anniversary party for the William Wylers. Billy Wilder asked Lee what it would take to get Ira working again, and Lee responded: "To be asked by someone he admires." Wilder believed he qualified, and Ira did not say no. The project was a

Wilder-I. A. L. Diamond adaptation of a French farce; its working title was *The Dazzling Hour*. The script centered on two amateur song-writers and their attempts to sell their material to a Las Vegas and Hollywood star (Dean Martin) who was temporarily stranded by motor trouble in their small desert town. Wilder said probably only three numbers would be needed: two novelty songs of the quality of "Doggie in the Window" and an Italian ballad—something strong like "Love Walked In." He was amenable to Ira's suggestions for a composer, assuming that Ira would probably pick either André Previn or Henry Mancini. Neither he nor Lee expected that Ira would suggest George. Ira (agreeing with Gertrude Stein that if you can do a thing easily—or have already done it—why bother?) now faced an intriguing problem: how to write three songs that would plausibly seem the work of amateurs and yet would not reflect upon George. He was determined that the songs must have a chance. So he immediately ruled out bad rhymes or forced construction: the songs must not be amateurish in structure but "perhaps just somewhat obvious." Meanwhile Wilder had come across "Blah, Blah, Blah" and said, "That's it!" But Ira insisted that that was precisely what It was not: 'Blah, Blah, Blah" is a standard, and he would not in conscience repeat that approach. Nor was he willing to write another "Someone at Last," where the humor came from overproduction.

Ira called Roger Edens, an old friend who had been the on-stage pianist for Ethel Merman in *Girl Crazy* and then gone on to become a film producer (*Funny Face* and *Hello Dolly*). Lee was delighted: "Roger is always tasty." He came on weekends and played through the manuscripts for Ira, taking down any changes Ira dictated. Ira thought that once he received the script he could decide the proper song for each marked spot. But then, to his discomfiture, he found that the script was not something prepared in advance nor was the story line itself precisely laid out. For the first time in his career he was called upon to write two novelty songs out of the blue and *they* would give the scriptwriters ideas for building the story! Ira's agent, Irving Lazar, read aloud to Wilder, Diamond, and Ira catchy titles from the listing of songs in *The Gershwin Years*. And when Wilder and Diamond heard "Does a Duck Love Water," they exclaimed that that was the kind of song wanted.

There is an old songwriter's joke about which comes first, the words or the music. The answer is, of course, the contract. A professional writes to specification, not on spec. For a musical-comedy lyricist—and Ira regards himself as such, not as a writer of popular songs—the song's situation is fundamental. Certainly songs are not restricted to the original situations that called them forth, and admittedly it would take expertise to show the appropriateness of "Love Walked In" and "Love Is Here to Stay" to *The Goldwyn Follies*. But Ira's working habits require a well-defined point of view. He thinks of lyrics as "lodgments"; and when *Kiss Me, Stupid* became a project of songs in a vacuum, Ira's spirits sank. Two of the three songs he provided, however, are well worth attention. Only "Sophia" is derivative and has lost whatever essential Gershwinality it possessed.

"Sophia" was, however, the song that came directly from a single source, "Wake Up, Brother, and Dance," which the Gershwins had written in 1936 for *Shall We Dance*. That song was a fine Astaire dance number and was printed (but not yet published) when the studio scrapped it and asked for a titular "Shall We Dance" as replacement. Ira thought that by changing "Wake Up"'s tempo into a waltz, altering its key, and canceling its original modulations he could make another "It's Amore," exactly the sort of imitation an amateur would think commercial. "When George wrote that song ["Wake Up, Brother, and Dance"] it reminded me a lot of an Italian song we used to hear on the East Side when I was a kid." When Ira had pointed this out to George, George modified the "Neapolitanesque" thematic line; but now the song was stripped of those Gershwinesque modulations and returned to its origins. Perhaps someday the original "Wake Up, Brother, and Dance" can yet be published.

"I'm a Poached Egg": Ira had long fancied the notion of a poached egg without a piece of toast as the perfect image of incompleteness and unhappiness. He had first begun writing it up in the early Twenties. When in 1940 he wrote *Lady in the Dark* he used the image in passing, in the verse to "It's Never Too Late to Mendelssohn"; but he felt that the notion was still worth complete development. And when he was going through George's manuscripts in 1945 with Kay Swift, he sang to her the main theme for the refrain that he and George had begun; Kay wrote it down as an eight-bar theme and put it among the unpublished manuscripts. This kind of catalogue song has always tickled Ira, and he thought he could solve his aesthetic dilemma in *Kiss Me, Stupid* (writ-

Leonore and Ira,
Beverly Hills,
October 1960. PHOTO
BY L. D. STEWART

ing for amateurs some songs that would remain Gershwin) by supplying two sets of lyrics: rather obvious ones for the film and wittier lines
for publication. For a bridge to the sprightly tune, he suggested to
Roger a theme from another early song, "Are You Dancing?" jumping
its rhythm slightly to liven it up. Inadvertently, the song came out as
thirty—not thirty-two—bars, for the "Are You Dancing?" strain was
not properly decelerated. By hastily inserting "slower and freely" below the bridge (in the proofs), Ira was able to smooth somewhat
what otherwise would have been a peculiar jerkiness in the transitions
and would have given, unintentionally, the song an amateur sound indeed.

But Ira's witty lyrics are not amateurish, and he never tired thinking
of new allusions and variations on the song's basic pattern. It was, by
the way, in writing this number that Ira said that for the second time in
his life he had gotten help from a rhyming dictionary: in looking up
rhymes for "toast" he found "hitching-post," and promptly tied the
lyric to it. When he was asked to do a female version for a promised
recording by Ella Fitzgerald he wondered about a third refrain. What

323

could he say about a poached egg he hadn't said before? The second
refrain had already produced a poached egg with egg upon its face. He
considered "A poached egg that's fallen on the floor," but that was
messy. Then he cleverly took another tack:

> I'm a girl-friend, without a thing to boast—
> Any egg-head would have me diagnosed
> As a poached egg without a piece of toast
> Each time I'm . . . without you.

At the Museum of the City of New York's Gershwin exhibition, one
of the most popular walls was the one which showed page after page of
Ira's lyrical notations for this song. Eventually Wilder and Diamond decided they wanted a number that wasn't quite so much of a novelty after all, and they would have liked it retitled "When I'm Without You."
But Ira, who had tried all his life to get a poached egg into a song, held
out; and the song is now out as he wanted.

But if there is a standard in *Kiss Me, Stupid*, it is "All the Livelong
Day (And the Long, Long Night)." (Ira wanted it "Love-Long Night"
but feared that would be thought vulgar.) Indeed, it was the opportunity to write another Gershwin ballad that might become a standard that
originally interested Ira in the film project. His first notion was to write
up ♯24 among the unpublished manuscripts, a tune with the working
title "Fifty-Second Floor." Ira considered calling it "All Time" and using rhymes like "all time" and "fall-time." By the time he had come to
write the film's ballad, however, he had switched to "Livelong Day,"
another fine blues of the Twenties, whose lead sheet he had dictated to
Kay Swift in the mid-Forties (♯57 among the unpublished mss.). The
distinctive verse music had come much earlier, from a three-day outing
to a summer camp in the Adirondacks. Bela Blau, one of Ira's boyhood friends, was a counselor there; and George, Ira, and Lou Paley had
gone up for a visit. "It was cold as hell," said Ira. "I slept in bed with
my clothes on—also a straw hat (as a gag). We wrote 'Phoebe' and
also a song, 'À vous toot dir veh, à vous,' a jingle which later came to
mind when I was writing *Of Thee I Sing*." George had always saved
the manuscript of "Phoebe" (dated August '21); both Lou Paley and
Ira had preserved among their own papers the lyric which they had
written together. Clearly it was not a song any of them took casually,

no matter how cold the circumstances of its inception. When the verse music was taken over for "Livelong Day," not a single note of it or its introduction was changed, although the publisher did transpose the key.

Anyone who studies the published song, "All the Livelong Day," will instantly see that George's fine musical phrase in the verse of "Phoebe" is incorporated into the refrain. That amalgam was made ingeniously. Kay Swift had marked on the manuscript of "Livelong"'s refrain, "figure need," and Roger Edens instantly sensed that no better figure could be found than that elusive whoo-whoo calling phrase in the verse. (Roger had a talent for enriched pauses and transitions; perhaps his finest work in this regard was the dancing vamp he supplied to "Singin' in the Rain"—a vamp which some think superior to the song.) To make logical the "amateur" source of "Livelong," Ira set up an old-fashioned lyric with a waffling on "you-oo-oo" and "do-oo-oo." The amateur's creation would not, therefore, be distinguished by its quality but by its imitativeness. But, from a Gershwin point of view, the song was not imitative. It was indeed a Twenties song in origin: it had just taken another forty years to get it finished. Ira's original Twenties lyric had read:

> I sit in Childs and order
>> Breakfast for one.
> I feel just like a boarder—
>> 'Magine my condition
>> When my one ambition
> Has, for oh, so long! been to hold you tight—
> All the livelong day and the long, long night.

If it was indeed to be left to him to devise script situations for songs, Ira thought of one that would be professionally logical and also might teach the public how songs are written. When lyricists—particularly those who do not know or read music—are given a tune to set, they may concoct a dummy lyric: words straight from the unconscious that sound like automatic writing but which do, nonetheless, set for the lyricist the pattern (accent, emphasis, and placement of rhymes) he must cut his words to. Ira thought it would be funny to have the amateur lyricist write a dummy lyric to "Livelong" and then have the

325

amateur composer sing that dummy lyric by mistake. Perhaps it was the innocence of the idea that disengaged Wilder, for the notion was not adopted. But Ira's dummy is a model of what a dummy might be:

When it's wintertime, many flowers droop.
> There is a saying old,
> Summer is not so cold.
Some like turtle better than onion soup.
> Ala kazam
> How's your wife, Sam?
> I'm what I am.
If we can laugh at trouble
> Ha Ha Ha Ha
Then trouble is a bubble
> Even in Nebraska,
> Hong Kong or Alaska.
So let's go outside and sit on the stoop.
When it's wintertime, many flowers droop.

By permission of Ira Gershwin

Ira would push his glasses back on his forehead and try out the lyric while wandering around 1021. Both he and Lee agreed that "I'm what I am" is a particularly good line.

But the movie itself was not good. From the beginning Ira had disliked the title. The studio hoped a Gershwin lyric would cleverly produce a better one, and Ira thought of *Lust for Lust, Lust Horizon, Get Lust,* and *Dino's Didoes*—they were all uncharacteristic of him, and they were no good. The picture, conceived almost without conception and structured with access only to easy vulgarity, tried to be farce; it became merely foul. Dean Martin, for whose voice the two ballads had been tailored, refused to record them; and the songs, though published, got no play. Though Ira insisted on writing songs to book, fortunately in time other songs have been liberated from their original confines. Perhaps such will yet happen with these: after all, the Gershwins had never been much for writing immediate hits. "The Man I Love," "I've Got a Crush on You," and "Love Is Here to Stay"—they all took years before they caught permanent hold of our awareness.

Lyrics

on Several Occasions

A SELECTION OF STAGE & SCREEN LYRICS
WRITTEN FOR SUNDRY SITUATIONS; AND NOW
ARRANGED IN ARBITRARY CATEGORIES. TO
WHICH HAVE BEEN ADDED MANY INFORMATIVE
ANNOTATIONS & DISQUISITIONS ON THEIR WHY
& WHEREFORE, THEIR WHOM-FOR, THEIR HOW;
AND MATTERS ASSOCIATIVE.

by Ira Gershwin, *Gent.*

New York: A L F R E D · A · K N O P F
1 9 5 9

Only an innocent confidence in the vindication of time sustained Ira on his longest project, the assembling of his book of lyrics for Alfred A. Knopf. As Ira's thoughts moved from the theater to the study, he looked back upon a life's work and wrote meditative essays, particularly upon the problems he and George had faced in writing songs to situation.

> I do not want to . . . end without giving the history of our collaboration . . . relating its origins, describing its phases, and indicating in this work in common, year after year, now the predominance of the elder brother over the younger, now the predominance of the younger over the elder.
> First of all, two absolutely different temperaments; my brother, a gay, exuberant, expansive nature; I, a melancholy, dreamy, introverted one, yet—what is odd—two minds receiving identical impressions from contact with the external world . . . But as these works appeared one after the other there was a fusion, an amalgam of our two styles, which united in the creation of a single style, one that was very personal.

327

No, that is *not* Ira writing about his work with George. It is Edmond
de Goncourt, writing on December 26, 1895—a little less than a year
before Ira's birth—about the years with Jules and that extraordinary
nineteenth-century fraternal collaboration. But Ira might have, with
justice, written those lines about himself and George; for their twentieth-century fraternal collaboration was equally remarkable; and much
of Ira's book was to describe, in bookish allusions, the peculiarities of
their relationship.

Ira always accepted Franklin P. Adams's judgment that he was not a
poet. (F.P.A. thought Oscar Hammerstein, 2nd, was the poet among
songwriters.) Ira thinks his own talent is for light verse. At the same
time he clearly had the poet's desire for his works to be collected together in one volume, where they could escape the impermanence of
flimsy sheet music. (When Ralph Barton had reviewed the lyrics of
Strike Up the Band [second version] he perhaps gave Ira incentive for
the project: "If they were printed in a book, I should buy it and find
something more than the accident of alphabetical arrangement in the
fact that it would be placed on my shelves next to the works of W. S.
Gilbert.") When Oscar Hammerstein published his own collection of
lyrics, its advertising maintained that there had never before been such
an undertaking. Ira pointed out otherwise. Harry B. Smith, in his *Stage
Lyrics*, had been the first to publish such a compilation. And his sort of
collection, where the lyrics were identified with those who had introduced them originally, was Ira's model.

Because his words were tied to music and performance, Ira was reluctant to take the poet's privilege and modify them for his collection,
even though there were occasional phrases that he knew he could improve. But published songs must, like all familiar material, not lose that
familiarity. With some, the frequent handling of material—family stories and accounts passing into legend—effaces its distinguishing features.
Ira, however, regards such stories and known lyrics as family plate—
best kept burnished in service. Only thus do they become legacies, rich
in the glow they cast. With unpublished songs and special material unknown to the public—particularly where the music itself was lost—he
felt more free; some of those lyrics in his book are, in their published
combinations, newly assembled or show lines from the Fifties.

Words By had been Ira's original title for the venture, for had not
George called him "Words"? But the phrase lacked panache. (And to

non-professionals the book might seem devotional literature.) At his most whimsical, Ira considered something of the Twenties, such as *A Bargain Basement of Lyrics*. But then came that happy moment when his eye fell upon Matthew Prior's *Poems on Several Occasions*, and he immediately thought *Lyrics on Several Occasions*. For had not every lyric been written for a specific place and time and book and voice? No matter the independence a song might achieve subsequently; it would always remind Ira of the occasion that constituted its milieu and gave it foundation.

He began work on August 3, 1955, by dictating a note for "The Babbitt and the Bromide." Thus the non-commerciality of the project was assured from the beginning, for no hit song that! (Louis Kronenberger had, in 1935, put that lyric into his *Anthology of Light Verse*, and Ira never forgot the honor.) Three years later, by mid-1958, Ira was still revising that original note—though, admittedly, he had been writing and rewriting dozens of other notes as well. And four years to the day, August 3, 1959, the index and corrected proofs were dispatched to Knopf. "If it were a child, he could talk on his own by now," said Ira.

The four years had not been spent in casually recording memories and dashing off observations. Ira never thought himself a prose writer; in his book he quoted M. Jourdain with amusement, a triumphant assertion that prose could indeed be natural and mastered. So working and reworking lines, he compressed them until they had the muscular sparseness of his lyrics. In such revision he occasionally forgot that sung lyrics had music to expand and relax the verbal force. *Lyrics on Several Occasions* is a "hard read" but a rewarding one—a book to be dipped into, read, and meditated upon, rather than something attempted straight through. For many years P. G. Wodehouse has written Ira annually of how he rereads the book; and praise from such a master is praise indeed. Ultimately the book is perhaps most interesting for its revelation of Ira's retrospective view of his life and craft. Particularly is this true of the categories he designed for his songs. Though *LOSO* stresses the facts of what Ira wrote and under which circumstances, those facts are not what most engages us in the book. What it shows is the lively and unique intelligence that formed those lyrics, a mind still perking along and, in reflection, ever capable of iridescent brilliance.

At the museum show, *GERSHWIN: George the Music/Ira the Words,* one of the most popular exhibits was a tile table made for Ira by Louis Calhern, the distinguished actor and Gershwin friend. We quote from the museum's catalogue description:

> At the center of the table stands Calhern's copy of Ira Gershwin's 1932 self-portrait, "My Body." Immediately surrounding it is a portrait of this lyricist's daily life—those objects which, to Calhern, summed up Ira Gershwin: a cigar-smoking songwriter who would occasionally venture, bow-tied, to the races or to a UCLA football game (for he and his brother, George, had, after all, adapted "Strike Up the Band for UCLA") but who more usually lived a contemplative life, sitting red-slippered, in his green armchair, surrounded by reference books and within handy reach of that remote-control box which was bringing him the world on television. The passions for golf and tennis had already cooled by 1954, when this table was made; there remained the pleasures of billiards and scrabble and the frustrations of poker.

In Ira's private world ("I live in an Ivory Tower—of course, it has a few doors!") not much has changed. The house itself at 1021 North Roxbury Drive has been pulled down and reassembled—this time as neo-Regency instead of California Spanish—and the slippers, armchair, and television have been replaced with other models. Scarves now serve for bow ties; but cigars and books and whimsical passions remain. If Ira is no longer in his Prince Bolkonski period, dyeing his underwear, making leather wallets, devising new and more complicated ways to tabulate his accounts, he has now mastered multiple concentration. He enjoys propping himself up on his reclining bed, turning on the remote TV and also switching on a transistor radio nearby. With lights ablaze around the bed, he strews open books, magazines, and newspapers in this land of Counterpane. And while confusion blares about, he calmly solves a Double-Crostic. "If you must live, you might as well live in California," he concludes.

To be surrounded with rhetoric is, for Ira, to be immersed in life. If every Gershwin song has a trick to it—and Ira insists it does—the trick is always conceptual and structural, verbal and musical. There is to be no tricking psychologically, no misleading of the mind by distortion of the heart. "I cry only in movies or at the theater," he says, pulling on his cigar. "It's artificiality that makes me cry. I can always

"... young girls sitting on fire escapes on hot summer nights ..." Martin Lewis's etching *The Glow of the City* (1930, 11⁷⁄₁₆ × 14³⁄₈″) captures the essence of George Gershwin's comment to S. N. Behrman and also the mood of the opening of the second movement of the *Concerto in F*. COLLECTION THE MUSEUM OF MODERN ART, NEW YORK

face reality." S. N. Behrman, while mentioning the "coarse, social texture" of the family's beginnings, also emphasized George and Ira's retained innocence—their vision that set them and their social gatherings apart from the notorious ones of their day. Behrman wrote in his *People in a Diary* that George "told me once that he wanted to write for young girls sitting on fire escapes on hot summer nights in New York and dreaming of love."

331

The Gershwins' creations mirror that idyllic vision we all would re-capture of the American experience. A Gershwin song has us willingly suspend our disbelief and voluntarily believe again that man's instincts and natural nature can bring him unto Truth and Beauty and Love. Ira has always disliked the forced response; and the old song, "You Made Me Love You," is for him almost unspeakable. Love in a Gershwin song is an aesthetic pleasure where one takes as much joy from the journey as from the destination.

Gershwin has been around so long that we forget it is a world invented and self-sustained, original as the name itself. *The Great Gatsby* immortalizes the process of these self-generated men, the Platonic creators of themselves. Certainly George shaped himself to the mold of his own devising. All attempts to account for either him or Ira fail. Their genes? Their Russian origins? Their Jewish tradition? Their second-generation ebullience and defensiveness? All are explanations that explain nothing. Sometime after George died, his mother Rose, smart and driving and somewhat warped in the heart, tried dictating her memoirs. They began by asserting she had always intended that George should be musical, and that when he was three she had already determined on lessons for him. The simplistic self-deception was insupportable and the autobiography abandoned; even Rose must have recognized that nothing in her could logically account for the genius of George and Ira.

The film, *Rhapsody in Blue*, perpetuated the myth of family. Its initial distortions eliminated the existence of Arthur and Frankie, George and Ira's brother and sister, and turned Morris Gershwin into a philosopher and wit to whom Ira was particularly close. Though whenever George was praised in the early Twenties, Morris would reply: "But have you met my son Izzy?" Ira himself never felt he knew his father until near the end when he had a perception of his character. What Ira found most difficult to accept was the way his father had been treated by his mother.

The family was a family of individuals, each going separately. Frankie well remembers how she almost had to raise herself. And the suggestion that there was a family harmony that brought them together, each attentive to the others' needs and wants, that is the myth Warner Brothers has, with economic reason, imposed upon generations. Clearly in that world where success rewarded itself and where failure went unattended, the genius that George possessed and that Ira husbands was not before, around, or after them. It built itelf in air and airs and miscible words. Cole Porter's legendary life centered upon parties, palaces, glittering shows, and song, all substantial as the substance they commemorated. The peculiarity of the Gershwin world is the peculiarity of Gatsby's; it is indeed material, palpable, enviable, occasionally accessible. But it is also like the lyrics of Ira: focused less on name brands that are the assurances of today, and more on eternals which are never quite clearly perceived. Ultimately the Gershwin world, created entirely of the will, is grounded in the mind, whereas that of others is founded on matter. These self-sustained worlds operate by their own logic and to their own rhythm; we may momently be caught up in one and, as in silent flight, lose awareness of gravity. But in time we return to ourselves, and that special timeless world continues. *There* is Art, to the degree that it is Art and not happenstance. "I guess I've always considered perfection, or as close as I could come to it, my armor," said Ira. "And I knew that even if the lyric failed, I had done my very best." And that is why he continues to take such a special pleasure in his work, and in the existence of George, and in himself.

Autobiographical poetry, "emotion recollected in tranquillity," too frequently confesses that no poem can recapture the experience it would commemorate. Only the Byronic have believed that that initial experience is nothing to the thrill which comes in turning deeds and emotions into words and in shaping the intensity of life upon paper. Ira's aesthetic pays no regard to either of those attitudes. For him, the original experience may not independently exist or be perceived; art to him is not reportage but invention. The moments given to invention are in themselves agonizing. But when he has produced a work, then life begins. (Remember the show he titled *Life Begins at 8:40.*) A good song can be heard with pleasure, ever and forever, never giving to anyone more than it always gives to its creator. When George died, Ira was inconsolable for days; and then he found himself putting upon the phonograph the *Shall We Dance* records where Fred Astaire sings to Johnny Green's orchestrations. And suddenly it was as though George were there; and Ira knew that he could go on, as long as he could hear the Gershwin sound. That is what is meant by *Gershwin*—melodic dreams and lyrical schemes so interfused that they are life. The personal charm of the brothers, the whimsicalities of temperament, these are

Ira in his music room in Beverly Hills attending to matters Gershwin.
PHOTO BY L. D. STEWART

diversions; what is important is upon paper and upon the air. And that is why—especially for us who are not Gershwins—an evening with Gershwin is a Gershwin evening and the willing aesthetic loss of our own identity.

When the first edition of this book was published, George Pallay, one of George's old friends who had been in California in 1937, wrote Ira that his records listed "I Love to Rhyme" as the last completed Gershwin song—not, as we had written, "Love Is Here to Stay." If by "completed," both verse and refrain are meant, then Mr. Pallay's records are correct. It is the *refrain* of "Love Is Here to Stay" that was the last work that George and Ira had completed together; and for Ira it was always to be George's last song. Especially he remembered telling George to put in the *and* notes, for they were to be the song's trick: "The radio *and* the telephone/*And* the movies that we know/May just be passing fancies—/*And* in time may go." (Italics added.)

In 1938, in a broadcast on the French radio, Vernon Duke revealed that it had been he who had supplied the music for the verses of some of George's *Goldwyn Follies* songs, including "Love Is Here to Stay." Duke emphasized that his contribution was unacknowledged. Ira was mystified: Duke's *Goldwyn Follies* contract and the records at ASCAP clearly stipulated payment. It was indeed true that there was no credit to Duke printed on the sheet music's verse music. But Ira was startled that Duke would want other than financial credit for so small a thing. And besides, as Ira would say, you can tell who really wrote the music: it was Ira himself who sang that particular verse to Duke and had him take it down. You can tell, said Ira, for the music is not very distinctive.

In later years Ira could not comprehend why he had titled the song "Love Is Here to Stay." He insists that in his mind it has always been "Our Love Is Here to Stay." And when, over twenty years later, he printed its words in *Lyrics on Several Occasions*, he wanted to make the correction but felt he couldn't. He was still believing that he had no right to touch a standard. A few years afterward, however, when he put the song itself in *The George and Ira Gershwin Song Book*, he finally did what he had always wanted to do; and he began with that warming pronoun.

The song marked for him the great dividing moment of his creative life. The refrain had been their last work together; and when he returned to California after George's funeral in New York, that verse was among the first matters attended to. For those aware of these circumstances, that verse to "Our Love Is Here to Stay" has always seemed the poignant summation of Ira's abiding feeling for George. Despite the loss of George's physical radiance, there could be no termination to their Gershwin years:

> The more I read the papers,
>   The less I comprehend
> The world and all its capers
>   And how it all will end.
> Nothing seems to be lasting,
>   But that isn't our affair;
> We've got something permanent—
>   I mean, in the way we care.

APPENDIX

THE WORKS OF
GEORGE AND IRA GERSHWIN

The following lists all the published works (indicated by *) of George and Ira Gershwin, as well as individual songs that were copyrighted but not published; it also mentions some of the musical-comedy numbers that were tried out on the road but did not survive the trip to New York. An asterisk before a show title indicates full score is published. For simplification, all of the songs that Ira wrote with his brother are listed under George's name; from 1920 through 1923, Ira published his lyrics under the pseudonym of Arthur Francis.

THE WORKS OF GEORGE GERSHWIN

1916

*When You Want 'Em, You Can't Get 'Em; When You've Got 'Em, You Don't Want 'Em (Lyric, Murray Roth)

THE PASSING SHOW OF 1916. Winter Garden Theatre, June 22, 1916.

*Making of a Girl (Lyric, Harold Atteridge; music, Sigmund Romberg and George Gershwin)

NOT USED: My Runaway Girl (Lyric, Murray Roth)

When the Armies Disband (Lyric, Irving Caesar)

Great Little Tune (Lyric, Irving Caesar)

1917

*Rialto Ripples (piano rag solo; music, George Gershwin and Will Donaldson)

We're Six Little Nieces of Our Uncle Sam (Lyric, Lou Paley)

1918

HITCHY-KOO OF 1918. Globe Theatre, June 6, 1918.

*You-oo Just You (Lyric, Irving Caesar)

LADIES FIRST. Broadhurst Theatre, October 24 ,1918.

*The Real American Folk Song (Lyric, Ira Gershwin)
*Some Wonderful Sort of Someone (Lyric, Schuyler Greene)

HALF PAST EIGHT. Empire Theatre, Syracuse, New York, December 9, 1918.

There's Magic in the Air (Lyric, Ira Gershwin)
Hong Kong
Ten Commandments of Love
Cupid

1919

GOOD MORNING, JUDGE. Shubert Theatre, February 6, 1919.

*I Was So Young (You Were so Beautiful) (Lyric, I. Caesar and Al Bryan)
*There's More to the Kiss than the X-X-X (Lyric, I. Caesar)

*O Land of Mine, America (Lyric, Michael E. O'Rourke) [Published in N.Y. *American*, Sunday, March 2, 1919]

THE LADY IN RED. Lyric Theatre, May 12, 1919.

*Something About Love (Lyric, Lou Paley)
*Some Wonderful Sort of Someone (Lyric, Schuyler Greene) revised edition

LA-LA-LUCILLE! Lyrics by Arthur J. Jackson and B. G. DeSylva; book by Fred Jackson; produced by Alex A. Aarons. At the Henry Miller Theatre, May 26, 1919. Cast: Janet Velie, John E. Hazzard, J. Clarence Harvey, and Helen Clark.

When You Live in a Furnished Flat
*The Best of Everything

*From Now On
It's Hard to Tell
*Tee-Oodle-Um-Bum-Bo
*Nobody but You
It's Great to Be in Love
*There's More to the Kiss than the Sound (Lyric, I. Caesar)
*Somehow It Seldom Comes True
The Ten Commandments of Love

NOT USED: *The Love of a Wife, Our Little Kitchenette. Money, Money, Money!, Kisses

DERE MABLE. Closed out-of-town.

*We're Pals (Lyric, I. Caesar)

Back Home (Lyric, Arthur Francis)

CAPITOL REVUE. Capitol Theatre, October 24, 1919.

*Swanee (Lyric, I. Caesar)
*Come to the Moon (Lyric, Ned Wayburn and Lou Paley)

MORRIS GEST MIDNIGHT WHIRL. Lyrics by B. G. DeSylva and John Henry Mears; revue produced by Morris Gest. At the Century Grove, December 27, 1919. Cast: Helen Shipman, Bessie McCoy Davis, Bernard Granville, and the Rath Brothers.

The League of Nations
Doughnuts
*Poppyland
*Limehouse Nights
Let Cutie Cut Your Cuticle
Baby Dolls

*LULLABY, for string quartet

1920

*Yan-Kee (Lyric, Irving Caesar)

ED WYNN'S CARNIVAL. New Amsterdam Theatre, April 5, 1920.

*Oo, How I Love to Be Loved by You (Lyric, Lou Paley)

GEORGE WHITE'S SCANDALS OF 1920. Lyrics by Arthur Jackson; book by Andy Rice and George White; produced by George White. At the Globe Theatre, June 7, 1920. Cast: Ann Pennington, Lou Holtz, George "Doc" Rockwell, Ethel Delmar, Lester Allen, George White, and the Yerkes Happy Six.

*My Lady
Everybody Swat the Profiteer
*On My Mind the Whole Night Long
*Tum On and Tiss Me
*Scandal Walk
*The Songs of Long Ago
*Idle Dreams

NOT USED: My Old Love Is My New Love

THE SWEETHEART SHOP. Knickerbocker Theatre, August 31, 1920.

*Waiting for the Sun to Come Out (Lyric, Arthur Francis)

BROADWAY BREVITIES OF 1920. Winter Garden, September 29, 1920.

*Spanish Love (Lyric, I. Caesar)
*Lu Lu (Lyric, Arthur Jackson)
*Snow Flakes (Lyric, Arthur Jackson)

PICCADILLY TO BROADWAY, an international revue by Glen MacDonough and E. Ray Goetz with additional music by William M. Daly, George Gershwin. With Johnny Dooley, Clifton Webb, Helen Broderick, and Anna Wheaton. [Toured: Detroit, St. Paul, etc., but probably closed while touring]

On the Brim of Her Old Fashioned Bonnet (Lyric, E. Ray Goetz)
The Baby Blues (Lyric, E. Ray Goetz)

BLUE EYES. Sam S. Shubert Theatre, February 1921

Wanting You (Lyric, Irving Caesar)

A DANGEROUS MAID. Lyrics by Arthur Francis; book by Charles W. Bell; produced by Edgar MacGregor. Opened in Atlantic City, March 21, 1921; closed in Pittsburgh, May 1921. Cast: Vivienne Segal, Amelia Bingham, Johnnie Arthur, Vinton Freedley, Juanita Fletcher, Creighton Hale.

*Just to Know You Are Mine
*Boy Wanted
*The Simple Life
*Dancing Shoes
*Some Rain Must Fall

NOT USED: Anything for You. The Sirens

SELWYN'S SNAPSHOTS OF 1921. Selwyn Theatre, June 1921. "A Travesty Revue in Two Acts," with Nora Bayes, Lew Fields, and DeWolf Hopper. (Both "On the Brim of Her Old Fashioned Bonnet" "Baby Blues" were borrowed from *Piccadilly to Broadway*). There was an additional Gershwin song.

Futuristic Melody (Lyric, E. Ray Goetz)

GEORGE WHITE'S SCANDALS OF 1921. Lyrics by Arthur Jackson; book by Arthur "Bugs" Baer and George White; produced by George White. At the Liberty Theatre, July 11, 1921. Cast: George White, Ann Pennington, Theresa "Aunt Jemima" Gardella, Olive Vaughan, Lester Allen, Bert Gordon.

OPENING: Mother Eve
*I Love You
*South Sea Isles
*Drifting Along with the Tide
*She's Just a Baby
*Where East Meets West

THE PERFECT FOOL. George M. Cohan Theatre, November 7, 1921.

*My Log-Cabin Home (Lyric, Irving Caesar and B. G. DeSylva)
*No One Else but That Girl of Mine (Lyric, Irving Caesar)

*Tomale (I'm Hot for You) (Lyric, B. G. DeSylva)
*Swanee Rose (Lyric, Irving Caesar and B. G. DeSylva) [Originally published as "Dixie Rose"]
*In the Heart of a Geisha (Lyric, Fred Fisher)

1922

THE FRENCH DOLL. Lyceum Theatre, February 20, 1922.

*Do It Again! (Lyric, B. G. DeSylva)

FOR GOODNESS SAKE. Lyric Theatre, February 20, 1922.

All to Myself (Lyric, Arthur Francis)
*Someone (Lyric, Arthur Francis)
*Tra-La-La (Lyric, Arthur Francis)

GEORGE WHITE'S SCANDALS OF 1922. Lyrics by B. G. DeSylva and E. Ray Goetz; book by George White and W. C. Fields; produced by George White. At the Globe Theatre, August 28, 1922. Cast: Winnie Lightner, Jack McGowan, George White, W. C. Fields, Lester Allen, Paul Whiteman's Orchestra.

Just a Tiny Cup of Tea
*Oh, What She Hangs Out (Lyric, B. G. DeSylva)
*Cinderelatives (Lyric, B. G. DeSylva)
*I Found a Four Leaf Clover (Lyric, B. G. DeSylva)
I Can't Tell Where They're from When They Dance
*I'll Build a Stairway to Paradise (Lyric, B. G. DeSylva and Arthur Francis)
*Across the Sea
*Argentina (Lyric, B. G. DeSylva)

*Where Is the Man of My Dreams
*Selection

BLUE MONDAY (Opera Ala Afro-American) (withdrawn after opening night). Original orchestration by Will H. Vodery. Reorchestrated by Ferde Grofé as *135th Street*, premiered December 29, 1925, at Carnegie Hall by Paul Whiteman and his Orchestra. Cast: Blossom Seeley, Jack McGowan, Charles Hart, Benny Fields, Francis Howard, and Austin Young.

OUR NELL. Music by George Gershwin and William Daly; lyrics by Brian Hooker; book by A. E. Thomas and Brian Hooker; produced by Hayseed Productions (Ed. Davidow and Rufus Le Maire). At the Bayes Theatre, December 4, 1922. Cast: Mr. and Mrs. Jimmie Barry, Emma Haig, Olin Howland, John Merkyl.

Gol-Durn!
*Innocent Ingenue Baby
The Cooney County Fair (Music, George Gershwin)
Names I Love to Hear
*By and By (Music, George Gershwin)
Madrigal
We Go to Church on Sunday (Music, George Gershwin)
*Walking Home with Angeline (Music, George Gershwin)
Oh, You Lady!
Little Villages
NOT USED: The Custody of the Child

*The Yankee Doodle Blues (Lyric, Irving Caesar and B. G. DeSylva)
The Flapper (Lyric, B. G. DeSylva)

1923

THE DANCING GIRL. Winter Garden, January 24, 1923.

*That American Boy of Mine (Lyric, Irving Caesar)

THE RAINBOW. Lyrics by Clifford Grey; revue by Albert de Courville, Edgar Wallace, and Noel Scott; produced by Albert de Courville. At the Empire Theatre, London, April 3, 1923. Cast: Grace Hayes, Stephanie Stephens, Earl Rickard, Ernest Thesiger, Jack Edge.

*Sweetheart (I'm So Glad That I Met You)
*Good-Night, My Dear
 Any Little Tune
*Moonlight in Versailles
*In the Rain
*Innocent Lonesome Blue Baby (Lyric, Brian Hooker and Clifford Grey; music, George Gershwin and William Daly)
*Beneath the Eastern Moon
*Oh! Nina
*Strut Lady with Me
*Sunday in London Town

GEORGE WHITE'S SCANDALS OF 1923. Lyrics by B. G. DeSylva, E. Ray Goetz, and Ballard MacDonald; book by George White and William K. Wells; produced by George White. At the Globe Theatre, June 18, 1923. Cast: Winnie Lightner, Tom Patricola, Lester Allen, Richard Bold, Beulah Berson, and the Tip Top Four.

 Little Scandal Dolls
*You and I
 Katinka
*Lo-La-Lo (Lyric, B. G. DeSylvâ)
*There Is Nothing Too Good for You (Lyric, B. G. DeSylva and E. Ray Goetz)
*Throw Her in High! (Lyric, B. G. DeSylva and E. Ray Goetz)
*Let's Be Lonesome Together (Lyric, B. G. DeSylva and E. Ray Goetz)
*The Life of a Rose (Lyric, B. G. DeSylva)
 Look in the Looking Glass
*Where Is She? (Lyric, B. G. DeSylva)
 Laugh Your Cares Away
*(On the Beach at) How've-You-Been (Lyric, B. G. DeSylva)
*Selection

LITTLE MISS BLUEBEARD. Lyceum Theatre, August 28, 1923.

*I Won't Say I Will but I Won't Say I Won't (Lyric, B. G. DeSylva and Arthur Francis)

NIFTIES OF 1923. Fulton Theatre, September 25, 1923.

*At Half Past Seven (Lyric, B. G. DeSylva)
*Nashville Nightingale (Lyric, Irving Caesar)

THE SUNSHINE TRAIL (film). Thomas H. Ince Production.

*The Sunshine Trail (Lyric, Arthur Francis)

1924

SWEET LITTLE DEVIL. Lyrics by B. G. DeSylva; book by Frank Mandel and Laurence Schwab; produced by Laurence Schwab. At the Astor Theatre, January 21, 1924. Cast: Constance Binney, Marjorie Gateson, Irving Beebe, Franklyn Ardell, Ruth Warren, and William Wayne.

 Strike, Strike, Strike
*Virginia
*Someone Believes in You
*The Jijibo
 OPENING: Quite a Party
*Under a One-Man Top
 The Matrimonial Handicap
 Just Supposing
*Hey! Hey! Let 'Er Go!
 Hooray for the U.S.A.
*Mah-Jongg
*Pepita
*Selection

NOT USED: You're Mighty Lucky, My Little Ducky. Sweet Little Devil. Be the Life of the Crowd

*RHAPSODY IN BLUE, for Jazz Band and Piano. (Orchestrated by Ferde Grofé.) Premiere: Aeolian Hall, February 12, 1924,

"An Experiment in Modern Music." Paul Whiteman and his Palais Royal Orchestra; George Gershwin, piano.

GEORGE WHITE'S SCANDALS OF 1924. Lyrics by B. G. DeSylva; book by William K. Wells and George White; produced by George White. At the Apollo Theatre, June 30, 1924. Cast: Winnie Lightner, Tom Patricola, the Elm City Four, the Williams sisters, Lester Allen, Richard Bold, Will Mahoney, and Helen Hudson.

Just Missed the Opening Chorus
*I Need a Garden
*Night Time in Araby
I'm Going Back
*Year after Year
*Somebody Loves Me (Lyric, B. G. De-Sylva and Ballard MacDonald)
*Tune In (to Station J.O.Y.)
*Mah-Jongg
Lovers of Art
*Rose of Madrid
I Love You, My Darling
*Kongo Kate

*PRIMROSE. Lyrics by Desmond Carter and Ira Gershwin; book by George Grossmith and Guy Bolton; produced by George Grossmith and J. A. E. Malone. At the Winter Garden Theatre, London, September 11, 1924. Cast: Margery Hicklin, Ernest Graham, Leslie Henson, Vera Lennox, Heather Thatcher, and Percy Heming.

Opening Chorus: Leaving Town While We May (Lyric, Desmond Carter)
Till I Meet Someone Like You (Lyric, Desmond Carter)
*Isn't It Wonderful (Lyric, Ira Gershwin and Desmond Carter)
*This Is the Life for a Man (Lyric, Desmond Carter)
When Toby Is out of Town (Lyric, Desmond Carter)
*Some Far-Away Someone (Lyric, Ira Gershwin and B. G. DeSylva) [same melody as "At Half Past Seven" from *Nifties of 1923*]
The Mophams (Lyric, Desmond Carter)
FINALE: Can We Do Anything? (Lyric, Ira Gershwin and Desmond Carter).
OPENING: Roses of France (Lyric, Desmond Carter)

Four Little Sirens (Lyric, Ira Gershwin)
Berkeley Square and Kew (Lyric, Desmond Carter)
*Boy Wanted (Lyric, Ira Gershwin and Desmond Carter)
*Wait a Bit, Susie (Lyric, Ira Gershwin and Desmond Carter)
Isn't It Terrible What They Did to Mary Queen of Scots (Lyric, Desmond Carter)
*Naughty Baby (Lyric, Ira Gershwin and Desmond Carter)
FINALE: It Is the Fourteenth of July (Lyric, Desmond Carter)
Ballet
I Make Hay When the Moon Shines (Lyric, Desmond Carter)
*That New-Fangled Mother of Mine (Lyric, Desmond Carter)
Beau Brummel (Lyric, Desmond Carter)

LADY, BE GOOD. Lyrics by Ira Gershwin; book by Guy Bolton and Fred Thompson; produced by Alex A. Aarons and Vinton Freedley at the Liberty Theatre, December 1, 1924. Cast: Fred and Adele Astaire, Walter Catlett, Cliff Edwards, Gerald Oliver Smith, Patricia Clarke, Alan Edwards, Phil Ohman and Victor Arden, duo-pianos.

OPENING: Seeing Dickie Home
*Hang on to Me
A Wonderful Party
The End of a String
We're Here Because
*Fascinating Rhythm
*So Am I
*Oh, Lady Be Good!
OPENING: The Robinson Hotel
*"The Half of It, Dearie, Blues"
Juanita
*Little Jazz Bird
Swiss Miss (Lyric, Arthur Jackson and Ira Gershwin)

NOT USED: *The Man I Love. Will You Remember Me?. Singin' Pete. Evening Star. The Bad, Bad Men. OPENING: Weather Man OPENING: Rainy Afternoon Girls. Laddie Daddy

USED IN LONDON PRODUCTION, 1926: *Something About Love (Lyric, Lou Paley). *I'd Rather Charleston (Lyric, Desmond Carter). OPENING: Buy a Little Button from Us (Lyric, Desmond Carter)

*SHORT STORY, for violin and piano (arranged by Samuel Dushkin). Originally called "Novelettes" and played by Samuel Dushkin, February 8, 1925, in a recital at the University Club, New York City.

TELL ME MORE. Lyrics by B. G. DeSylva and Ira Gershwin; book by Fred Thompson and William K. Wells; produced by Alex A. Aarons. At the Gaiety Theatre, April 13, 1925. Cast: Alexander Gray, Emma Haig, Phyllis Cleveland, Lou Holtz.

*Tell Me More!
Mr. and Mrs. Sipkin
When the Debbies Go By
*Three Times a Day
*Why Do I Love You?
How Can I Win You Now?
*Kickin' the Clouds Away
Love Is in the Air
*My Fair Lady
In Sardinia
*Baby!
The Poetry of Motion
Ukulele Lorelei

NOT USED: Shop Girls and Mannikins. Once. I'm Somethin' on Avenue A. The He-Man

USED IN LONDON PRODUCTION: *Murderous Monty (and Light-Fingered Jane) (Lyric, Desmond Carter). Love, I Never Knew (Lyric, Desmond Carter)

*CONCERTO IN F, for piano and orchestra. Premiere: Carnegie Hall, December 3, 1925. Walter Damrosch conducting the New York Symphony Society; George Gershwin, piano.

TIP-TOES. Lyrics by Ira Gershwin; book by Guy Bolton and Fred Thompson; produced by Alex A. Aarons and Vinton Freedley. At the Liberty Theatre, December 28, 1925. Cast: Queenie Smith, Allen Kearns, Harry Watson, Jr., Andrew Tombes, Jeanette MacDonald, Lovey Lee, Amy Revere, and Robert Halliday, with Ohman and Arden at the pianos.

Waiting for the Train
*Nice Baby! (Come to Papa!)
*Looking for a Boy
Lady Luck
*When Do We Dance?
*These Charming People
*That Certain Feeling
*Sweet and Low-Down
Our Little Captain
Harbor of Dreams
*Nightie-Night
Tip-Toes

NOT USED: *Harlem River Chanty. Gather Ye Rosebuds. Dancing Hour. Life's Too Short to Be Blue. We. *It's a Great Little World!

SONG OF THE FLAME. Music by George Gershwin and Herbert Stothart; lyrics and book by Otto Harbach and Oscar Hammerstein II; produced by Arthur Hammerstein. At the Forty-Fourth Street Theatre, December 30, 1925. Cast: Tessa Kosta, Greek Evans, Dorothy Mackaye, Hugh Cameron, Guy Robertson, the Russian Art Choir.

*Midnight Bells (Music, George Gershwin)
Far Away
*Song of the Flame
Women's Work Is Never Done
*The Signal (Music: George Gershwin)
*Cossack Love Song (Don't Forget Me)
Tar-Tar
*You Are You
*Vodka

1926

AMERICANA. Belmont Theatre, July 26, 1926.

*That Lost Barber Shop Chord (Lyric, Ira Gershwin)

OH, KAY! Lyrics by Ira Gershwin; book by Guy Bolton and P. G. Wodehouse; produced by Alex A. Aarons and Vinton Freedley. At the Imperial Theatre, November 8, 1926. Cast: Gertrude Lawrence, Oscar Shaw, Victor Moore, the Fairbanks twins.

The Woman's Touch
Don't Ask!
*Dear Little Girl (I Hope You've Missed Me)
*Maybe
*Clap Yo' Hands
 OPENING: Bride and Groom
*Do-Do-Do
*Someone to Watch over Me
*Fidgety Feet
*Heaven on Earth (Lyric, Ira Gershwin and Howard Dietz)
*Oh, Kay (Lyric, Ira Gershwin and H. Dietz)

NOT USED: *Show Me the Town. What's the Use?. When Our Ship Comes Sailing In. OPENING: The Moon Is on the Sea. The Sun Is on the Sea. Stepping with Baby. Guess Who (to tune of "Don't Ask!"). Ain't It Romantic. Bring on the Ding Dong Dell.

*PRELUDES FOR PIANO. Five preludes were premiered by George Gershwin at the Hotel Roosevelt, December 4, 1926; on January 16, 1927 at Symphony Hall, Boston, he played six preludes—both times in concerts given with Mme. Marguerite D'Alvarez. Three preludes were published: I. *Allegro ben ritmato e deciso;* II. *Andante con moto e poco rubato;* III. *Allegro ben ritmato e deciso.* Two other preludes were the basis of Dushkin's transcription, *Short Story.* A sixth prelude remains in manuscript.

1927

STRIKE UP THE BAND. Lyrics by Ira Gershwin; book by George S. Kaufman; produced by Edgar Selwyn. At the Shubert Theatre, Philadelphia, September 5, 1927. Cast: Herbert Corthell, Vivian Hart, Roger Pryor, Edna May Oliver, Lew Hearn, Jimmie Savo, Morton Downey.

Fletcher's American Cheese Choral Society
*Seventeen and Twenty-One
Typical Self-Made American
Meadow Serenade
The Unofficial Spokesman
Patriotic Rally
*The Man I Love
*Yankee Doodle Rhythm
*Strike Up the Band!
 O, This Is Such a Lovely War
 Hoping That Someday You'll Care
*Military Dancing Drill
 How About a Man Like Me
 Homeward Bound
 The Girl I Love
 The War That Ended War

FUNNY FACE. Lyrics by Ira Gershwin; book by Fred Thompson and Paul Gerard Smith; produced by Alex A. Aarons and Vinton Freedley. At the Alvin Theatre, November 22, 1927. Cast: Fred and Adele Astaire, Allen Kearns, Victor Moore, William Kent, and Betty Compton. Ohman and Arden at the pianos.

OPENING: We're All A-Worry, All Agog
When You're Single
Those Eyes
Birthday Party
*High Hat
*Let's Kiss and Make Up
*Funny Face
*'S Wonderful
*The World Is Mine
 FINALE: Come Along, Let's Gamble
 OPENING: If You Will Take Our Tip
*He Loves and She Loves
 The Finest of the Finest
*My One and Only (What Am I Gonna Do)
 Tell the Doc
 Sing a Little Song
 In the Swim
*The Babbitt and the Bromide
*Dance Alone with You

NOT USED: *How Long Has This Been Going On? Once. Acrobats. Aviator. When You Smile. Dancing Hour. Blue Hullabaloo.

1928

ROSALIE. Lyrics by P. G. Wodehouse and Ira Gershwin; book by William Anthony McGuire and Guy Bolton; produced by Florenz Ziegfeld. At the New Amsterdam Theatre, January 10, 1928. Cast: Marilyn Miller, Jack Donahue, Gladys Glad, Frank Morgan, and Bobbe Arnst. Sigmund Romberg collaborated on the score; the following songs are by George Gershwin alone:

Show Me the Town (Lyric, Ira Gershwin)
*Say So!
Let Me Be a Friend to You (Lyric, Ira Gershwin)
*Oh Gee!-Oh Joy!
New York Serenade (Lyric, Ira Gershwin)
*How Long Has This Been Going On? (Lyric, Ira Gershwin)
*Ev'rybody Knows I Love Somebody (Lyric, Ira Gershwin; same tune as "Dance Alone with You" in *Funny Face*)

NOT USED: *Rosalie (Lyric, Ira Gershwin). *Beautiful Gypsy (Lyric, Ira Gershwin; same melody as "Wait a Bit, Susie" in *Primrose*, 1924). *Yankee Doodle Rhythm (Lyric, Ira Gershwin). When Cadets Parade (Lyric, Ira Gershwin). Follow the Drum (Lyric, Ira Gershwin). I Forget What I Started to Say (Lyric, Ira Gershwin). You Know How It Is. The Man I Love (Lyric, Ira Gershwin)

TREASURE GIRL. Lyrics by Ira Gershwin; book by Fred Thompson and Vincent Lawrence; produced by Alex A. Aarons and Vinton Freedley. At the Alvin Theatre, November 8, 1928. Cast: Gertrude Lawrence, Clifton Webb, Mary Hay, Walter Catlett, Paul Frawley, and Ferris Hartman.

Skull and Bones
*I've Got a Crush on You
*Oh, So Nice
According to Mr. Grimes
Place in the Country
*K-ra-zy for You
*I Don't Think I'll Fall in Love Today
*Got a Rainbow

*Feeling I'm Falling
*What Are We Here For?
*Where's the Boy? Here's the Girl!

NOT USED: OPENING: This Particular Party. What Causes That?. Treasure Island. Goodbye to the Old Love, Hello to the New. A-Hunting We Will Go. Dead Men Tell No Tales. I Want to Marry a Marionette

*AN AMERICAN IN PARIS, an orchestral tone poem. Premiere: Carnegie Hall, December 13, 1928. Walter Damrosch conducting the New York Symphony Society orchestra.

1929

SHOW GIRL. Lyrics by Gus Kahn and Ira Gershwin; book by William Anthony McGuire and J. P. McEvoy; produced by Florenz Ziegfeld. At the Ziegfeld Theatre, July 2, 1929. Cast: Ruby Keeler Jolson, Eddie Foy, Jr., Frank McHugh, Jimmy Durante, Lou Clayton, Eddie Jackson, Barbara Newberry, and Harriet Hoctor.

Happy Birthday
My Sunday Fella
FINALETTO: How Could I Forget
Lolita
*Do What You Do!
One Man
*So Are You!
*I Must Be Home by Twelve O'Clock
Black and White
*Harlem Serenade
An American in Paris Blues Ballet
Home Blues
Follow the Minstrel Band
*Liza (All the Clouds'll Roll Away)

NOT USED: *Feeling Sentimental. At Mrs. Simpkin's Finishing School. Adored One. Tonight's the Night! I Just Looked at You. I'm Just a Bundle of Sunshine. Minstrel Show. Somebody Stole My Heart Away. Someone's Always Calling a Rehearsal. I'm Out for No Good Reason To-night. Home Lovin' Gal. Home Lovin' Man

*In the Mandarin's Orchid Garden (Lyric,
Ira Gershwin)

1930

*STRIKE UP THE BAND. Lyrics by
Ira Gershwin; book by Morrie Ryskind,
based on a libretto by George S. Kaufman; produced by Edgar Selwyn. At the
Times Square Theatre, January 14, 1930.
Cast: Bobby Clark, Paul McCullough,
Blanche Ring, Dudley Clements, Gordon
Smith, Kathryn Hamill, Helen Gilligan,
Doris Carson, and Jerry Goff.

Fletcher's American Chocolate Choral Society Workers
*I Mean to Say
*Soon
A Typical Self-Made American
A Man of High Degree
The Unofficial Spokesman
Three Cheers for the Union!
This Could Go on for Years
If I Became the President
*Hangin' Around with You
FINALETTO: He Knows Milk
*Strike Up the Band!
OPENING: In the Rattle of the Battle
Military Dancing Drill
*Mademoiselle in New Rochelle
*I've Got a Crush on You
How About a Boy Like Me?
*I Want to Be a War Bride
Unofficial March of General Holmes
OFFICIAL RESUME: First There Was Fletcher
Ring a Ding a Ding Dong Bell

*GIRL CRAZY. Lyrics by Ira Gershwin;
book by Guy Bolton and John McGowan;
produced by Alex A. Aarons and Vinton
Freedley. At the Alvin Theatre, October
14, 1930. Cast: Ginger Rogers, Allen
Kearns, William Kent, Willie Howard,
Ethel Merman, and the Red Nichols Band.

The Lonesome Cowboy
*Bidin' My Time
*Could You Use Me?
Broncho Busters
Barbary Coast
*Embraceable You

FINALETTO: Goldfarb! That's I'm!
*Sam and Delilah
*I Got Rhythm
OPENING: Land of the Gay Caballero
*But Not for Me
*Treat Me Rough
*Boy! What Love Has Done to Me!
When It's Cactus Time in Arizona

NOT USED: The Gambler of the West. And
I Have You. Something Peculiar (Lyric,
Lou Paley). You Can't Unscramble Scrambled Eggs

WRITTEN FOR THE 1932 FILM VERSION:
*You've Got What Gets Me

1931

DELICIOUS. Lyrics by Ira Gershwin;
screenplay by Guy Bolton and Sonya
Levien; produced by Winnie Sheehan; released by Fox Film Corporation, December 3, 1931. Cast: Janet Gaynor, Charles
Farrell, Mischa Auer, and El Brendel.

*Blah-Blah-Blah
*Delishious
*Somebody from Somewhere
*Katinkitschka
You Started It

DREAM SEQUENCE: "We're from the *Journal*,
the *Warheit*, the *Telegram*, the *Times*; We
specialize in interviews and crimes."
Manhattan Rhapsody
NOT USED: Thanks to You. *Mischa, Yascha, Toscha, Sascha

*OF THEE I SING. Lyrics by Ira Gershwin; book by George S. Kaufman and
Morrie Ryskind; produced by Sam H.
Harris. At the Music Box, December 26,
1931. Cast: William Gaxton, Victor Moore,
Lois Moran, George Murphy, Grace
Brinkley, Florenz Ames, Dudley Clements,
Ralph Riggs, and June O'Dea.

*Wintergreen for President
Who Is the Lucky Girl to Be?
The Dimple on My Knee
*Because, Because

348

FINALETTO: Never Was There a Girl So
    Fair
Some Girls Can Bake a Pie
*Love Is Sweeping the Country
*Of Thee I Sing
Here's a Kiss for Cinderella
I Was the Most Beautiful Blossom
OPENING: Hello, Good Morning
*Who Cares? (So Long as You Care for
    Me)
Garçon, S'il Vous Plait
*The Illegitimate Daughter
The Senatorial Roll Call
Jilted
I'm About to Be a Mother (Who Could
    Ask for Anything More?)
Posterity Is Just Around the Corner
Trumpeter, Blow Your Golden Horn
FINALE ULTIMO: On That Matter No One
    Budges

NOT USED: Call Me Whate'er You Will

1932

*SECOND RHAPSODY, for orchestra
with piano ("Finished May 23, 1931").
Premiere: Symphony Hall, Boston, January
29, 1932. Serge Koussevitzky conducting
the Boston Symphony Orchestra;
George Gershwin, piano.

*CUBAN OVERTURE (*Rumba*), for orchestra.
Premiere: Lewisohn Stadium, August
16, 1932. Albert Coates conducting
the New York Philharmonic-Symphony
orchestra.

*PIANO TRANSCRIPTIONS OF
EIGHTEEN SONGS. Published in
George Gershwin's Songbook (New
York: Simon and Schuster, September,
1932); illustrated by Alajálov. A limited
edition of three hundred copies was issued
by Random House in May 1932, each volume
being signed by George Gershwin
and Alajálov and containing a slipped-in
copy of "Mischa, Yascha, Toscha, Sascha,"
which had not been previously published.
(Because the song had been written in the

early 1920s, however, the lyric is signed:
"Arthur Francis.") The songs, which were
printed both in their original sheet-music
arrangements and with George Gershwin's
new transcriptions, are: "Swanee," "Nobody
But You," "I'll Build a Stairway to
Paradise," "Do It Again," "Fascinating
Rhythm," "Oh, Lady Be Good," "Somebody
Loves Me," "Sweet and Low Down,"
"That Certain Feeling," "The Man I Love,"
"Clap Yo' Hands," "Do Do Do," "My One
and Only," " 'S Wonderful," "Strike Up
the Band," "Liza," "I Got Rhythm," and
"Who Cares?"

1933

PARDON MY ENGLISH. Lyrics by Ira
Gershwin; book by Herbert Fields; produced
by Alex A. Aarons and Vinton
Freedley. At the Majestic Theatre, January
20, 1933. Cast: Lyda Roberti, Jack
Pearl, George Givot, Carl Randall, and
Barbara Newberry.

Three Quarter Time
*Lorelei
Pardon My English
Dancing in the Streets
*So What?
*Two Waltzes in C
*Isn't It a Pity?
*My Cousin in Milwaukee
Hail the Happy Couple
The Dresden Northwest Mounted
*Luckiest Man in the World
FINALE: What Sort of Wedding Is This?
Tonight
*Where You Go I Go
*I've Got to Be There
FINALE: He's Not Himself

NOT USED: Freud and Jung and Adler. Together
at Last. OPENING: Bauer's House.
Poor Michael! Poor Golo!. Fatherland,
Mother of the Band

LET 'EM EAT CAKE. Lyrics by Ira
Gershwin; book by George S. Kaufman
and Morrie Ryskind; produced by Sam H.
Harris. At the Imperial Theatre, October

21, 1933. Cast: William Gaxton, Victor
Moore, Lois Moran, and Philip Loeb.

Wintergreen for President
Tweedledee for President
*Union Square
Down with Everything That's Up (pub-
    lished as an "Interlude" in "Union
    Square")
Shirts by the Millions
Comes the Revolution
*Mine
Climb Up the Social Ladder
Cloistered from the Noisy City
What More Can a General Do?
*On and On and On
Double Dummy Drill
*Let 'Em Eat Cake
*Blue, Blue, Blue
Who's the Greatest——?
No *Comprenez*, No *Capish*, No *Versteh!*
Why Speak of Money?
No Better Way to Start a Case
Up and at 'Em! On to Vict'ry
Oyez, Oyez, Oyez
That's What He Did
I Know a Foul Ball
Throttle Throttlebottom
A Hell of a Hole
Let 'Em Eat Caviar
Hanging Throttlebottom in the Morning

NOT USED: First Lady and First Gent

*Till Then (Lyric, Ira Gershwin)

1934

*"I GOT RHYTHM" VARIATIONS,
for orchestra and piano solo. Premiere:
Symphony Hall, Boston, January 14, 1934.
Charles Previn conducting the Leo Reisman Symphonic Orchestra; George Gershwin, piano.

1935

*PORGY AND BESS. Lyrics by DuBose
Heyward and Ira Gershwin; libretto by
DuBose Heyward; produced by the
Theatre Guild. At the Alvin Theatre, Oc-
tober 10, 1935. Cast: Todd Duncan, Anne
Wiggins Brown, John W. Bubbles, War-
ren Coleman, Ruby Elzy, Abbie Mitchell,
Eddie Matthews, Georgette Harvey, J.
Rosamond Johnson, Helen Dowdy, Ray
Yeates, Ford L. Buck, the Eva Jessye
Choir.

OVERTURE

ACT I
Scene 1: Summertime; A Woman Is a
    Sometime Thing; Street Cry (Honey
    Man); They Pass by Singing; Crap
    Game Fugue (Oh Little Stars); Crown
    and Robbins' Fight
Scene 2: Gone, Gone, Gone; Overflow;
    My Man's Gone Now; Train Song
    (Leavin' fo' the Promis' Lan')

ACT II
Scene 1: It Take a Long Pull to Get
    There; I Got Plenty o' Nuttin'; Woman
    to Lady; Bess, You Is My Woman Now;
    Oh, I Can't Sit Down
Scene 2: It Ain't Necessarily So; What
    You Want with Bess?
Scene 3: Time and Time Again; Street
    Cries (Strawberry Woman, Crab Man);
    I Loves You, Porgy; Storm Music
Scene 4: Oh, de Lawd Shake de Heaven;
    A Red Headed Woman; Oh, Doctor
    Jesus

ACT III
Scene 1: Clara, Don't You Be Down-
    hearted
Scene 2: There's a Boat Dat's Leavin'
    Soon for New York
Scene 3: Oh, Where's My Bess?; I'm on
    My Way

NOT USED: ACT I, *Scene* 1: Jazzbo Brown
piano music. ACT II, *Scene* 1: Buzzard Song;
I Hates Yo' Struttin' Style; *Scene* 2: I
Ain' Got No Shame; *Scene* 4: Oh, Hevn'ly
Father (Six Prayers). ACT III, *Scene* 3: Oc-
cupational Humoresque (Good Mornin',
Brother; Sure to Go to Heaven); Lone-
some Boy

Complete score published October 1935 in limited edition of 250 copies by Random House and signed by George Gershwin, DuBose Heyward, Ira Gershwin, and Rouben Mamoulian.

1936

Doubting Thomas (Lyric, Albert Stillman)
*King of Swing (Lyric, Albert Stillman)
*Strike Up the Band for U.C.L.A. (Lyric, Ira Gershwin)

CATFISH ROW, SUITE FROM "PORGY AND BESS," for orchestra. Premiere: Academy of Music, Philadelphia, January 21, 1936. Alexander Smallens conducting the Philadelphia Orchestra.

I. Catfish Row
II. Porgy Sings
III. Fugue
IV. Hurricane
V. Good Morning, Brother

THE SHOW IS ON. Winter Garden Theatre, December 25, 1936

*By Strauss (Lyric, Ira Gershwin)

1937

SHALL WE DANCE. Lyrics by Ira Gershwin; screenplay by Allan Scott and Ernest Pagano; produced by Pandro S. Berman; released by RKO, May 7, 1937. Cast: Fred Astaire, Ginger Rogers, Edward Everett Horton, Eric Blore, Jerome Cowan, and Harriet Hoctor.

*(I've Got) Beginner's Luck
*Let's Call the Whole Thing Off
*Shall We Dance
*Slap That Bass
*They All Laughed

*They Can't Take That Away from Me
*Walking the Dog, instrument interlude [Published as Promenade]

NOT USED: *Hi-Ho!. Wake Up, Brother, and Dance

A DAMSEL IN DISTRESS. Lyrics by Ira Gershwin; screenplay by P. G. Wodehouse, Ernest Pagano, and S. K. Lauren; produced by Pandro S. Berman; released by RKO, November 19, 1937. Cast: Fred Astaire, George Burns, Gracie Allen, Joan Fontaine, Reginald Gardiner, and Ray Noble.

*A Foggy Day
*I Can't Be Bothered Now
*The Jolly Tar and the Milk Maid
*Nice Work If You Can Get It
 Put Me to the Test
 Sing of Spring
*Stiff Upper Lip
*Things Are Looking Up

NOT USED: Pay Some Attention to Me

1938

THE GOLDWYN FOLLIES. Lyrics by Ira Gershwin; screenplay by Ben Hecht; produced by Samuel Goldwyn; released by Goldwyn-UA, February 23, 1938. Cast: Adolphe Menjou, the Ritz Brothers, Zorina, Kenny Baker, Andrea Leeds, Helen Jepson, Ella Logan, Phil Baker, Bobby Clark, Jerome Cowan, Edgar Bergen and Charlie McCarthy.

*I Love to Rhyme
*I Was Doing All Right
*Love Is Here to Stay
*Love Walked In

NOT USED: *Just Another Rhumba. Exposition: idea for a ballet (By George Balanchine and Ira Gershwin)

*Dawn of a New Day (Lyric, Ira Gershwin [song of the New York World's Fair])

The Works of George and Ira Gershwin

THE SHOCKING MISS PILGRIM. Lyrics by Ira Gershwin; screenplay by George Seaton; produced by William Perlberg; released by 20th Century-Fox. Cast: Betty Grable, Dick Haymes, Anne Revere, Allyn Joslyn, and Gene Lockhart.

*Aren't You Kind of Glad We Did?
*The Back Bay Polka
*Changing My Tune
 Demon Rum
*For You, For Me, For Evermore
*One, Two, Three
 Stand Up and Fight
 Sweet Packard
 Waltzing Is Better Sitting Down
 Welcome Song

NOT USED: Tour of the Town

KISS ME, STUPID. Lyrics by Ira Gershwin; screenplay by Billy Wilder and I. A. L. Diamond; produced and directed by Billy Wilder; released through United Artists. Cast: Dean Martin, Kim Novak, Ray Walston, Felicia Farr, and Cliff Osmond.

*All the Livelong Day (and the Long, Long Night)
*I'm a Poached Egg
*Sophia

1968

"Hi-Ho!"; "facsimile edition of the song [including a copy of the published song as well as photostats of both musical and lyric mss.] . . . prepared for Friends of the Theatre & Music Collection of the Museum of the City of New York to commemorate a special exhibition: *GERSHWIN: GEORGE the Music/IRA the Words.*" 250 copies, signed by Ira Gershwin; copies 1–25 also bear George Gershwin's signature on canceled checks.

THE SONGS OF IRA GERSHWIN
(Exclusive of Those Written with His Brother George):

1920

PICCADILLY TO BROADWAY

 Who's Who with You? (Music, Vincent Youmans)
 Mr. and Mrs. (Music, Vincent Youmans)
 [Note: both these songs were later used in *Two Little Girls in Blue*]

1921

TWO LITTLE GIRLS IN BLUE. Music by Vincent Youmans and Paul Lannin; book by Fred Jackson; produced by A. L. Erlanger. At the Cohan Theater, May 3, 1921. Cast: Madeline and Marion Fairbanks, Oscar Shaw, and Fred Santley.

OPENING: We're Off on a Wonderful Trip
Wonderful U.S.A. (Music, Paul Lannin)
When I'm with the Girls (Music, Vincent Youmans)
Two Little Girls in Blue
The Silly Season
*Oh Me! Oh My! (Music, Vincent Youmans)
*You Started Something (Music, Vincent Youmans)
FINALE: We're Off to India
OPENING: Here, Steward
*Dolly (Lyric, Arthur Francis and Schuyler Greene; music, Vincent Youmans)
*Who's Who with You? (Music, Vincent Youmans)
*Just Like You (Music, Paul Lannin)
There's Something about Me They Like (Lyric, Arthur Francis and Fred Jackson; music, Vincent Youmans)
*Rice and Shoes (Lyric, Schuyler Greene and Arthur Francis; music, Vincent Youmans)
FINALE: She's Innocent
*Honeymoon (When Will You Shine for Me?) (Music, Paul Lannin)
I'm Tickled Silly

NOT USED: Summertime (Music, Paul Lannin). Happy Ending (Music, Paul Lannin). Make the Best of It. Little Bag of Tricks. Utopia (Music, Vincent Youmans). Slapstick (Music, Paul Lannin). Mr. and Mrs. (Music, Vincent Youmans)

1922

PINS AND NEEDLES. Shubert Theatre, February 1, 1922.

*The Piccadilly Walk (Lyric, Arthur Francis and Arthur Riscoe, music, Edward A. Horan)

FOR GOODNESS SAKE. Lyric Theatre, February 20, 1922.

*French Pastry Walk (Lyric, Arthur Jackson and Arthur Francis; music, William Daly and Paul Lannin) (NOT USED)

MOLLY DARLING. Liberty Theatre, September 1, 1922.

*When All Your Castles Come Tumbling Down (Music, Milton E. Schwarzwald)

FASCINATION. Metro picture, 1922.

*Fascination (Lyric, Arthur Francis and Schuyler Greene; music, Louis Silvers)

1923

GREENWICH VILLAGE FOLLIES (5th Annual Production). Winter Garden Theatre, September 20, 1923.

*Hot Hindoo (Music, Lewis Gensler)

NIFTIES OF 1923. Fulton Theatre, September 25, 1923.

*Fabric of Dreams (Lyric, B. G. DeSylva and Arthur Francis; music, Raymond Hubbell)

1924

TOP HOLE. Fulton Theatre, September 1, 1924.

*Imagine Me without My You (And You without Your Me) (Music, Lewis E. Gensler)
Cheerio! (Music, Lewis E. Gensler)

BE YOURSELF. Music by Lewis Gensler and Milton Schwarzwald; book by George S. Kaufman and Marc Connelly; produced by Wilmer and Vincent. At the Sam H. Harris Theatre, September 3, 1924. Cast: Jack Donahue and Queenie Smith.

*I Came Here (Lyric, Marc Connelly, George S. Kaufman, and Ira Gershwin; music, Lewis Gensler)

*Uh-Uh! (Lyric, Marc Connelly, George S. Kaufman, and Ira Gershwin; music, Milton Schwarzwald)

*The Wrong Thing at the Right Time (Lyric, George S. Kaufman, Marc Connelly, and Ira Gershwin; music, Milton Schwarzwald)

All of Them Was Friends of Mine (Lyric Marc Connelly and Ira Gershwin)

They Don't Make 'Em That Way Any More

THE FIREBRAND. Morosco Theatre, October 15, 1924.

*The Voice of Love (Music, Russell Bennett and Maurice Nitke)

1925

CAPTAIN JINKS. Martin Beck Theatre, September 8, 1925.

*You Must Come over Blues (Music, Lewis E. Gensler)

A NIGHT OUT. Closed out-of-town.

*I Want a Yes Man (Lyric, Clifford Grey, Irving Caesar, and Ira Gershwin; music, Vincent Youmans)

1926

AMERICANA. Belmont Theatre, July 26, 1926.

*Blowin' the Blues Away (Music, Philip Charig)

*Sunny Disposish (Music, Philip Charig)

1928

THAT'S A GOOD GIRL. Lyrics by Douglas Furber, Ira Gershwin, and Desmond Carter; music, Joseph Meyer and Philip Charig; book by Douglas Furber; produced by Jack Buchanan. At the Lewisham Hippodrome, March 19, 1928. Starred Jack Buchanan.

OPENING: What to Do?

*The One I'm Looking for (Lyric, Ira Gershwin and Douglas Furber)

*Chirp-Chirp

*Sweet So-and-So (Lyric, Ira Gershwin and Douglas Furber)

*Let Yourself Go! (Lyric, Ira Gershwin and Douglas Furber)

OPENING: Week-end

NOT USED: Before We Were Married. Day after Day. There I'd Settle Down. Why Be Good?

1930

THE GARRICK GAIETIES. Guild Theatre, June 4, 1930.

*I Am Only Human after All (Lyric, Ira Gershwin and E. Y. Harburg; music, Vernon Duke)

SWEET AND LOW. Forty-Sixth Street Theatre, November 17, 1930.

*Cheerful Little Earful (Lyric, Ira Gershwin and Billy Rose; music, Harry Warren)

*In the Merry Month of Maybe (Lyric, Ira Gershwin and Billy Rose; music, Harry Warren)

1931

THE SOCIAL REGISTER. Fulton Theatre, November 9, 1931.

*The Key to My Heart (Music, Louis Alter)

1934

LIFE BEGINS AT 8:40. Lyrics by Ira Gershwin and E. Y. Harburg; music by Harold Arlen; sketches by David Freedman; produced by the Messrs. Shubert. At the Winter Garden, August 27, 1934. Cast: Bert Lahr, Ray Bolger, Brian Donlevy, and Luella Gear.

OPENING: Life Begins
Spring Fever
*You're a Builder Upper
My Paramount-Publix-Roxy-Rose
*Shoein' the Mare
Quartet Erotica
*Fun to Be Fooled
C'est la Vie
*What Can You Say in a Love Song?
*Let's Take a Walk around the Block
Things
All the Elks and Masons
I Couldn't Hold My Man
It Was Long Ago
I'm Not Myself
Life Begins at City Hall

NOT USED: I Knew Him When. I'm a Collector of Moonbeams. Weekend Cruise (Will You Love Me Monday Morning, as You Did on Friday Night?)

1936

ZIEGFELD FOLLIES OF 1936. Music by Vernon Duke; sketches by David Freedman; produced by the Messrs. Shubert. At the Winter Garden Theatre, January 30, 1936. Cast: Fanny Brice, Josephine Baker, Gertrude Niesen, Harriet Hoctor, Eve Arden, Judy Canova, and Bob Hope.

Time Marches On!
He Hasn't a Thing except Me
*My Red-Letter Day
*Island in the West Indies
*Words without Music
The Economic Situation
Fancy, Fancy
Maharanee
*The Gazooka
*That Moment of Moments
Sentimental Weather

Five A.M.
*I Can't Get Started
Modernistic Moe (Lyric, Ira Gershwin and Billy Rose)
Dancing to Our Score

NOT USED: Please Send My Daddy Back Home. Does a Duck Love Water?. I'm Sharing My Wealth. Wishing Tree of Harlem. Why Save for That Rainy Day?. Hot Number. The Last of the Cabbies. The Ballad of Baby Face McGinty. Sunday Tan

*I Used to Be Above Love (Music, Vernon Duke)

1938

GOLDWYN FOLLIES OF 1938. Samuel Goldwyn—United Artists Production, 1938.

*Spring Again (Music, Vernon Duke)

*No Question in My Heart (Music, Jerome Kern)
*Once There Were Two of Us/Now That We Are One (Music, Jerome Kern)

1939

*Baby, You're News (Lyric, Ira Gershwin and E. Y. Harburg; music, Johnny Green)

1941

*LADY IN THE DARK. Music by Kurt Weill; play by Moss Hart; produced by Sam H. Harris. At the Alvin Theatre, January 23, 1941. Cast: Gertrude Law-

rence, Danny Kaye, Victor Mature, Macdonald Carey, and Bert Lytell.

GLAMOUR DREAM: Oh Fabulous One, Huxley, One Life to Live, Girl of the Moment
WEDDING DREAM: Mapleton High Choral, This Is New, The Princess of Pure Delight
CIRCUS DREAM: The Greatest Show on Earth, The Best Years of His Life, Tschaikowsky, The Saga of Jenny
CHILDHOOD DREAM: My Ship

NOT USED:
WEDDING DREAM: Unforgettable. It's Never Too Late to Mendelssohn.
CIRCUS DREAM: No Matter under What Star You're Born. Song of the Zodiac
CHILDHOOD DREAM: Bats about You
HOLLYWOOD DAY-DREAM: The Boss Is Bringing Home a Bride. Party Parlando. In Our Little San Fernando Valley Home

*Honorable Moon (Lyric, Ira Gershwin and E. Y. Harburg; music, Arthur Schwartz)

1943

NORTH STAR. Music by Aaron Copland; screenplay by Lillian Hellman; produced by Samuel Goldwyn; RKO release. Cast: Walter Huston, Walter Brennan, Eric von Stroheim, Anne Baxter, Jane Withers, and Farley Granger.

Can I Help It?
Loading Song (From the Baltic to the Pacific)
Loading Time at Last Is Over
*No Village Like Mine
Song of the Fatherland (Text of V. Lebedev-Kumach adapted by Ira Gershwin; music of I. Dunayevsky transcribed by Aaron Copland)
*Song of the Guerrillas
Wagon Song
*Younger Generation

NOT USED: Workers of All Nations

1944

COVER GIRL. Music by Jerome Kern; screenplay by Virginia Van Upp; produced by Arthur Schwartz; Columbia release. Cast: Rita Hayworth, Gene Kelly, Lee Bowman, and Phil Silvers.

*Cover Girl
*Long Ago And Far Away
*Make Way for Tomorrow (Lyric, Ira Gershwin and E. Y. Harburg)
*Put Me to the Test
The Show Must Go On
*Sure Thing
Who's Complaining?

1945

WHERE DO WE GO FROM HERE?. Music by Kurt Weill; screenplay by Morrie Ryskind; produced by William Perlberg; 20th Century-Fox release. Cast: Fred MacMurray, Joan Leslie, and June Haver.

Morale
*The Nina, the Pinta, the Santa Maria
*If Love Remains
*Song of the Rhineland
*All at Once
It Happened to Happen to Me

NOT USED: Woo, Woo, Woo, Woo, Manhattan

THE FIREBRAND OF FLORENCE. Music by Kurt Weill; libretto by Edwin Justus Mayer and Ira Gershwin; produced by Max Gordon. At the Alvin Theatre, March 22, 1945. Cast: Lotte Lenya, Earl Wrightson, Beverly Tyler, and Melville Cooper.

SONG OF THE HANGMAN: One Man's Death Is Another Man's Living
CIVIC SONG: Come to Florence
ARIA: My Lords and Ladies
*FAREWELL SONG: (There'll Be) Life, Love and Laughter
*LOVE SONG: You're Far Too Near Me

THE DUKE'S SONG: Alessandro the Wise
FINALETTO: I Am Happy Here
*THE DUCHESS' SONG: Sing Me Not a Ballad
MADRIGAL: When the Duchess Is Away
TRIO: I Know Where There's a Cozy Nook
NIGHT MUSIC: The Nighttime Is No Time for Thinking
TARANTELLA: Dizzily, Busily
CAVATINA: The Little Naked Boy
LETTER SONG: My Dear Benvenuto
MARCH OF THE SOLDIERS OF THE DUCHY: Just in Case
*ODE: A Rhyme for Angela
CHANT OF LAW AND ORDER: The World Is Full of Villains
TRIAL BY MUSIC: You Have to Do What You Do Do
DUET: Love Is My Enemy
CIVIC SONG: Come to Paris

NOT USED: I Had Just Been Pardoned. Master Is Free Again

1946

PARK AVENUE. Music by Arthur Schwartz; book by Nunnally Johnson and George S. Kaufman; produced by Max Gordon. At the Shubert Theatre, November 4, 1946. Cast: Byron Russell, Ray McDonald, Martha Stewart, Arthur Margetson, Leonora Corbett, Robert Chisholm, Marthe Errolle, Mary Wickes, and David Wayne.

Tomorrow Is the Time
*For the Life of Me
The Dew Was on the Rose
*Don't Be a Woman If You Can
Nevada (Western version)
*There's No Holding Me
There's Nothing Like Marriage for People
Hope for the Best
My Son-in-Law
The Land of Opportunitee
*Good-bye to All That
Stay as We Are

NOT USED: Heavenly Day. The Future Mrs. Coleman. Nevada (waltz version)

1949

THE BARKLEYS OF BROADWAY. Music by Harry Warren; screenplay by Betty Comden and Adolph Green; produced by Arthur Freed; MGM release. Cast: Fred Astaire, Ginger Rogers and Oscar Levant.

Call on Us Again
Manhattan Down Beat
*My One and Only Highland Fling
*Shoes with Wings on
Swing Trot
These Days
Weekend in the Country
*You'd Be Hard to Replace

NOT USED: The Courtin' of Elmer and Ella. Minstrels on Parade. Natchez on the Mississip'. The Poetry of Motion. Second Fiddle to a Harp. Taking No Chances on You. There Is No Music

1953

GIVE A GIRL A BREAK. Music by Burton Lane; screenplay by Albert Hackett and Frances Goodrich; produced by Jack Cummings; MGM release. Cast: Marge and Gower Champion and Debbie Reynolds:

Applause! Applause!
Give a Girl a Break
*In Our United State
*It Happens Every Time
Nothing Is Impossible

NOT USED: Ach, Du Lieber Oom-Pah-Pah. Dream World. Woman, There Is No Living with You

1954

*A STAR IS BORN. Music by Harold Arlen; screenplay by Moss Hart; produced by Sidney Luft; Transcona-Warner Brothers release. Cast: Judy Garland,

James Mason, Jack Carson, and Charles Bickford.

The Works of George and Ira Gershwin

*Gotta Have Me Go with You
*The Man That Got Away
*Here's What I'm Here for
*It's a New World
*Someone at Last
*Lose That Long Face
 The Commercial (Calypso)

NOT USED: Dancing Partner. Green Light Ahead. I'm off the Downbeat

THE COUNTRY GIRL. Music by Harold Arlen; screenplay by George Seaton; produced by William Perlberg; Paramount release. Cast: Bing Crosby, Grace Kelly, and William Holden.

 Commercial
*Dissertation on the State of Bliss (or Love and Learn)
 It's Mine, It's Yours
 The Land Around Us
*The Search Is Through

AN INFORMAL DISCOGRAPHY

E. J. in collaboration with KAY SWIFT

Recordings of the handful of the "serious" Gershwin multiply; at last count there were at least eighteen versions of the *Rhapsody in Blue*, ranging from a thumpy piano roll by the composer (a point in its favor) to a piano accompanied by the Moog (not a point in its favor).

The Gershwin collector is confronted by a myriad of dilemmas. The hope is that this discography, complete (in the sense that all works are touched on) and yet selective (only worthwhile, or unique, recordings are considered), will prove useful, especially to the young adventurer in the world of the Gershwins. One guiding premise is that no one, no matter how devoted an admirer, needs eighteen recordings of the *Rhapsody in Blue*. Our purpose was to wade through these and find those few—or that one—that approach a nearly perfect performance. The word "definitive" has been much abused in the field of Gershwin and will not be employed; what we were seeking was that performance that best caught the spirit and style of Gershwin and accomplished this with musicality.

Why not, then, review the recordings with the help of Kay Swift, a good friend of the Gershwins from about the mid-Twenties and a composer herself? She has written such concert works as the orchestral song cycle *Reaching for the Brass Ring*, *Theme and Variations for Cello and Orchestra*, and *Man Have Pity on Man*, for voices and orchestra. She has composed theater music (*Paris '90*) as well as such popular songs as "Fine and Dandy" and "Can't We Be Friends?", among others. With a solid musical background—one of her teachers was Charles Martin Loeffler (a Gershwin fan)—her knowledge of the works of Gershwin is unique. She was frequently present when he worked, served as a sounding board for newly completed pieces, and played the second piano part (substituting for the orchestra) for the tryout of new works or in the performance of older favorites—including Bach and Brahms, by the way.

359

Kay Swift's insights into the authentic performances of the larger works, as well as of the songs, is exceptional, as is her musical memory. She knows the correct tempos as well as those Gershwinesque rhythmic nuances and harmonic shadings that were so distinctly his and which are essential to a good performance of his music. This has nothing to do with "symphonic jazz" or "the American idiom," terms generally employed pejoratively by critics reviewing recordings of Gershwin by a non-American pianist. Gershwin's work has transcended the Jazz Age and dated idioms; he succeeded in vanquishing the composer's most formidable enemy: time.

Merely playing the *Rhapsody in Blue* with a jazzy zip and exaggerated emphasis on ricky-tick effects does not make it idiomatically true. Then too, there's the other approach, the solemn one—after all, it *is* "serious music"— so that the joy and delight with which GG infused his music are dissipated and the effect is ponderous and humorless.

In our record listening sessions I did not inform Kay who played what. She is not a record collector (curious: most musicians are not), nor was she familiar with the recordings; in some instances she wasn't even aware of their existence. This eliminated unconscious prejudgment.

We began with the larger works and listened to them in order of composition; this was interesting for its own sake, for in the course of an afternoon we traversed the musical development of George Gershwin, an impressive experience. Crucial to most of the concert pieces is the very opening; GG had a remarkable theatrical flair that he applied to these works, *vide* the opening of the *Rhapsody in Blue*, the *Concerto in F*, the "Walking theme" of *An American in Paris*, for example. The method was this: we listened to the openings of several versions of the same work and when Kay sensed that we had come upon one that came closest in tempo, spirit, and, most importantly, the pianist's handling of the solo, we would hear that recording through for total effect. If all, or most, of the elements held up we knew we had the most desirable performance.

While the emphasis is upon modern—especially available—recordings, historic out-of-print records are listed also. The record industry being what it is these days, there is always the possibility that such rarities might become available again. Now and again the record companies need to be reminded of what they have in their vaults, although, sad to say, the historic importance means little to them. Still there is the remote chance that a demand may create a supply. Rare-record dealers may have some of the out-of-print discs (both 78s and LPs), but their prices are all too often fanciful. Thus the emphasis on those records that can be acquired without excessive expenditures of effort or cash.

The songs present a special problem in that one could fill a house with recordings in order to obtain this or that rendition of this or that song. Only those albums completely devoted to Gershwin songs—with an exception or

two—are included to keep the discography of reasonable length. Unfor-
tunately the two outstanding song collections, "Ella Fitzgerald Sings the
George and Ira Gershwin Song Books" (on Verve) and "The Gershwin
Years" (Decca), have gone out of print.

The discography which follows takes the following, rather eccentric,
form: The first part of the first major section covers all of the so-called
"serious" Gershwin, including those few works not yet recorded—this is
because, perhaps, if a record company executive chances to be browsing for
off-beat material (a likely story!) it might give him an idea. It is in this section that those works readily available may be found. The second part
covers those few musicals that have been preserved on records, and the third
is devoted to song collections. The second major section covers several
"historic records," a surprising number of which may still be found. The
final major section is given over to what we call "esoterica," namely piano
rolls, very early disc recordings, and radio broadcasts, in the vain hope that
someone just might have recorded them or studios saved their reference
copies—another unlikely story!

THE "SERIOUS" GERSHWIN

I. THE CONCERT WORKS

LULLABY, for string quartet (ca. 1920)

Precise dating of this little (about eight minutes) piece is difficult, but it
was undoubtedly done primarily as a harmony exercise in late 1919 or early
1920 for Kilenyi. This was GG's first semi-public excursion into "serious"
music and his only attempt at writing for string quartet. Curiously, near the
end of his life he spoke of trying this genre again, but the idea got no farther than a few sketches. Ira Gershwin recalls that *Lullaby* was frequently
performed by some of George's "many musician friends before—sometimes
after—they'd get down to the more serious business of classical quartets and
quintets. I attended three of these intimate sessions and could see and hear
that 'Lullaby' was invariably welcomed."

No proper recording of *Lullaby* has been made (though it has been performed by both the Juilliard and Kohon String Quartets). Larry Adler, the
harmonica virtuoso, first brought the work to light in 1963 when he performed it at the Edinburgh Festival with a quartet. He recorded it, in a
transcription for harmonica and string orchestra, in an album entitled

Discovery (RCA Victor LSC-2986), along with two unpublished Gershwin songs. These are entitled, for the album's purpose (just as *Lullaby* is called "Lullabye Time," heaven knows why), "Three Quarter Blues" and "Merry Andrew." In the listing of unpublished manuscripts the former is Gershwin Melody ♯32–Waltz and was generally referred to by Ira as "Irish Waltz"; this was the title known also to Kay. "Merry Andrew," Gershwin Melody ♯43–Comedy Dance is believed to have been used in *Rosalie* and was recalled by Ira when he and George were working on *Shall We Dance* and needed a song for Fred Astaire. The opening idea was adapted by George and eventually became "They All Laughed." The album has since been deleted. The performance of *Lullaby* itself, despite the overblown instrumentation, is true to the mood of the piece; Adler performs the first violin part and the strings, led by Morton Gould, fill in for the rest of the quartet.

BLUE MONDAY, one-act "opera" (1922)

A problematic work which some consider a harbinger of *Porgy and Bess* and others regard as minor, even inferior, Gershwin. Whatever the view, Gershwin fans have long been awaiting a recording of this short (about a half hour) "opera." It was not a composition upon which GG lavished much work, nor did he do much with it when it was revived as *135th Street* by Paul Whiteman three years later. Nor has it gone unperformed since: it was in the original print of the film *Rhapsody in Blue* (even at times in the television showings); it was done in the early days of television with a good deal of fanfare (something roughly along the lines of "Great Rediscovered Gershwin Opera Saved for Posterity!") and with scant reaction. It has been done now and again in concert form. It is not vintage Gershwin, though musically it is easier to take than its book, recitative, and the DeSylva lyrics. The purely instrumental passages are quite interesting (though not orchestrated by George) in a Twenties kind of "This Is Jazz" style—and there are two good songs, "Has Anyone Seen My Joe" (based on the theme of *Lullaby*) and "Blue Monday Blues"; the spiritual "I'm Going to See My Mother" is better left unmentioned. Perhaps a suite from *Blue Monday* would be a possibility; a full-scale recording would hardly serve the Gershwin cause.

RHAPSODY IN BLUE, for piano and orchestra (1924) (Orchestrated by Ferde Grofé)

Auditioning several interpretations of the *Rhapsody in Blue* successively was a revelation—and both of us have heard it, quite literally, hundreds of times. The generally critic-approved version is Leonard Bernstein's (Columbia MS-7518, collected with the *Preludes* played by Oscar Levant; the last movement of the *Concerto*, by André Previn and Andre Kostelanetz; *An American in Paris*, by the Philadelphia Orchestra with Ormandy; and the *Porgy and Bess Symphonic Picture* by the same; the album is entitled *Gershwin's Greatest Hits*; the *Rhapsody* is also coupled with *An American in Paris* by Bernstein on MS-6091). When Bernstein's interpretation of the *Rhapsody* is compared with some of the others it emerges as rather lifeless. Kay found the entire approach "too sentimental" and lacking in that brashness and impetus that it requires. And Bernstein, as soloist, tends now and then to moon over a phrase as if infatuated with the sound of his own cadenza. The Earl Wild-Boston Pops, Arthur Fiedler approach comes much closer (RCA Victor LSC-2367), as does André Previn's recording (in which he conducts the London Symphony: Angel S-36810); Kay found his piano performance "excellent." However, there are some unnecessary cuts, which spoils the effect. There is a fine, sensitive performance by Philippe Entremont with Ormandy and the Philadelphia Orchestra (Columbia MS-7013); the soloist is in better fettle than the orchestra—or is it the conductor?—as far as Gershwinisms go. The recording is remarkably sharp and clear. The finest all-around interpretation, however, is that of Werner Haas—"most like George"—with the Monte Carlo Orchestra led by Edo de Waart. An unlikely combination on paper, perhaps, but superb via the loudspeakers. This is the recording of the *Rhapsody in Blue* to have; along with it comes also the *Concerto in F* and "*I Got Rhythm*" *Variations* (Philips 6500118). A very good *Rhapsody in Blue*, with Morton Gould at the piano and conducting, may be obtained—and very inexpensively—in *Gershwin's Biggest Hits* (RCA Victrola VICS-1669). This was lifted out of an album, pre-stereo, called *The Serious Gershwin*, and while the recording may be slightly dated the performance is authoritative and finely detailed. Gould was a special favorite of George's; I recall seeing a letter GG had written to Eva Gauthier (this was when we were doing the original research for the book) in which he suggested that young Morton Gould serve as his proxy as piano soloist when she presented a revival of their history-making "Recital of Ancient and Modern Music for Voice" (which did not come off after all). Also, when Kay had completed a ballet and found herself too involved to orchestrate it, George suggested that she get Morton Gould for the job; he was then about twenty-one years old. If Gershwin knew his Gould, it is equally true that Gould knows his Gershwin. Also included in this album is Bennett's *Symphonic Picture* from *Porgy and Bess* (in true stereo), which Bennett himself conducts; Leonard Pennario doing the *Second Prelude*; and Leonard Bernstein's early recording of *An American in Paris*, a very lean and energetic performance and very good.

SHORT STORY, for violin and piano (1925) (Arranged by Samuel Dushkin)

Years ago, sometime about the mid-Thirties, there was a 78-rpm recording of this rather little-known piece issued by the Gramophone Record Shop (GP-794) in New York, a wonderful place which no longer exists. George frequently bought his records there. The violin soloist on the recording was Samuel Dushkin, who had, with GG's co-operation, stitched together a couple of the manuscript *Preludes, Andantino con fantasia* and *Allegretto scherzando*. These "titles" are analogous with those assigned to the three published *Preludes*. It is known that George began work on these pieces in January 1925 and that Dushkin performed *Short Story* in February. Then, in December of 1926, George presented five *Preludes* (and in January 1927, six) at the Marguerite D'Alvarez recital; whether or not the two pieces that comprised *Short Story* were among them is not certain. But they probably were. *Short Story* was not one of George's favorites among his works. When his first biographer Isaac Goldberg inquired about it, the composer's reaction was dismissive: "I really don't know what you want with it," he said. A query about other small piano pieces was similarly repudiative. "I may have written one or two novelettes which you ask about," he informed Goldberg, "but they were never published and are not worth bringing up." This was, of course, a wholesome, self-critical attitude when it appeared that George Gershwin had a long, productive life ahead of him. But as it turned out, even so slight and uncharacteristic a work (sounding like imitation Gershwin) as *Short Story* has its value.

CONCERTO IN F, for piano and orchestra (1925)

As with the *Rhapsody in Blue* the preferred recorded performance of the *Concerto* is that by Haas and de Waart on Philips. We had listened first to two openings (Previn: "Not bad"; Wild-Fiedler: "Better") and then the spirited de Waart: "The tempos are just right"; and after listening to Haas through most of the recording: "He hasn't done one thing wrong." The "feel" of the performance is right and does not bear down self-consciously on the "jazz" elements and is thoroughly musical. The work is approached as if it were a standard (which, in fact, it really is) concerto and not an excursion into musical slumming, nostalgia, or gimmickry; there is, in short, no condescension—just a very straightforward, no-nonsense, authentic interpretation. Again the Haas touch is very Gershwinesque: sure, deft, and, as Kay observed, "sensitive and yet masculine." The *Concerto* must stand as one of the outstanding American works for piano and orchestra—and is certainly the most viable of its time, not just another Jazz Age novelty.

Not that George was ever completely satisfied with its structure; on reflection, he found it at times "too sequential," with one idea leading to another rather obviously with too much reliance on repetition ("melodic sequence," technically) to get from one point to the other. Still this is a perfectly legitimate musical device and, in the *Concerto*, is most prevalent in the last movement. But it is the totality of the *Concerto* that counts and which has contributed to its long life. The "structural weaknesses" that contemporary critics pointed out (and of which GG was fully aware) seem not to have been permanently damaging. Inspiration is its own reward. Interestingly, in the Haas-de Waart recording, the solo trumpet (which is supposed to be muted) is blended into the orchestra, without losing its voice, however. The effect is poetically nocturnal, as it should be; most recordings bring the trumpet up front and distort the effect.

Kay's conclusion as the work closed: "I'd forgotten what a pleasure the *Concerto* is because I have heard it so badly played."

Entremont also does well at the piano, with Ormandy (Columbia MS-7013), in a generally fine performance.

PRELUDES FOR PIANO (1926)

The genesis of the *Preludes* is covered in the main text and under *Short Story* in the discography. Though George played six in public, he chose to publish only three; the one stray one, "Sleepless Night," is not inferior—in fact, is a beauty. But in slow song form, its mood is close to that of the second published *Prelude* and would have upset the form that George planned for the three, a kind of classic "fast-slow-fast" suite.

"It's very easy to ruin the *Preludes*," Kay observed; "they're not foolproof at all." (She was present, incidentally, when George composed what is now the first *Prelude*, helped to notate it, after which GG made a clean copy himself.) They are not, indeed, foolproof nor are they among the better-known Gershwin; they are subtle and elusive. The tendency of most pianists is to play the two fast pieces too fast and the slow middle one too slowly. This is true of such brilliant performances as those by Frank Glazer (Concert Disc 217) and Leonard Pennario (RCA Victor LSC-5001). The very best recorded version is that by George's friend Oscar Levant, who practically reproduces the composer's own way of playing the captivating pieces (Columbia MS-7518; this album also brings with it Bernstein's *Rhapsody in Blue*, a movement from the *Concerto*, and Ormandy's *American* and *Porgy and Bess* suite).

AN AMERICAN IN PARIS, for orchestra (1928)

The title page reads: "*An American in Paris*"/ *a Tone Poem*/ *for Orchestra*/ *Composed and Orchestrated*/ *by*/ *George Gershwin*/ *Begun early in 1928*/ *Finished November 18, 1928*. Perhaps subconsciously George wished to stress the fact that he had both "Composed and Orchestrated" the *American* because there were those, among them some of his friends who should have known better, who doubted that he had orchestrated the *Concerto in F*. A great deal of the *American* orchestration was done at the Warburg farm in Greenwich, Connecticut, and Kay, then Mrs. James Warburg, heard much of the work in progress as it was being completed and then, in company with the Gershwin family, attended the premiere at Carnegie Hall. It was during this performance that Morris Gershwin took out his watch and, upon hearing the final bars of the *American*, said "Exactly twenty minutes." (He had a curious sense of musical evaluation: the longer the work, the more important it must be.) Probably the rendition he heard, conducted by Walter Damrosch, was a bit on the long side.

When Kay and George looked in on the Friday afternoon performance later in the week and stood in the back of the hall, George moaned, "Oh, no —he's [Damrosch] starting to bend his knees." This was an indication, to GG at least, that the conductor would take the work at too pedestrian a pace. After the concert he unobtrusively took Kay's arm and they slipped out of Carnegie Hall and took a walk. Eventually they briskly walked along Madison Avenue where George noticed "two lovely English bracelets which he bought for me; I still have them. And thanks to Walter Damrosch and his bent knees."

The *American* has become a standard, even familiar, composition and no one treads through it as warily as once Damrosch was wont. Both Arthur Fiedler with the Boston Pops (RCA Victor LSC-5001) and Eugene Ormandy with the Philadelphia Orchestra (Columbia MS-7518) do reasonably well by it; Fiedler may hurry too much, having done the piece so often, and Ormandy, though slick, may be a bit careful. Leonard Bernstein's version with the New York Philharmonic (Columbia MS-6091) has plenty of verve, is a spirited performance, and is blessed with excellent recording (so, for that matter, are the others). But the most satisfactory approach is that of André Previn with the London Symphony (Angel S-36810), although the opening "Walking theme" may be taken a bit too briskly. Kay found the total performance most "tasteful with just the right tempo in the Blues." (It might be mentioned here that Maestro Previn is no favorite interpreter of Gershwin to either of us, primarily because of what he did to the Gershwin orchestrations for the film version of *Porgy and Bess*.) As with all the other recent recordings, this one is very sharp and crystal-clear and, what with the right handling, bringing out all the singing and bubbling details, Kay was moved to inquire, "How could anyone doubt that George was a great orchestrator?"

SECOND RHAPSODY, for piano and orchestra (1931)

There is no recording currently listed in the record catalogues of this work, a misfortune, for it is a most interesting one. There was an excellent performance in the recent past (recent enough to have been done in genuine stereo) which, though withdrawn, may very well appear again. This was in an album entitled *Gershwin by Starlight* (Capitol SP-8581) which also included an unfortunately "transcribed" *Cuban Overture*, a not bad *Porgy and Bess* medley for piano and orchestra, and a fine "*I Got Rhythm*" *Variations*. Pianist Leonard Pennario is excellent and he is given apposite backing by conductor Alfred Newman.

The background of the *Second Rhapsody*'s creation may be found in the main text, but it might be mentioned that since the first edition of the book a very fine print of the film *Delicious* materialized one day (literally), making it possible to compare (if only fleetingly) the film's "Manhattan Rhapsody" and the final composition. Rather surprisingly a great deal of the *Second Rhapsody* was used, practically a capsule version with all the main themes—if memory serves—intact. The songs were quite dreadfully done, excepting Janet Gaynor's wistful "Somebody from Somewhere." And no less an authority than Alfred Simon concurred that the piano accompanist for several of the songs may very well have been the composer; another pianist, obviously, played the *Second Rhapsody* sequence. This was background music for the lonely immigrant girl (Janet Gaynor) wandering forlornly through the canyons of Manhattan.

Besides the arresting opening "rivet theme," the *Rhapsody* is characterized (as is the first *Rhapsody*) by a broad middle melody—but with a great difference. The romanticism of the *Rhapsody in Blue* has been supplanted by what George called "a horizontal theme," an idea extended over ten bars. It is a theme of great breadth and one that Kay found "philosophically contemplative." The *Second Rhapsody* marked the advent of the truly mature Gershwin.

The rehearsal recording mentioned in Goldberg still exists. GG conducts the orchestra from the piano and, while the orchestra may sound rather uneasy with the new score, George's playing is splendid: sensitive yet full of vitality and assured. The piano sound is very good for 1931 though the orchestra sounds rather muddy. One copy of this disc was once stored in the record library at NBC with this label copy: "Special Record of NBC/ MRC 69986-1/Second Rhapsody/Concert Orchestra conducted by George Gershwin." This recording seems to have vanished from the NBC library. George's copy is in the Gershwin Archives and another appears to have ended up in the International Piano Library, New York.

CUBAN OVERTURE, for orchestra (1932)

This is a problem work whose performance even gave GG trouble (but then its first performance occurred in the open air of Lewisohn Stadium, which may have dispersed, and thus spoiled, the effect). We both agree that there has been—to date—only one really right recording of it and that is the one by Howard Hanson and the Eastman-Rochester Orchestra (Mercury SR-90290). Sadly, this recording has been withdrawn. The only available one presents a distorted, rather overblown view by Arthur Fiedler and the Boston Pops (RCA Victor LSC-2586). The emphasis on bravura is an impressive exemplification of orchestral virtuosity, but the total effect is one of strain (the finale even sounds as if the tape has been speeded up, the orchestra plays so fast) and it simply does not work. Considering how George had intended to invoke some "feel" of the Cuban bands he heard during his visit to Havana, treating the *Cuban Overture* as a grand orchestral excursion seems inappropriate. It might better be approached as a chamber piece, with rather gruff string tone, a bite in the brass (Cuban style), and the percussion instruments up front as he originally suggested. Kay, by the way, considers this "his sexiest composition." I'm not quite certain what she means by that—and I didn't ask.

PIANO TRANSCRIPTIONS OF 18 SONGS (1932)

This collection of Gershwiniana was prepared for the now long out-of-print *George Gershwin's Songbook* and was dedicated to Kay Swift. The composer also presented her with the original manuscript (very neat, very sure), which, in turn, she presented to the George Gershwin Collection in the Library of Congress. To date there has been only one recording: by Leonid Hambro on the now defunct Walden Records. While the interpretations, a bit on the slow side, are not absolutely George-like, they are sprightly and vivacious and give a good idea of what the composer had in mind when he set the music down. The *Transcriptions* might be regarded as tiny études in which GG's style of playing was notated, so far as that was possible. As with classic jazz performers, he had a highly personal way of interpreting his songs which eluded strict notation. In these pieces he attempted to define those characteristics—melodic, rhythmic, and harmonic—that came to be inimitably and irreplaceably "Gershwinesque." The *Transcriptions* served as the musical base for George Balanchine's ballet *Who Cares?* (1970). For this purpose those pieces used were orchestrated, which rather canceled out their original function. For those who have not been able to find, or to afford, the rare *Songbook*, the *Transcriptions* themselves have been published by Warner Brothers (New World Music) under the title of *Gershwin at the Keyboard*.

[TWO WALTZES IN C, for piano (1933)

These are the "contrapuntal waltzes" from *Pardon My English* referred to in the main text. Kay remembers playing this piece (for it is a single work) on two pianos with George. Each played one of the waltzes singly and then played them simultaneously (contrapuntally, to be technical). The result is quite exhilarating. One of the few, so far, unrecorded Gershwin pieces. Thus the brackets.]

"I GOT RHYTHM" VARIATIONS, for piano and orchestra (1934)

"George wrote this partly," Kay observed, "because he had become rather sick of playing the *Rhapsody* or the *Concerto*." And, it might be added, there was little clamor for the *Second Rhapsody*.

The result was a pianistically pyrotechnical little showpiece for himself, for which he concocted one of his most ingenious orchestrations. Kay regards the *Variations* "the best-orchestrated" of all his compositions for orchestra, i.e., excluding *Porgy and Bess*. The "program" is clearly stated in the title and it is musically straightforward—rather "intellectual" Gershwin showing how skillfully and wittily he could manipulate a single theme. There are two recorded *Variations*, both very good. The one by Wild and Fiedler (RCA Victor LSC-2586), though, must take second place to the Haas-de Waart performance on Philips (6500118). The playing of the *Variations* is fine, but the recording also brings with it the excellent *Rhapsody in Blue* and *Concerto in F*.

PORGY AND BESS, opera in three acts (1935)

By now this masterpiece has come to be regarded as an important American opera, if not in the United States at least in practically all the rest of the world. Its creation has been covered comprehensively in the main text; little more need be added to that. Only one "complete" recording has been made—the word is in quotes because there are cuts. Still, there is more music preserved on the recording than was heard in the original production when it opened in New York.

Although the recording (Odyssey 3260018E) is rather aged (pre-stereo) it is very good technically and musically it is splendid. For the sessions Goddard Lieberson assembled many members of the original cast (except the principals, who were unavailable). The singing is uniformly good and the conducting, by Lehman Engel, is exactly right. So is the price, by the way, for this three-record set.

A fine excerpt album is also available with powerful singing by Leontyne

Price and William Warfield, two of the stars of the famed Blevins Davis-Robert Breen touring company. But the real highlight of the album (RCA Victor LSC-2679) is the presence of John W. Bubbles, the original "Sportin' Life" of the 1935 production.

CATFISH ROW (*Suite from "Porgy and Bess"—1936*)

This is GG's own suite from his opera. The new title was supplied by Ira Gershwin to distinguish it from the well-known, oft-recorded "symphonic picture" arranged by Robert Russell Bennett. The composer's handling of the material is richer, for it appears from the content that, though he used several of the obvious songs, he chose to preserve much of the purely orchestral music, some of which was eliminated before the New York opening. For example: the "Jazzbo Brown piano music," which is a bridge between the Overture and "Summertime"; an especially effective section is a lashing fugue (underscoring for the murder of Crown by Porgy). There is also the storm music, which was also used by Bennett but is often—and inexplicably—cut from many of the recorded versions. There is a wonderful finale which opens with the atmospheric "occupational humoresque" (which had also been cut in 1935). So it may be said that *Catfish Row* (in a sense Gershwin's last large work, though admittedly a kind of scissors and paste job) contains much fresh—and good—Gershwin for the record collector, not to mention the concertgoer or even those who have seen a performance of *Porgy and Bess.*

One recording was made by the Utah Symphony conducted by Maurice Abravanel (originally Westminster WST-14063; reissued as Music Guild MS-167; both withdrawn). The performance was quite good though Kay particularly noted certain problems with intricate syncopations. Still, the performance, and the recording, was worthwhile while it lasted.

Catfish Row, strangely, has yet to be presented in New York, despite the fact that André Kostelanetz purported to do this at Lincoln Center. The result, and the recording that followed, was such a butchering that it could not have been called *Catfish Row,* but just another medley of "top hits" from *Porgy and Bess.*

PROMENADE ("Walking the Dog," from *Shall We Dance,* 1936)

The amusing, sprightly, dog-walking sequence from *Shall We Dance* has always been a favorite among Gershwin fanciers partly because of its caustic (though subtle) commentary by George on overblown Hollywood scoring and mainly because of its captivating musical ideas. Since no complete manuscript was found among George's papers, the little piece lay fallow for a number of years until it was possible to piece it together from the film's soundtrack, from a rediscovered page of the second piano part, and from the very good memory of Hal Borne, who had served as rehearsal pianist to Rogers and Astaire during the shooting of the film. The first recording ever of *Promenade* (the new title by Ira) was included in the deluxe album of Gershwiniana by Ella Fitzgerald in an orchestral performance by Nelson Riddle on the Verve label. Later it was included in an album entitled *Gershwin Wonderland* (Columbia CS-8933) by André Kostelanetz—also since withdrawn. Both performances were very good, though the orchestral forces rather canceled George's satiric point; even so, they do not overwhelm the piece. The Kostelanetz album was notable also for a *Girl Crazy Overture* (which included "Land of the Gay Caballero"). GG's own *Porgy and Bess Suite, Catfish Row*, unfortunately was represented only in excerpt form, which is difficult to fathom. The performances, as customary under Kostelanetz, were brilliant.

II. MUSICALS

LADY, BE GOOD (1924): See under "Historic Recordings" below.

OH, KAY! (1927)

Only three complete (virtually if not actually) George and Ira show scores have been recorded and only one is still reasonably available. The best done, the charming *Oh, Kay!*, seems to have slipped out of the catalogue. Of all the show re-creations produced by Goddard Lieberson this one most delightfully evoked the period and the flavor of the show itself, complete even to a two-piano team as part of the orchestra. It might be noted that all the songs that were used in the show may be heard in the album. An especially endearing highlight: the fittingly entitled "Dear Little Girl." The album number was Columbia OS-2550.

FUNNY FACE (1927): See under "Historic Recordings" below.

GIRL CRAZY (1930)

Also produced by Lieberson for Columbia (CSP COS-2560), this album, though generally splendid, is marred somewhat by the mannered singing of the "star," Mary Martin. In fact, the vocal high point of the album is

Louise Carlyle's powerful "Sam and Delilah." Unfortunately, it was decided to delete the satirical "Goldfarb! That's I'm!" and the instrumental "Land of the Gay Caballero" (once recorded by André Kostelanetz as part of a *Girl Crazy Overture* on Columbia CS-8933, now withdrawn). The complex of letters in *Girl Crazy's* catalogue number means that, while it is out of general circulation, it may still be obtained by ordering it directly from Columbia Special Products, Special Service Collectors' Series, 51 West 52nd Street, New York, N.Y. 10019. Hopefully the *Oh, Kay!* will also one day be available under this plan.

OF THEE I SING (1931)

This score is a cornucopia of musical/lyrical invention and the fact that a full-length recording of it (and of its precursor, *Strike Up the Band*, as well as its sequel, *Let 'Em Eat Cake*) is not a standard entry in the record catalogue is a cultural misdemeanor. The one recording of *Of Thee I Sing* was available for a time in the Fifties and featured the cast of the 1952 revival (Capitol S-350). The singing of the principals, excepting the sweet-voiced Betty Oaks as Mary Turner, leaves, shall we say with a cliché, a bit to be desired. But for all that, the total effect is spirited with much fine singing from the chorus. The orchestra, conducted by Maurice Levine, is excellent also and the recording was truly filled with fine music making and a good idea of what the Gershwins were striving for comes through; but it is time for another, even better, recording of this score, one of the glories of our musical history.

Unfortunately the recording derived from the October 1972 television production of *Of Thee I Sing* (Columbia S 31763) does not fill the gap left by the deletion of the Capitol recording, whatever its demerits. Although a surprising amount (considering this was television) of music and lyrics was retained from the original, there were infelicitous cuts ("Some Girls Can Bake a Pie," "Here's a Kiss for Cinderella," and "Hello, Good Morning," among others) plus the interpolation of "Mine" from *Let 'Em Eat Cake*. But the essential Gershwin was missing which is its chief *raison d'être*. Kay was disturbed by the new orchestrations, cuts, and the harmonic violence done to GG's original conceptions and L.D.S. "thought it very corny" (that is, the TV production itself and all that went with it). E.J. found it "shoddy," although the singing of stars Carroll O'Connor (roughly whiskey baritone) and Cloris Leachman (roughly post-ingenue) was rather likable, if not great. Besides, for the time being, this is all we have. But it must be approached with reservations (including laugh-tracks), Heaven help us.

LADY IN THE DARK (1941)

There is more to say for this recording than against it. The pros: more music and lyrics than on any other recording and the use of Kurt Weill's original orchestrations (Columbia COS-2390; if not available at your dealer, order from Columbia Special Products as noted in *Girl Crazy* entry, above). Lehman Engel handles the chorus and orchestra knowingly, and Risë Stevens and Adolph Green, re-creating the roles originally portrayed by Gertrude Lawrence and Danny Kaye respectively, are surprisingly good. It is the essence of the recording, with its remarkable showlike feeling, that makes this album so delightful and the cons not even worth mentioning.

A STAR IS BORN, film score (1954)

The album contains one of the best scores ever written for a film, music by Harold Arlen and lyrics by Ira, and, happily, is sung by its star, Judy Garland. All the Gershwin-Arlen songs used in the film may be heard in the album (Harmony 11366). The one quibble (the fault of the film-makers, not the record producers) is the inclusion of a concocted medley under the title of "Born in a Trunk," a rather obvious autobiographical bit of corn. This "socko" closing of the first part of the movie displaced the excellent Gershwin-Arlen "I'm Off the Downbeat." Despite this—for "Born in a Trunk" introduces a number of good songs from another era: "I'll Get By," "Peanut Vendor," "Swanee," etc.—this is a cherishable album. Columbia has withdrawn its full-priced version and reissued it on the inexpensive Harmony label.

III. SONG COLLECTIONS

FRED ASTAIRE: NOTHING THRILLED US HALF AS MUCH (Epic FLS-15103)

Originally this album was entitled *The Best of Fred Astaire*, and may well belong in the "Historic Recordings" section that follows. No matter; what is important is that it assembles a dozen songs, mainly from the film musicals of the latter Thirties and recorded at the time. Most of the songs are by the Gershwins—songs from *Shall We Dance* (accompaniment by Johnny Green, at the piano, and his orchestra) and from *A Damsel in Distress* (accompaniment by the Ray Noble band). These are no less than wonderful—even the band sound, slightly dated but fresh, is hauntingly evocative; Johnny Green's piano is beautifully idiomatic and Fred Astaire's singing is—of course—impeccable.

ELLA FITZGERALD SINGS THE GEORGE AND IRA GERSHWIN SONG BOOKS (Verve MG V-4029-5)

This musical and lyrical treasure trove was originally released in 1959 complete with a fancy box and a handsome booklet (by none other than L.D.S.). Ira revised several of the lyrics for Miss Fitzgerald especially for this album. With the deluxe set there was also a bonus record with orchestral versions of the *Preludes* and a so-called *Ambulatory Suite*, with orchestration by Nelson Riddle, using *Promenade* ("Walking the Dog"), the "Swiss Soldiers' March" from *Strike Up the Band*, and "Fidgety Feet" from *Oh, Kay!*

No less than fifty-nine songs are included on the five records, among them such rarities as "The Real American Folk Song," "Just Another Rhumba," "By Strauss," "Somebody from Somewhere," "Boy Wanted," and "You've Got What Gets Me," from the first filmed *Girl Crazy*.

THE GERSHWIN YEARS (Decca DXSB-7160)

The idea of this three-record set was to present the songs chronologically, and was a good one—by arranger-conductor George Bassman. Sadly, however, the album was withdrawn by Decca Records, but there is hope for its being reissued on Decca's inexpensive label, Vocalion. This must be one of the finest Gershwin collections ever recorded. The singing and the orchestrations (now and then, perhaps, a bit Hollywoodian) are generally authentic and more traditional, say, than in the Ella Fitzgerald collection. These two sets really complement one another. Beginning with the first published song, "When You Want 'Em," Bassman leads soloists, chorus, and orchestra through a rich vein of Gershwin up to the final songs for *The Goldwyn Follies*. There are some off-beat selections: "Rialto Ripples," for example, and the lovely "Some Wonderful Sort of Someone," plus "I Was So Young," "I Won't Say I Will," "High Hat," "Oh, So Nice," "Where's the Boy?", "Feeling I'm Falling," "Do What You Do!", and "Mine" presented as an excerpt from *Let 'Em Eat Cake*.

GEORGE GERSHWIN REVISITED (Painted Smiles 1357)

The idea of this collection, though not original, is an admirable one: to concentrate on Gershwin rarities. This is fine, provided the songs are done right; otherwise they would be better undone than done in—as is generally the case with the enterprises of Ben Bagley, producer of the various "Revisited" albums. The songs range wonderfully from the very early—"Tra-La-La," for example—through the posthumous: "Back Bay Polka" and "Changing My Tune." But Bagley, King (the term is used advisedly) of Instant Kamp, though he avers a profound devotion for the songs of the great American songwriters, proceeds to controvert that with a perverse assemblage of "artists" to do the songs (not all of which should of necessity be done) and then tops it all off with what must be the most tasteless liner annotations in the history of the phonograph record. That would be bearable (no one has to read the stuff), but too often the songs are so badly done or so obviously travestied that the point of the album is canceled out. This particular set has some fine singing by Barbara Cook, Bobby Short, and even by amateur singer Tony Perkins; and there are a number of little-known, particularly early, songs. Alas, and a definite lack, there are no other recordings of most of these songs.

IRA GERSHWIN REVISITED (Painted Smiles 1353)

This collection is afflicted with the same problem as the George album above: the heavy hand of Ben Bagley. Again the emphasis is on neglected songs—some of the very best from the late Forties and early Fifties (excepting those from *A Star Is Born*, of course). Songs with music by George are mainly early ones again—including "On My Mind the Whole Night Long," for which Ira did not do the lyric. There are songs from *Give a Girl a Break* (music by Burton Lane)—but, having heard composer and lyricist do them, I feel the performances on this album sound like parody. There are songs too by Kurt Weill, Harry Warren, Phil Charig, and Vernon Duke. How nice to have them but would that they had been done better. There is some good singing by Margaret Whiting and Blossom Dearie. Wrong tempos, wrong phrasings, other misfortunes spoil the musical as well as lyrical content of the songs. But, again, there being no other recordings of these songs, we are stuck with this imperfect album.

'S WONDERFUL, 'S MARVELOUS, 'S GERSHWIN (Daybreak 2009)

This is the soundtrack of the television production which starred Jack Lemmon as well as the talents of Fred Astaire, Leslie Uggams, Larry Kert, Robert Guillaume, Linda Bennett, and Peter Nero (Ethel Merman, also on the show, does not sing on the record). Here is a generous collection of Gershwiniana (though no surprises, no attempt at presenting anything too unfamiliar) rather vitiated, as was the show itself, by Lemmon's pointless impersonations of various people associated with GG's career. Nor was the singing always right, particularly on the distaff side. Musically, however, the material is well done and the high point—as it was on the show—is Fred Astaire's easygoing medley.

375

HISTORIC RECORDINGS

This is a kind of catchall section in which recordings of real historic interest are mingled with those now out of circulation or those which, if available, are of rather limited technical quality and of interest to the truly devoted Gershwin collector. Interestingly, about half are still readily obtainable; these are marked with an asterisk (*).

*RHAPSODY IN BLUE

Included in an album entitled *Paul Whiteman*, Volume 1 (RCA Victor LPV-555), this is the 1927 recording (there being an earlier 1924 one) of the *Rhapsody* abridged to fit on two sides of a twelve-inch 78-rpm record. Present on the recording—with one, according to gossip, major exception—are most of the original members of the Whiteman band that introduced the work at Aeolian Hall three years before. George is at the piano, the sound is not bad at all, and the performance has a fine dated quality. The exception mentioned is Paul Whiteman; according to one source, on the day of the recording GG and PW were not in agreement about how the work should be done. They reached an impasse and Nathaniel Shilkret took over for Whiteman. Included also, among other Whiteman items, is a jaunty "I'll Build a Stairway to Paradise," as the band played it in the *Scandals* of 1922.

*RHAPSODY IN BLUE

The composer's complete piano roll version (Archive of Piano Music X-914) of the *Rhapsody* as well as several popular song rolls. There is no doubting that GG cut these rolls and that his touch is evident, but a pianola roll is a pianola roll and not a live performance. These were made from the Duo Art rolls so do reproduce better than most the nuances of George's playing—though one can never be certain whether or not the tempos have been tampered with. Still, a souvenir from another time.

RHAPSODY IN BLUE

The same piano rolls again, plus five popular rolls, though the outstanding feature of this recording, *George Gershwin at the Piano* (Movietone 71009, deleted), is the transfers from sound film of a *Strike Up the Band* rehearsal and a newsreel performance of "I Got Rhythm." The rehearsal sequence has GG playing "Hangin' Around with You," "Strike Up the Band," and accompanying Clark and McCullough in "Mademoiselle in New Rochelle," as well as exchanging banter with Bobby Clark.

*CONCERTO IN F (excerpt from first movement)

This is a fragment from the only commercial recording of the *Concerto* issued in the composer's lifetime (on Columbia 50139-D, 50140-D, and 50141-D) as interpreted by Paul Whiteman and his orchestra with Roy Bargy at the piano. George was unhappy with this album: besides the cuts required to fit it onto the six twelve-inch sides, Whiteman had Ferde Grofé reorchestrate the work. Where Grofé's touch in the *Rhapsody* had been a happy one (George had conceived it with the Whiteman band and soloists in mind and suggested much of the scoring), the tampering with the *Concerto* orchestration was a retrogression. Bargy does a creditable job at the piano, but the Whitemanesque posturings of the orchestra sound rather ludicrous. Bix Beiderbecke, according to legend, is supposed to have participated in this recording but is not heard on this excerpt. It is in a fascinating album entitled *The Original Sound of the "Twenties"* (Columbia C3L-35); included also is GG's recording of "Someone to Watch Over Me."

AN AMERICAN IN PARIS

The first recording of this work, made in February 1929, was performed by the RCA Victor Symphony Orchestra with Nathaniel Shilkret (RCA Victor LPT-29; coupled with the 1927 "Whiteman" *Rhapsody*). This is a thoroughly delightful performance, the first complete recording of a Gershwin work and one in which he—as well as the famous taxi horns he brought back from Paris—participated. GG may be heard contributing a few bars on the celesta in a brief transitional passage about halfway through. For years the label stated that he was at the piano, which must have mystified many. The recording is one well worth reviving.

*LEVANT PLAYS GERSHWIN

George's old friend (and others) perform the *Rhapsody in Blue* (originally Columbia X-251) with Ormandy and the Philadelphia Orchestra and the *Concerto in F* (originally Columbia M-512) with Kostelanetz and the Philharmonic-Symphony Orchestra of New York; a bonus is the fine Rodzinski-conducted *An American in Paris* (originally Columbia X-246). All of these have been gathered and electronically rechanneled for stereo on Columbia CS 8641 (not necessarily an improvement, but it does keep these performances in the current catalogue). Suffice it to say that Levant plays with more style and authority than either of his accompanying orchestras.

PRELUDES FOR PIANO

George recorded the *Preludes*, and the Andante from the *Rhapsody in Blue*, during one of his trips to England. The twelve-inch disc was eventually issued here by Columbia Records (originally 50107-D, later 7192-M). The piano sound is quite good and the performance of the *Preludes* confirms George's unsentimental approach, particularly in the second. Though slow, compared with the first and third, it is done with a brisk touch and a steady forward-moving rhythm. Even the middle section is accomplished without that lagging tempo that so many later pianists seem to have adopted.

SECOND RHAPSODY/"I GOT RHYTHM" VARIATIONS/ PRELUDES

What a treasure this was for the Gershwin collector when it was released in the early days of the long-playing record! Not only the *Preludes* but two Gershwin rarities performed to perfection by Oscar Levant with Morton Gould, himself a fine Gershwin interpreter, conducting. A ten-inch LP (Columbia ML-2073), it eventually went the way of all such dimensioned discs. This was sad, for these are really excellent performances and should be available—perhaps combined with the material on the *Levant Plays Gershwin* album.

PORGY AND BESS

Four days after the premiere of *Porgy and Bess* Victor recorded an album of excerpts under the supervision of the composer and led (in all but one song) by the show's conductor Alexander Smallens; also on hand were the Eva Jessye Choir and the opera's orchestra. But there the parallels ended, for the vocalists were Lawrence Tibbett and Helen Jepson of the Metropolitan Opera and not Todd Duncan and Anne Brown of the Alvin Theatre. This casting was undoubtedly GG's wish, for he certainly had the Metropolitan in mind during those years he worked on *Porgy*. In a letter to Heyward he described Todd Duncan, his choice for the role of Porgy, "as the closest . . . to a colored Lawrence Tibbett I have ever heard."

The singing by all is very good; interestingly one of the songs done by Tibbett is "The Buzzard Song," which had been cut from *Porgy* just a few days before in Boston. The album was originally released on four 78-rpm records and then, briefly in 1959, on a Victor "budget" label, RCA Camden (CAL-500), which was eventually, and unfortunately, withdrawn.

*PORGY AND BESS

This album is the original cast recording of the 1942 revival with virtually the same cast as the first production, the major substitution being Avon Long for John W. Bubbles as Sportin' Life. Most of the other fine singers that GG had a hand in choosing (with the sad exception of the late Ruby Elzy) may be heard: Todd Duncan, Anne Brown, Edward Matthews, Helen Dowdy, William Woolfolk, the Eva Jessye Choir and the orchestra conducted by Alexander Smallens. This album—Decca 79024—is a must for every Gershwin collection, for it is a landmark in the American musical theater as well as in the history of the phonograph record; it is a first of its kind. The sound, though gimmicked for "stereo(?)," is still good.

*LADY, BE GOOD

During the London run of this show George recorded several of the songs with the stars, Fred and Adele Astaire. These recordings, plus others with orchestra, make up one side of this delightful album (Monmouth-Evergreen 7036). The Gershwin performances are "Fascinating Rhythm," "I'd Rather Charleston," "Hang On to Me," and "Half of It Dearie, Blues." Included also, but with orchestra, are the title song (rather excruciatingly sung by William Kent), "So Am I" by Adele Astaire and George Vollaire, and the Astaires in "Swiss Miss."

It is only fair to warn potential buyers that these recordings were cut ca. 1926 and the transfers were made from surviving shellac discs and not from the original masters (which vanished sometime around the Second World War). Even so, they sound remarkably good and, best of all, the piano sound is a pleasant surprise. All the vigor and thrust, not to mention imaginativeness, of GG's keyboard manner come through vividly—and the Astaires are charming. (The reverse side of the record contains a number of songs Astaire recorded later.) Note: If you cannot obtain this recording from your local dealer, write directly to Monmouth-Evergreen Records, 1697 Broadway, New York, N.Y. 10019.

*TIP-TOES

Eight selections sung by the original cast of the 1926 London production, among them Dorothy Dickson, Laddie Cliff, and Allen Kearns, the latter re-creating the role he had in the original New York production (he later appeared in *Funny Face* and *Girl Crazy*). The transfers from the old shellacs are well done; the few bumps (from nicks in the originals) are not distressing and the "presence" of the vocalists is quite good. Neither of the

379

leads is an outstanding singer, but the treatment of the songs is true to the style and period. The outstanding factor of this album is the number of lesser-known songs: "These Charming People," "Nice Baby," "It's a Great Little World" (cut from the original '25 production), "When Do We Dance," and the gently satirical but charming "Nightie Night." This album (Monmouth-Evergreen 7052) contains songs from Vincent Youmans' *Wildflower* (also English production) on the reverse side. The usual informative, impeccable liner notes by Stanley Green are an asset.

*FUNNY FACE

Side one of this album (Monmouth-Evergreen 7037) is virtually an original (English) cast album complete with principals (the Astaires again), juvenile, comics, chorus, and orchestra; side two brings George in solo piano renditions of songs from *Funny Face* as well as *Tip-Toes*. The title song and "The Babbitt and the Bromide" are done by the Astaires; Adele and Bernard Clifton do "He Loves and She Loves" and "'S Wonderful"; Fred Astaire does "My One and Only" and, with chorus, the marvelous "High Hat" (no little of the marvel can be attributed to the orchestration, including the duo pianos of Fray and Braggiotti). Leslie Henson and a quartet do the little-known but caustically brilliant "Tell the Doc." The side brings a special bonus in the form of a comedy sketch by Henson and Sydney Howard that is a theatrical period piece and a classic "of its kind."

On the reverse GG plays from this show: "Funny Face," "'S Wonderful," and "My One and Only"; from *Tip-Toes:* "Looking for a Boy," "Sweet and Low Down," "That Certain Feeling," and "When Do We Dance?" Again the recordings are scratchy, or dim—or both, but, also again, the effort is worth it and the spirit comes through, especially in the piano sides. Interestingly, when Ira visited Moscow in 1956 during the *Porgy and Bess* tour, one of his Russian musical hosts displayed one of his most treasured records, George's performance of "Looking for a Boy."

NOTE: The *Lady, Be Good* and *Funny Face* albums assemble nearly all the solo piano recordings cut by GG excepting four sides from *Oh, Kay!*: "Clap Yo' Hands"/"Do, Do, Do" issued on English Columbia 4538 and American Columbia 809-D; and "Maybe"/"Someone to Watch Over Me," English Columbia 4539, U.S. Columbia 812-D. "Someone to Watch Over Me," as noted already, is included in Columbia's *The Original Sound of the "Twenties"* (Columbia C3L-35).

*GERTRUDE LAWRENCE

The full title of this cherishable album is *Gertrude Lawrence: Songs from Two of Her Greatest Starring Vehicles: George and Ira Gershwin's "Oh, Kay!" and Cole Porter's "Nymph Errant"* (Monmouth-Evergreen 7043). Not much Gershwin, however; only three songs: "Someone to Watch Over Me" and two duets (with Harold French, of the London Production), "Do, Do, Do" and "Maybe." The rendition of "Someone to Watch Over Me" has never been as exquisitely done as on this recording; the verse is a joy. Though slender pickings for Gershwinites, this one song makes the album a treasure; the Porter songs are worth having too.

*LADY IN THE DARK

Another Gertrude Lawrence treasure trove, songs from Ira's and Kurt Weill's successful musical of 1941 (the second side is devoted to Weill's "folk opera," *Down in the Valley;* RCA Victor LPV-503). Miss Lawrence's sides were produced shortly after the show opened in New York, something she did with a great deal of reluctance. She was unhappy because Hildegarde had recorded several songs first; perhaps she did not like the sound of her voice, for it is strained and a little fractured here and there. What is important, much of the material she did in the show is preserved in this album and, cracks and all, is most affectingly done. An evocative and entrancing album.

*LEE WILEY SINGS GEORGE GERSHWIN AND COLE PORTER

This album brings together two of those memorable Lee Wiley albums from the late Thirties and early Forties in which she sang songs by the masters of popular music (she also did Harold Arlen and Rodgers and Hart, also phonographically revived by the enterprising Bill Borden of Monmouth-Evergreen). Not only were the songs invariably unhackneyed and intelligently sung (with an ineffable womanly quality), the accompaniment was provided by some of the best jazz men around at the time. The Gershwin songs are "How Long Has This Been Going On?" "My One and Only," "Sweet and Low Down," " 'S Wonderful" (alas, sung *"It's* wonderful . . ."), "I've Got a Crush on You" (sung at about half tempo, which began the practice; this is really a 2/4 rhythm number), "Someone to Watch Over Me" (accompanied by Fats Waller at the organ), "Sam and Delilah," and "But Not for Me" (Monmouth-Evergreen 7034). Among the musicians are, besides Waller, Pee Wee Russell, Max Kaminsky, Bud Freeman, Eddie Condon, Artie Shapiro, George Wettling, Joe Bushkin, Sid Weiss, and (on the Porter side) Bunny Berigan.

*EDDIE CONDON & CO.–GERSHWIN PROGRAM (1941–1945)

A dozen freewheeling, relaxed, Condon-directed interpretations, a reminder that Gershwin music has inspired jazz musicians for at least half a century. There are also vocals by Lee Wiley and Jack Teagarden, piano solos by Jess Stacy and Joe Sullivan, as well as some lovely trumpeting by Bobby Hackett (Decca 79234). While the songs are, in general, the standards, it is refreshing to hear them in the Condon "Nicksieland Jazz" style. The range is from "Swanee" through "I'll Build a Stairway to Paradise" and "The Man I Love" to "Summertime" in a previously unreleased performance by Sullivan. Interesting point: you can recognize the tunes; this lady and these men loved Gershwin too.

TRYOUT

Recordings used as a tool for songwriters are generally called "demos," demonstration recordings prepared by (often but not always) composer and lyricist as a guide to producer, director, singers, and musical director. Thus is the song, as actually conceived by its creators, set down in authentic form in terms of phrasing, tempo, emphasis—most of which, thereupon, is ignored by all concerned. Back in 1953 the no longer extant Heritage Productions Corp. issued an album entitled *Tryout* (H-0051) which presented several demos which had been made by Ira and Kurt Weill. The latter is at the piano and, from time to time, joins Ira in the vocalizing, besides contributing his own solos. Suffice it to say, neither songwriter aspired to the Met, or even the Palace, but their approach is fascinating.

The Gershwin-Weill material was gleaned from their film score for *Where Do We Go from Here?* and includes the long take-off on opera, "The Nina, the Pinta, the Santa Maria," as well as "Song of the Rhineland" and "Manhattan," which was not heard in the film. (The rest of the disc is devoted to Weill's presentation of songs from his show—with Ogden Nash—*One Touch of Venus.*) This album is a priceless collection for anyone seriously interested in popular song. Incidentally, a set of similar demos exists of the superior score done by Ira and Kurt Weill for *The Firebrand of Florence*, though it has never been made generally available.

ESOTERICA

I. PIANO ROLLS

As was noted in the main text, George Gershwin began augmenting his income as a teen-ager by cutting piano rolls during the heyday of the pumping parlor piano. At last count there were more than a hundred issued under his name as well as his pianola pseudonyms James Baker, Fred Murtha, and Bert Wynn. A good number of these rolls are being preserved by collectors and several have been issued commercially on long-playing records.

Thanks to the industry of two Australian friends, B. G. C. Whelen and Frank Bristow; an American Gershwin devotee, Alan Dashiell; and a pianola expert, Mike Montgomery, we have a reasonably good idea of George's piano roll output.

It is, of course, possible to argue about the true merits of a piano roll performance, particularly those that have been "enhanced" by stylus with additional figurations to filigree the sound (that characteristic fast tremolo that has become known as "red light treble"). It is true that the precise touch (although the exact notes are there) and certainly shadings and nuances of tone, amplitude are simply not present in most piano rolls. But in the performance of popular songs it was George who once said, "To play American popular music most effectively one must guard against the natural tendency to make too much use of the sustaining pedal. Our study of the great Romantic composers has trained us in the method of the legato, whereas our popular music asks for staccato effects, for almost stenciled effects. The rhythms of American popular music are more or less brittle; they should be made to snap, and at times to crackle. The more sharply the music is played, the more effective it sounds."

With this in mind, it might be claimed that, within certain limits, the piano rolls may well be representative of GG's playing and approach—the playing is crisp and driving (though this at times may have been added by speeding up the tempo of the reproducing piano). But, as time went by, there was an attempt at perfecting the rolls and a playback piano that would allow for certain nuances of performance: the result was the Duo-Art, which was a remarkable instrument and which was, indeed, capable of reproducing a performance difficult to discern from that of the pianist himself. Luckily, George recorded the complete *Rhapsody in Blue* for Duo-Art.

What follows is not a complete list of all the Gershwin piano rolls (a subject for the specialist), but rather those rolls that George cut of his own music.

1916

"When You Want 'Em, You Can't Get 'Em . . ." - - - - Universal 202865

Metro Art 202864

Rialto Ripples - Universal 202935

Metro Art 202934

1917

"Waiting for the Sun to Come Out" - - - - - - - - - Melodee 203733

1919

"Tee-Oodle-Um-Bum-Bo" - - - - - - - - - - - - - - Universal 3517

Melodee 3517

"From Now On" - - - - - - - - - - - - - - - - - - - Universal 3543

Melodee 3543

"Nobody But You" - - - - - - - - - - - - - - - - - - Universal 3549

Melodee 3549

"I Was So Young, You Were So Beautiful" - - - - - - Universal 3557

Melodee 3517

Duo-Art 10033

1920

"Come to the Moon" - - - - - - - - - - - - - - - - - Melodee 3701

"Swanee" - Melodee 3707

Duo-Art 1649

"Limehouse Nights" - - - - - - - - - - - - - - - - - Melodee 3739

Duo-Art 0541

"Poppyland" - Melodee 3741

"On My Mind the Whole Night Long" - - - - - - - - Melodee 203577

"Idle Dreams" - Melodee 203579

"Scandal Walk" - - - - - - - - - - - - - - - - - - - Melodee 203583

1921

"Drifting Along with the Tide" - - - - - - - - - - - - Duo-Art 17445

1924

"So Am I" - Duo-Art 102625

Rhapsody in Blue

Part 1 - Duo-Art 68787

Part 2 - Duo-Art 70947

"Kickin' the Clouds Away" - - - - - - - - - - - - - - Duo-Art 713122

"Sweet and Low Down" - - - - - - - - - - - - - - Duo-Art 713214
Melodee 47175

"That Certain Feeling" - - - - - - - - - - - - - - Duo-Art 713216
Melodee 47178

While this note may properly belong in the Historic Recordings section, it seems more appropriate here. An album has been released by Klavier Records entitled *George Gershwin Plays Gershwin and Kern* (KS-122) and is undoubtedly the best of the piano roll transfers. Ten rolls in all: six of them Gershwin songs ranging from "Tee-Oodle-Um-Bum-Bo" and "I Was So Young . . ." (both 1919) through "Kickin' the Clouds Away" (1925). There are three early Kern songs and one by Walter Donaldson, all dating from 1920. While there is evidence of some slippage because of a worn roll on a couple of the songs, it is not too obtrusive and only one, "I Was So Young," appears to have been tickled up with the typical tremolo of the pianola; altogether, however, the recording is very good and the tempos seem right (though "Drifting Along with the Tide" might be a bit fast). Outstanding are "So Am I" and "Kickin' the Clouds Away," the first a ballad and the latter a rhythm tune, and both beautifully characteristic of the Gershwin style in sound (i.e. harmonically), nuance (phrasing and touch) and vivacity (rhythm). Together with the Archive of Piano Music collection, with its complete *Rhapsody in Blue*, this album provides a fine compilation of the Gershwin piano roll output. Klavier Records may be reached at 5652 Willowcrest Ave., North Hollywood, California 91601.

II. VERY EARLY RECORDINGS

In 1920 George was a member of the Vernon Trio (GG, piano, Bert Ralton, alto sax, and Eddie King, banjo). On July 28, 1920, the group recorded at the Victor studios two songs, "Kismet" and "Chica" (which was perhaps the "Mexican Dance" to which George refers in his London letter to Ira and which later became "Tomale"). The record was never released.

Then on October 14 the trio recorded again at Victor (with Ralton doubling on oboe), doing "Kismet" again and "Ping Pong Poo" (each four times); on November 11 they had another go at these pieces, "Kismet" five times and "Ping Pong Poo" four, but to no avail, for these recordings were never issued either.

George was also recorded with the Van Eps Trio, but the information on these is not as definite as with the Vernon Trio; it is possible that George is the pianist on these recordings: "Teasin' the Cat" (Victor 18226, recorded ca. December 1916—which seems rather early); "A Bunch of Rags" (Victor 16667; recorded November 22, 1920); and "Palm Beach Rag" (Melodisc 701; recorded "early 1920").

And that's it. The tragedy of the Gershwin phonographic experience is that when he was most active the recording industry was nearly dormant. This fact is what makes the English recordings so priceless, whatever their technical quality. In a civilization that prizes documentation, often settling for poor photography—a bad snapshot being preferable to no photo at all—crumbling manuscripts and other papers, how sad that no one thought to preserve more of George's inimitable playing style by recording it, despite the poor equipment (it was still the best of its time) and the lack of outlets for a financial gain. The historic value, especially as more time passes, will grow immeasurably—like the precious faded snapshot, the only link between our time and a time and a world long gone.

III. GERSHWIN RADIO BROADCASTS

George flourished during radio's halcyon period—which contributed so grievously to the temporary near-extinction of the phonograph record. He was often a guest on popular radio shows and, in 1934, presided over his own program. It was the practice, even in the early days, to make reference lacquers (often sixteen inches in diameter) of broadcasts and it is just possible that some of these still exist.

While this survey is by no means complete, it is a reasonable cross section of GG's radio activities and may lead enthusiasts on searches that may well unearth some treasures.

The earliest mention I have been able to find of a GG broadcast was the NBC Everready Hour (WEAF) on December 14, 1926; he appeared again on the same program on December 27 (this may well have been the twenty-eighth, which would have made it the following week; but in those days programming was more informal than it later became).

On December 8, 1929, he appeared with Wendall Hall and his Majestic Music Makers in an hour-long CBS broadcast devoted to his music. He was piano soloist in *Rhapsody in Blue* and played "Clap Yo' Hands," "Fascinating Rhythm," "Do, Do, Do," "My One and Only," "Say So," "So Are You," and "Liza."

He was a guest on Walter Damrosch's "Music Appreciation Hour" (NBC) on August 3, 1931, during which he presented the second movement of the *Concerto in F*. And also via NBC he appeared at least three times as a guest on the Rudy Vallee Hour: November 10, 1932, October 26, 1933, and November 9, 1933.

Beginning on February 19, 1934, his own program, "Music by Gershwin," was heard over WJZ on Monday and Friday evenings from 7:30 to 7:45 P.M. This series ran till around June when George left for Charleston and points south to work on *Porgy and Bess*. GG introduced the *"I Got Rhythm" Variations* to his radio audience (after he had returned from his tour) and had recordings made; this was done on extremely delicate Celluloid-like material which would not stand up over any long period of time. George's own copy became very warped, although the Gershwin Archives has it preserved on tape.

The second series of "Music by Gershwin" (WABC) began on September 30, 1934, and ran through December 30, 1934, and was heard on Sunday evenings from 6 to 6:30 P.M. Many of the scripts, but no recordings, of these shows are preserved in the Gershwin Archives. Producer of the show was Edwin Byron, who collaborated on the scripts with Finis Farr.

George's last program at Lewisohn Stadium was broadcast over WOR on Thursday evening, July 9, 1936, from 8:30 to 10:30 P.M. (his last appearance, the following evening, was not broadcast). With Alexander Smallens conducting, George was soloist in both the *Rhapsody in Blue* and the *Concerto in F; An American in Paris* was conducted by Smallens, and Anne Brown, Ruby Elzy, Todd Duncan, and the Eva Jessye Choir presented songs from *Porgy and Bess*.

BIBLIOGRAPHY

L. D. S.

THE PUBLISHED SOURCES

Any research on George and Ira Gershwin must begin with Isaac Goldberg's *George Gershwin: A Study in American Music* (N.Y.: Simon & Schuster, 1931; rptd., supplemented by Edith Garson; N.Y.: Frederick Ungar, 1958). That biography resulted from a letter of August 2, 1929, from Grace Morse, a literary agent, to Isaac Goldberg, a Harvard professor. Miss Morse wrote that she had "what amounts to an order from the Curtis Publishing Company for several articles about Mr. Gershwin." She wondered about Goldberg's ghosting articles for George, "stating his views as to what the modern music meant, what people were striving for, who were doing it both successfully and unsuccessfully, what it would amount to in the future, etc. . . . Mr. Gershwin himself admires your work and would prefer collaborating with you to anyone else I may choose, and he has authorized me to approach you." A series of three articles for the *Ladies' Home Journal* was planned, following editor Graeme Lorimer's suggestions: "he wants the mother and father theme practically cut out, adhering strictly to the material having to do with Gershwin's musical education and career . . . Lorimer was interested in the Art angle also. (A sketch by Gershwin of something or someone would be a good illustration.)" The articles appeared in the *Journals* for February, March, and April 1931; the book itself considerably expanded them.

Although Goldberg did ghost one Gershwin article—the "Introduction" signed by George to Goldberg's *Tin Pan Alley: A Chronicle of the American Popular Music Racket* (N.Y.: John Day, 1930)—he received full titular credit for his biography of the composer, as well as the co-operation of the Gershwin family. John McCauley, a New York researcher, did

389

most of the interviewing of George and Ira, sending reports to Oxford, Massachusetts, where Goldberg lived and wrote.

The immense importance of the book is its reported conversations with, and opinions by, George. Historically the book also has a residual charm; its snappy, flashy, twenty-three skiddoo style mirrors in prose the chrome and polish of George's contemporary penthouse at 33 Riverside Drive. After George's death, Goldberg announced plans to update his biography, but he died July 14, 1938; his essay for the Armitage anthology (cf. below) was his final Gershwin work. In 1957 when Miss Garson was commissioned to supplement Goldberg's biography, she wisely made no alterations in the text itself, and in her supplement she does not attempt to duplicate Goldberg's whimsical style. Hers is a clear and factual account of the final years of George's life; and thus the book remains an invaluable source for any study of the Gershwins.

Another biographer, Merle Armitage, also had met the Gershwins in the Twenties, but he did not become involved with George until 1936, after the composer and his brother had come to Beverly Hills. Armitage was an impresario who sponsored George's final concerts, February 10 and 11, 1937, at the Los Angeles Philharmonic Auditorium. He also was the first to revive *Porgy and Bess*, when he brought the company to the West Coast in February 1938. Although Armitage attended many Gershwin opening nights, his main interest is in George's concert compositions and folk opera; his books place Gershwin in the milieu of Frank Lloyd Wright, Edward Weston, John Marin, and Martha Graham; and there are frequent allusions to Spinoza, Stravinsky, and Paul Tillich. Certainly if Goldberg saw George as the delightfully brash young man who came out of the ghetto and blazed through Tin Pan Alley, Armitage always saw George as Artist, a man of rare and refined taste.

After George's death, Armitage brought out his first Gershwin publication: *George Gershwin* (London, N.Y., Toronto: Longmans, Green, 1938), a collection of essays rich in Gershwin lore; most were commissioned, some were reprinted from earlier sources. Undoubtedly the most important work in the collection is Ira Gershwin's "My Brother," which was written for the book and is Ira's first retrospective view of George. (Some twenty years later, Ira's "Foreword" to, and "Marginalia on Most of the Songs" in, *The George and Ira Gershwin Song Book* [N.Y.: Simon & Schuster, 1960] would be another valuable survey of his brother's achievement.) The thirty-six contributors to the Armitage volume include Paul Whiteman, Ferde Grofé, Todd Duncan, Irving Berlin, Arnold Schoenberg, George Antheil, Jerome Kern, Harold Arlen, and Henry Botkin. The book also reprinted two essays by George and provided photographs of several of his own paintings. Two later Armitage books also have interesting insights into the Gershwins: *George Gershwin, Man and Legend* (N.Y.: Duell, Sloan & Pearce, 1958) and Armitage's autobiography, *Accent on Life* (Ames, Ia.:

Iowa State University Press, 1965). Armitage's Gershwin books build by accretion, and each tends to reprint material Armitage had published earlier; so one must hunt for modification of his insights.

Biographers of the Gershwins who have drawn heavily upon *The Gershwin Years* include: Robert Payne, *Gershwin* (N.Y.: Pyramid Books, 1960; London: Robert Hale, 1960), whose peculiarly emphasized ethnic attack sees Gershwin only as a sexual athlete or as "a musician who at his best either consciously or unconsciously drew his inspiration from the deep wells of Jewish lamentation"; Robert Rushmore, *The Life of George Gershwin* (N.Y.: Crowell-Collier, 1966), a pleasantly compiled biography for the young; and Edward Jablonski, *George Gershwin* (N.Y.: Putnam, 1962), whose straightforward account appeared in the "Lives to Remember" series for teen-agers.

I would prefer omitting mention of David Ewen's work on the Gershwins, for I do not consider it to be serious. As a Gershwin has said, "The trouble with Ewen is that he thinks a work completed is a work well done"; and scholars are here advised to verify Ewen's facts before relying upon them. His *The Story of George Gershwin*, a biography with invented conversations for an audience of young people, was first published in 1943. In 1956 he brought out his *A Journey to Greatness: The Life and Music of George Gershwin*. In 1970 appeared his *George Gershwin: His Journey to Greatness*, "an authorized, definitive biography." Mr. Ewen does not reveal the source of his commission; certainly it was neither Ira Gershwin nor the trustees of the Rose Gershwin Estate.

The autobiographies of those who personally knew the Gershwins invariably have interesting comments. Perhaps the most familiar of these works is Oscar Levant's first book, *A Smattering of Ignorance* (N.Y.: Doubleday, 1940). The section for Gershwin fans is "My Life: or the Story of George Gershwin." (Serious students will also wish to consult Irving Kolodin's *The Musical Life* [N.Y.: Knopf, 1958], which reveals the source of some of those anecdotes.) Two additional volumes have appeared under Levant's name: *The Memoirs of an Amnesiac* (N.Y.: Putnam, 1965) and *The Unimportance of Being Oscar* (N.Y.: Putnam, 1968)—which wits said proved the importance of having been the right Oscar. Levant's first book made self-proclaimed neurosis amusing. In the disorganized and tragic later works, wisecracks try to wallpaper over the fissures of disintegration.

In his *Memoirs*, Levant complained that *The Gershwin Years* "was so controlled that they read me out of it. I was the Trotsky of the Gershwin ménage." Levant will always have, for the history of our time, an interest —especially a clinical one. His position in the Gershwin world is, however, something other than that publicly assumed; and in writing *The Gershwin Years* we attempted to retain George's evaluation. In 1935, when George had Siqueiros paint the portrait of the composer in a concert hall, George had Siqueiros put in the first row of the otherwise anonymous audience all those who were central to the composer's consciousness: his parents, his two brothers and his sister and their spouses, Emily and Lou Paley, Kay Swift, Bill Daly, Mabel Schirmer, Leopold Godowsky, Sr., and De. Gregory Zilboorg. Oscar is indeed in the picture. But in writing *The Gershwin Years* we could find little evidence that justified a better position than that which George had assigned him: second row, at the end.

Vernon Duke, a peculiarly contentious, opinionated, and gifted man, whose dapper elegance gave him brittle brilliance, was in and out of the Gershwin world until the middle Fifties, when, in fancied slight ("my capacity for indignation is the bane of my existence"), he dropped away from it. His *Passport to Paris* (Boston: Little, Brown, 1955), which he had wanted to call *April in Paris*—but not if that meant repairing his ruptured relationship with Yip Harburg—is full of facts and quickly dispatched opinions. There were two gods in Duke's life: Prokofiev and George Gershwin, and this book chronicles his devotion and indebtedness to Gershwin. The well-indexed book is structured around that transformation of Vladimir Alexandrovitch Dukelsky into Vernon Duke, a name given him by George Gershwin. Many months after Duke had stopped visiting the Ira Gershwins, he sent them an announcement of the wedding of "Vernon A. Duke." Since that was not precisely the name he had professed adopting permanently, we wondered whatever the "A." could stand for. "Arch, probably," said Ira laconically. A fine composer, a valuable book.

S. N. Behrman's *People in a Diary* (Boston: Little, Brown, 1972); Behrman's first essay on the Gershwins appeared in the May 25, 1929, *New Yorker*. (It is reprinted in Armitage.) These many years since the Thirties Behrman has been trying to put George and Ira into words that would please him; he has often said that George was possible, Ira almost impossible, to capture in prose. Of all those who knew George, only Behrman observed the composer's "knack for making enigmatic remarks," and he suggests that George had a sensitivity to language that few appreciated. Behrman's own ability to re-create the ambiance of the period is extraordinary. *People in a Diary* paid *The Gershwin Years* its highest compliment when Behrman took our title for his own recollections of the Gershwins and used the Hirschfeld frontispiece, which Edward Jablonski had commissioned, for his own illustration of the brothers.

The autobiographies of Fred Astaire, Gertrude Lawrence, Ethel Merman, Lillian Hellman, and Dwight Taylor are worth examining for Gershwin lore. Miss Hellman has only a paragraph in her *An Unfinished Woman* (Boston: Little, Brown, 1969), pp. 73–74, but it is an imperishable vignette of George near the very end of his life. Mr. Taylor's *Joy Ride* (N.Y.: Putnam, 1959) has a chapter about an evening with George and Lindbergh: "these two idols of the contemporary scene were caught together for a brief period in time, never to be forgotten." Mr. Taylor depicts George as modest, kind, and tactful—a portrait occasionally lost sight of in the gallery of the energetic man.

Nor should one overlook the essential portrait of George in Ira's *Lyrics on Several Occasions* (N.Y.: Knopf, 1959). All other accounts build from George in social situations; only Ira's portrait continually emphasizes the personality of the man-at-work, and that is, after all, what is primary. Similarly, *Lyrics on Several Occasions* is the best of all portraits of Ira. (Those who prefer concrete visuality may also look to Arthur Knight and Eliot Elisofon's *The Hollywood Style* [London and Toronto: Macmillan, 1969], a photographic tour of the present 1021 North Roxbury Drive, Beverly Hills, with occasional glimpses of Ira in his immurement.)

Critical books and social histories which valuably inform, especially about George: Gilbert Seldes, *The Seven Lively Arts* (N.Y.: Harper, 1924), completed the month *Rhapsody in Blue* premiered. Seldes observes the emerging talent of George and praises especially "Swanee." (Ten years later, Seldes modified that judgment, finding "Swanee" "simple although synthetic." His 1934 *Esquire* assessment, "The Gershwin Case," is reprinted in Armitage's *Gershwin*.) In 1924 Seldes had feared that the song-to-be-sung was being superseded by the song-to-be-played: "we are now full in the jazz age and darkness has set in." To Henry O. Osgood, *So This Is Jazz* (Boston: Little, Brown, 1926), the *Rhapsody* and *Concerto* showed that that darkness had presaged a glorious dawn. Osgood's book is full of biographical facts (culled from his interviews with George) and critical analyses of the concert works; several pages of the scores are reprinted and discussed. Charles G. Shaw, *The Low-Down* (N.Y.: Holt, 1928) has a biographical chapter listing George's whimsical traits, hobbies, and habits: the statistical evidence of genius in its daily life.

John Tasker Howard, *Our American Music: Three Hundred Years of It* (N.Y.: Crowell, 1931; 4th ed., 1965) was the first full-scale study to put George into a historical context. The first edition is filled with Howard's early praise for, and appreciation of, the composer. (Howard had attended the Palais Royal dress rehearsal of the Aeolian Hall concert and here reports on it.) In 1931, Howard preferred the "natural charm" of the *Rhapsody* to the more polite *Concerto* (where George "was a little too mindful of his musical manners") and *An American in Paris*. He also speculated about the influence of jazz upon George and his presumed inability to "rise above his subjective feeling for it and make it something bigger." The fourth edition re-evaluates the *Concerto* and *American* and gives a full account of George's later work; but the revision lacks the contemporaneity and intellectual excitement of the original edition. (Howard's other valuable work, *Our Contemporary Composers* [N.Y.: Crowell, 1941], quotes and discusses many critics' reactions to George; Howard especially praises George's effect upon other composers.)

Bibliography

Gilbert Chase, *America's Music from the Pilgrims to the Present* (N.Y.: McGraw-Hill, 1955) investigates George's relationship to jazz and emphasizes his ability to synthesize known materials. Chase's study—in the tradition of Howard's but perhaps more rigorously intellectual in approach —believes in George's "genius" and the greatness of *Porgy and Bess*: "Gershwin was a composer of the people and for the people, and his music will be kept alive by the people." H. Wiley Hitchcock, *Music in the United States: A Historical Introduction* (Englewood Cliffs, N.J.: Prentice-Hall, 1969) covers much the same ground, *accelerando*. Gershwin gets one and a half pages; Hitchcock does not highly regard *Porgy and Bess* as opera and restricts George's genius to the writing of songs. The *Preludes* are praised as "unpretentious but charming trifles, among the very best 'household music' of the 1920's."

The most technical of such studies are undoubtedly the following two: Wilfred Mellers, *Music in a New Found Land* (London: Barrie and Rockcliff, 1964; N.Y.: Knopf, 1965) has two tightly packed pages on the structured brilliance of "The Man I Love," showing how statement is made and reinforced both lyrically and musically. A chapter is given to *Porgy and Bess*, which "like the operas of Mozart and Verdi, is at once a social act, an entertainment, and a human experience with unexpectedly disturbing implications. Historically it is a work of immense, if as yet only potential significance."

Alec Wilder's *American Popular Song: The Great Innovators, 1900–1950* (N.Y.: Oxford University Press, 1972) catalogues the immediacy of the author's responses. Wilder, himself a composer of several pop standards, professes interest only in the music; but the lyrics keep entering his pages, and it is clear his sounder instincts oppose the separation of music from words in a successful song. His study, which is confined to published sheet music, tries to free the songs from their associations with story and performer. By so blinding himself to published scholarship, Wilder makes free with facts and occasionally draws conclusions which established evidence refutes. (Cf. his remarks on the verse to "Love Is Here to Stay" and the lyric to Kern's "Bill.") Wilder's professed interest is "innovations"; he therefore finds it difficult to be a Gershwin fan—and he is not. (He complains about George's "characteristic repeated note device," though he confesses it "usually works very well." But what is "characteristic" cannot, alas, be "innovative.") This is a casual and not unpleasing book; but it is to be read more for the expressions of Wilder's taste than for historically accurate accounts of the material. His assumption that quality is explainable—and his defeat at accounting for the singularity of the Gershwins—reminds me of Alban Berg's remark to an embarrassed George Gershwin in Vienna. George had been playing for Berg when he suddenly realized the one-sidedness of the situation and its intellectual, as well as social, imbalance. "Mr. Gershwin, music is music," reassured the composer, who was fascinated by George's pianism. Only occasionally is Alec Wilder content with so simply profound a conclusion.

For those who wish to see the Gershwins in the context of their professional world, there are few better sources than the scrupulously factual books of Stanley Green: *The World of Musical Comedy* (N.Y.: Barnes, 1960; rev. ed., 1968) and *Ring Bells! Sing Songs! Broadway Musicals of the 1930's* (New Rochelle, N.Y.: Arlington House, 1971). The latter is a particularly handsome folio, giving "the evaluations and receptions at the time of the original presentations" with special attention to the performers and the *mise en scène*. The book is happily historical and reproduces production photos, contemporary ads, newspaper headlines, and the covers of sheet music; it concludes with valuable appendices on "all 175 productions shown in New York between January 1, 1930, and December 31, 1939."

And finally, for those interested in the origins, and something of the production history, of fifty-three Gershwin songs, there is my *The Gershwins: Words upon Music* ([Beverly Hills, Calif.:] Verve Records, 1959), which draws upon the Gershwin archives and George's notebooks; it was issued as part of the *Ella Fitzgerald Sings the George and Ira Gershwin Song Books* package.

THE GERSHWIN ARCHIVES

L. D. S.

THE PUBLIC ARCHIVES

When Rose Gershwin died in 1948, her will stipulated that George's manuscripts of his concert works—those final ink holograph copies which the composer had so proudly prepared and had had especially bound—should be left to the Library of Congress. Thus, *Rhapsody in Blue, Concerto in F, An American in Paris, Second Rhapsody, Cuban Overture*, and *Porgy and Bess* began the Gershwin archive in our national library. The two major manuscripts not in Mrs. Gershwin's possession—the eighteen piano transcriptions from *George Gershwin's Song Book* (dedicated to Kay Swift) and the *"I Got Rhythm" Variations* (dedicated to Ira)—had been given by George to the dedicatees (both of whom subsequently donated those manuscripts to the Library of Congress). In the early Fifties Ira gave the Library George's copy of a Satie score bought in Paris; and that modest gift began what has since become an annual donation, the totality of which will be appreciated by all future generations.

Ira has given the Library George's holograph scores of *Of Thee I Sing* and *Let 'Em Eat Cake*, the holographs of several songs (including "Oh, Lady Be Good" and "By Strauss"), and rough drafts for arias and themes from *Porgy and Bess*. He has given the Library some Frank Saddler orchestrations of Gershwin songs—orchestrations that George had saved and studied with Milton Ager; notebooks of George's studies with Joseph Schillinger; phonograph records that George owned, and books inscribed by famous composers; George's financial statements (which alone reveal which songs sold and which did not, for statistics and critical histories seldom agree); scripts of Gershwin films and musicals; and the rosewood desk that George had designed and ordered built in the early Thirties, the desk on which he wrote so much of *Porgy and Bess*. What enriches these gifts is Ira's annotation of every item, telling what he remembers of its circumstances in George's life.

When Ira was nearing the end of writing his *Lyrics on Several Occasions*, Harold Spivacke, then Chief of the Music Division of the Library, visited Ira and reminded him that the Gershwin archive was to contain Ira as well as George. Until that moment, Ira had not been possessive of his own manuscripts; and he, who had treasured every scrap left by his brother, had usually discarded his own rough drafts as fast as they had been corrected and recopied. Fortunately the drafts of *Lyrics on Several Occasions* were retrievable (I had been circumventing their route to the wastebasket); the complete manuscript was properly assembled, and thus one can see some indication of how in the Fifties Ira's head and hand worked together. The *Kiss Me, Stupid* manuscripts have also been reserved for the Library; those random drafts of earlier lyrics that yet remain in Ira's possession will eventually join the Library's collection. Ira's contribution of his own material has been particularly rich in correspondence. The letters exchanged with Kurt Weill during the writing of *Lady in the Dark*, for instance, have not merely been put into chronological order. By writing amusing explanations for each letter, Ira has provided an intramural view of what really went on in the writing of that show.

Gershwin friends and other members of the Gershwin family have also enriched the Library of Congress archive. Dr. Albert Sirmay presented it with the *Porgy and Bess* typed libretto that DuBose Heyward had prepared for George. (It is annotated in the handwriting of George, DuBose, and Ira.) Kay Swift has given the Library some Gershwin manuscripts; and Arthur Gershwin has presented the collection with a scrapbook of national editorials and obituaries that his mother had ordered compiled on the death of George. Arthur has also given the Library many of the signed celebrity photographs which George had framed: photographs inscribed by Alban Berg, Pirandello, Damrosch, DuBose Heyward, Molnar, Lehar, Toch, Schoenberg, Gloria Swanson, the Astaires, Gertrude Lawrence, *et al*.

The Library of Congress is, however, primarily a library; while space was gladly made to accommodate George's desk and George's oil portrait of Schoenberg, it was not equipped to handle material better suited for a museum. For that reason, Lee and Ira Gershwin decided in 1967 to make the Museum of the City of New York the repository for the other physical material that is such valuable evidence of George's existence and worth.

Before the Gershwin archives were established there, the Museum's Theatre and Music Collection had already many Gershwin items. Howard Dietz's collection of his own memorabilia at the museum included the final holograph draft of "Slap That Bass." When the museum inherited William Auerbach-Levy's collection of his own drawings and paintings, it acquired not only some fine caricatures of George and Ira but a splendid oil portrait of George at the piano, which Auerbach-Levy had painted in 1926; it is probably the most poetically compelling of all the composer's portraits.

The best index to the museum's Gershwin archive is the catalogue for its 1968 exhibition: *GERSHWIN: George the Music/Ira the Words*. It is expected that the museum will inherit Ira's own collection of family memorabilia which was part of that exhibit. Meanwhile, gifts already made include: George's first rosewood desk, which he designed for the 33 Riverside Drive penthouse (and upon which he worked on *Strike Up the Band*, *Girl Crazy*, and *Of Thee I Sing*), his autographed fountain pen, the dummy practice keyboard he carried with him on his 1934 concert tour, and the baton he used in his last concerts. One of the most poignant of the museum's possessions is the silver cigarette lighter which George gave Ira on the opening of *Girl Crazy*: "To IRA The words From GEORGE The music." It was this lighter which gave title to the Gershwin exhibition.

Like the Library of Congress, the museum is also a fine research facility; it has a complete run of Gershwin sheet music (including "In the Heart of a Geisha"), a fine program file of performances, and numerous photographs of the Gershwins and their world. The archives of many actors and actresses, which have been given to the museum, also contain much of Gershwin interest.

Smaller, but still valuable, collections of Gershwin material exist at other institutions. The George Gershwin Memorial Collection of Music and Musical Literature, established by Carl Van Vechten at Fisk University, is the oldest of such Gershwin collections. The Gershwin archive at the Academic Center Library, Humanities Research Center, University of Texas at Austin, contains a few George Gershwin manuscripts, as well as Ira's lyric drafts for *A Star Is Born*. The manuscripts for the first edition of *The Gershwin Years* are also in the Texas collection. The Isaac Goldberg collection at Harvard University has letters from George Gershwin.

IRA'S PRIVATE ARCHIVE

Despite all the gifts made to libraries and museums, Ira Gershwin's archive of material on his and his brother's lives and works is considerable; and for those interested in the working habits of the Gershwins it remains the richest of all storehouses. Ira retains the bound copies of his own songs; he also has the run of George's compositions which George himself had had bound. (Neither George nor Ira was fussy about first issues, however; and Ira's files contain published versions which predate the bound ones. George kept no Capitol Theatre cover at all of his first big hit, "Swanee," for instance—only the edition with Jolson's picture.)

In 1953, when I began arranging the Gershwin archives, I started with the scrapbooks which had been put together all those years in a catch-as-catch-can fashion. Although the reassembled scrapbooks do not contain every clipping that appeared about the brothers (in reorganizing the materials I discovered that an earlier reorganization had destroyed a number of clippings), their presentation of material in chronological order now clearly establishes the Gershwin story as seen by the contemporary press. (Many of those clippings are so fugitive, it is unlikely that the collection could ever be duplicated.) Ira also has the correspondence that his brother received and saved, together with carbons of those answers George made when he had a secretary. Ira's own more extensive correspondence has retained from the past twenty years carbons of most of his more important answers. The items in the collection that arouse most curiosity and speculation, however, are the unpublished manuscripts and George's collection of paintings.

On February 14, 1964, when Murray Schumach of the New York *Times* went to interview Ira about the *Kiss Me, Stupid* songs, Ira knew that there would be an inevitable question about George's unpublished manuscripts—the composer's legendary trunk. So he prepared in advance a quip about the new film score: "It's not top drawer, but it's not bottom drawer either—though it *is* out of a drawer. (Today there are no porters and no trunks—only drawers.)" It was an amusing disclaimer, but Ira has never had a gift for delivering the prearranged remark—his best conversation has always come impromptu. Schumach did not publish the joke; but on February 17 the New York *Times* did have a front page story about George's unpublished music: not only the three *Kiss Me, Stupid* songs but fourteen other unpublished (and unlyricized) compositions which had been sent to George Balanchine for a possible Gershwin ballet. The story announced "that there is a much larger storehouse of Gershwin compositions in the composer's notebooks, which date back to 1920." Immediately there came an international reaction, as though the existence of George's unpublished music had not been previously disclosed. But the public forgets. On April 20, 1946, Philip Scheurer in the Los Angeles *Times* ("Gershwin Left Unused Hit Legacy") had spoken about this material; and on January 1, 1947, *Variety* had captioned a similar account: "Several Posthumous Geo. Gershwin Scores Will Be Available."

Ira has disliked enumerating the precise contents of the drawers that hold this musical legacy. Besides the numerous completed songs, there are many phrases and fragments which could be logically developed but which, in their present state, recall only to him elusive tunes that George once played on the piano. Isaac Goldberg correctly described George's practice: "His note books rarely show a completed page. . . . He does not employ any private system of musical shorthand, depending a great deal upon a remarkable memory that seems able to draw at will upon any of his thousand songs, not to speak of his major compositions. A mere jotting is enough to recall to him a complicated harmonization." Fortunately George had attentive listeners to the work not written up: both his brother and, until the Gershwins went West in 1936, Kay Swift. When Ira and Kay worked in the mid-Forties on *The Shocking Miss Pilgrim*, Kay wrote out many of these tunes that had theretofore been cryptically alluded to in the notebooks.

Early in his cataloguing of George's completed tunes, Ira assigned numbers to a series of manuscripts. (The numbered catalogue by no means includes all the unpublished Gershwin songs. "Wake Up, Brother, and Dance," "Sing of Spring," "Pay Some Attention to Me," "Put Me to the Test," *et al.* listed in *The Gershwin Years* "Works of George and Ira Gershwin" as "Not Used" also are among the Gershwin papers and have not been assigned numbers; nor were the subsequently published "Real American Folk Song," "Hi-Ho!," "Harlem River Chanty," "Waltzes in C," or "Just Another Rhumba" among the numbered works.)

The numbers begin with ♯17, for reasons Ira cannot recall. (Perhaps the sixteen published Gershwin songs from the 1936–37 films account for those missing numbers.) ♯17 is "Sleepless Night," Ira's title for what could also be a prelude. (The fact that Ira could never decide which way to treat the music has kept it in the drawer.) ♯18 ("Ossining: 'You Got Me Flying High'") through ♯50 ("Ask Me Again") are completed, but unused, tunes which were probably copied by the publisher's copyist in 1938. All have dummy titles; ♯s 32 and 43 have been recorded but not published. Although most of these were never written up in final form, ♯44 ("Ain't It Romantic") is a haunting song written for, but not used in, *Oh, Kay!* (Rodgers and Hart's subsequent song, "Isn't It Romantic?," which was heard in the 1932 film *Love Me Tonight*, has kept Ira from releasing his lyric, since it might seem imitative.)

When Kay Swift began copying other songs from the notebooks, and writing down still others that notebook entries recalled to her and Ira, she continued the numbering system. ♯51 was "Gold Mine"—and that became, of course, "For You, For Me, For Evermore." ♯52 is the verse music to that refrain. Kay Swift's additions to the numbered catalogue run through ♯76. ♯s 77 through 104 have been arbitrarily assigned to earlier manuscripts, often those in George's own hand. ♯81 is "We're Six Little Nieces of Our Uncle Sam," that charming sextette that George and Lou Paley wrote in 1917–18. ♯85 ("Under the Cinnamon Tree") remains from the abortive *East Is West.* ♯92 ("Knitting Song") once opened the second act of *Strike Up the Band.* There is even a breathless rag (♯103: "I Want Somebody"). As one who has listened to all of these numbers many times, I should add that I personally find them invariably interesting, often enchanting. But Ira's acute ear and high standards keep him from carelessly releasing anything that George himself had not given final approval. Perhaps someday all of these works will be available; meanwhile, that they exist is assurance that the world has not heard its last new Gershwin song.

GEORGE'S COLLECTION OF PAINTINGS

The Gershwin
Archives

If there was a catalogue made of the paintings, drawings, and sculpture in George's collection at the time of his death, that catalogue has disappeared. There remain only estimates of the size and quality of the collection. Although he had bought some Bellows lithographs in the Twenties and had acquired some small works at the Arthur B. Davies auction, he did not begin collecting with passionate enthusiasm until the early Thirties. Then, through the discerning eye and taste of his painter cousin, Henry A. Botkin, who was living in France, he was able to buy major works by twentieth-century painters. The Gershwin-Botkin correspondence is a fascinating revelation of how a collection could be put together; each Botkin letter carefully describes several available works, pointing out the advantages of each; and each Gershwin letter selects the one or two pictures thought indispensable and asks for more.

Family tradition says that George's most expensive painting was a Max Weber oil. The work that would today command the highest interest is probably the Picasso oil, "L'Absinthe," which had first been shown at the Vollard Exhibition in 1901. When George came to California in the fall of 1936 he had some of his favorite paintings shipped West, the Picasso among them. After George's death that painting went to his mother, Rose; in her will she stipulated that it be sold as an asset of her estate. It was bought by John Hay Whitney; since 1956 it has been in the collection of Mr. and Mrs. William B. Jaffe of New York. (The only other Picasso George owned was a small unsigned drawing, ca. 1906, of a nude boy riding bareback; this emerged from the bottom of a trunk at Arthur Gershwin's in 1966. The drawing had come from the collection of Leo Stein, and the Gershwin family had forgotten its existence.)

Although the Gershwin family has since come to appreciate the taste and value of George's collection, when the collection was being formed several members were embarrassed and critical: so much money spent conspicuously in a depression on matters "not necessary." But George bought wisely, with daring and with conviction. He had particularly a fondness for great painters in uncharacteristic moments. Thus a fine Utrillo is not a Parisian scene but windmills on the island of Ouissant; the two Pascins are not nude whores but a fellow painter, and a lovely small girl holding a kitten; a Derain is a portrait of Kisling, executed egg-eyed manner.

After George's death, most of the paintings which had been sent him in 1936 in California remained with Ira. Later the paintings that had been left in storage in New York were divided among the family, and several were given to museums. (A Kokoschka impression of the pyramids and a large Siqueiros of a torture victim went to the Museum of Modern Art.) Ira still retains two oils and two drawings by Modigliani, and oils by Derain, Utrillo,

Pascin, Soutine, Chagall, de Segonzac, Rouault, Masson, and Thomas Hart Benton. Arthur's collection includes a Utrillo, a Pascin, a Bombois, and a splendid Siqueiros self-portrait, as well as Noguchi's bronze head of George. Frankie—who is, herself, a fine painter—has a Gauguin self-portrait, some Rouaults, a beautiful Chagall. Ira and Arthur possess a large number of paintings and drawings by George, as the picture credits in *The Gershwin Years* so evidently acknowledge; and Frankie has one of George's best oils: his portrait of Siqueiros.

The Santa Barbara Museum of Art received, through Ira, half a dozen paintings from George's collection, including a Kandinsky, a Tchelitchew, a Siqueiros, and the John Carroll "Negro nude" that George particularly prized. The University of Texas has title to the largest of the Siqueiros oils, "Portrait of George Gershwin in a Concert Hall," but Ira retains possession of the work for his lifetime. The Library of Congress has, besides George's oil portrait of Arnold Schoenberg, Henry Botkin's evocative watercolors of Folly Beach, of George's room at 1019 North Roxbury Drive, and of George at the piano in the living room of that house. The National Portrait Gallery in Washington, D.C., has George's oil self-caricature as well as his oil portrait of DuBose Heyward. The Museum of the City of New York has numerous oils, watercolors, and drawings by both George and Ira; it also has some humorous pastels that Will Cotton did of the Gershwin brothers.

Many oils, watercolors, and drawings by George Gershwin remain in private collections. Harold Arlen owns George's oil of Jerome Kern. Emily Paley has, among several Gershwin works, George's largest oil: the portrait he did of her in Mexican costume. Harold Arlen, Samuel Goldwyn, Vincente Minnelli, and Alexander Smallens all own self-portraits by George. And Mabel Schirmer has two fine colored-pencil drawings of Paul Mueller: the same pose in two different styles (one, almost Fauve). There have, over the past fifteen years, come into several hands some telephone doodles that George made during the Thirties. These had been secretly collected by Paul Mueller, who gave them to Ira after George's death. Ira has had some of the more interesting of these telephone "portraits" framed, together with a canceled-check signature of George's. And these he has given to friends, relatives, charities, and university collections. Thus the personal evidence of George Gershwin as artist is, through Ira's generosity, widely spread indeed.

INDEX

Index

408